TRUST

Also by Iyanla Vanzant

BOOKS

Forgiveness: 21 Days to Forgive Everyone for Everything

Peace from Broken Pieces: How to Get Through What You're Going Through

Tapping the Power Within: A Path to Self-Empowerment for Women

In the Meantime: Finding Yourself and the Love You Want

Acts of Faith: Daily Meditations for People of Color

One Day My Soul Just Opened Up: 40 Days and 40 Nights
Toward Spiritual Strength and Personal Growth

Until Today!: Daily Devotions for Spiritual Growth and Peace of Mind

Don't Give It Away!: A Workbook of Self-Awareness
and Self-Affirmations for Young Women

Living Through the Meantime: Learning to Break the Patterns
of the Past and Begin the Healing Process

Yesterday, I Cried: Celebrating the Lessons of Living and Loving

The Value in the Valley: A Black Woman's Guide Through Life's Dilemmas

Every Day I Pray: Prayers for Awakening to the Grace of Inner Communion

Faith in the Valley: Lessons for Women on the Journey to Peace

The Spirit of a Man

CDs/DVDs

Peace From Broken Pieces

Living From Your Center

In the Meantime: Music That Tells the Story

Giving to Yourself First

Finding Faith

Giving Thanks

CARD DECKS

Until Today Cards: A 50-Card Deck

Tips for Daily Life Cards: A 50-Card Deck

Please visit the distributor of SmileyBooks: Hay House USA: **www.hayhouse.com**®;
Hay House Australia: **www.hayhouse.com.au**; Hay House UK: **www.hayhouse.co.uk**;
Hay House South Africa: **www.hayhouse.co.za**; Hay House India: **www.hayhouse.co.in**

TRUST

MASTERING THE FOUR ESSENTIAL TRUSTS

IYANLA Vanzant

SMILEYBOOKS

Distributed by Hay House, Inc.
Carlsbad, California • New York City
London • Sydney • Johannesburg
Vancouver • Hong Kong • New Delhi

Library of Congress Control Number: 2015950389

Hardcover ISBN: 978-1-4019-4398-1
Digital ISBN: 978-1-4019-4484-1

10 9 8 7 6 5 4 3
1st edition, December 2015
Printed in the United States of America

This book is dedicated to:

Every child whose inherent trusting nature has been knowingly or unknowingly violated by someone he/she loved and trusted

Every woman whose heart has been betrayed by people who simply didn't value the trust she placed in them

Every man whose confidence, self-worth, and agency has been diminished because of his race or stature, because society has deemed him to be untrustworthy

Every person who may believe that trust is something you give and receive because he/she does not understand it is a state of mind and being

To us all I say, *Lean not on your own understanding because we really do not know what anything is for.*

Contents

INTRODUCTION

ALL RIGHT . . . DON'T BELIEVE ME!

Grandma Mary

How does a newborn baby know that when it sucks on a nipple, something good will come out? It doesn't know. What it does is *trust*. I never forget this wisdom because it taught me that no matter how old I am or how much I think I know, each day that I awake, I am like a newborn baby who trusts in life.

Over the years, what I have learned about trust is that we, like the newborn, do it all of the time without even thinking about it. Trust is what we do each day, when we get out of our bed and put our clothes on. It is the thing that makes it possible for us to keep putting one foot in front of the other.

I trust that my body will sustain me; that people will support me; and that what I need, want, and desire I can and will eventually have. I trust that I can leave my home and return to find it standing. I trust that my children and grandchildren will be safe from harm as they move throughout their day. I trust that my partner really does love me and that we will become stronger together as the years pass.

When trust is present, against all odds we enroll in school with no guarantee that we will find a job. It is trust that makes "not enough" money enough to do what we need to do. Trust turns rejection, abandonment, disappointment, and loneliness into motivations rather than a deterrents. Trust moves us beyond what is wrong and what is missing into taking any next best step that will make a difference. We demonstrate trust in ourselves, in God, in others, and in life without thinking about it because trust is a natural, inherent part of who we are as human beings.

The problem with trust begins when we start thinking about it and decide that trust means we are vulnerable. That's when we choose whom to trust and what to trust, and when we make the choice not to trust based on our untested beliefs. If and when anything shifts or shows up differently than we expected it would, our trust is fractured. Once that happens, we get angry with ourselves for being stupid enough to trust, angry with God for messing up our fantasies about life, and angry with whoever or whatever has been injected in our lives to disturb our expectations.

Clearly there are some innate challenges that come with trust. We can never really know what someone will or will not do after we declare and demonstrate trust for them. By the same token, we never know what each day will bring or remove from our life experience. What I have come to understand and embrace wholeheartedly is that when I trust myself, God, others, and the process of life—moment by moment, without thinking about it—if something happens that violates my trust, I always have the option, power, and ability to make a choice to do something about it or not.

We are born with total trust. Doctors and nurses release us as innocent, vulnerable beings from hospitals and birthing centers, assuming that we will be protected and provided for in loving and appropriate ways. They have a very limited awareness or knowledge of the adults who will shape the minds and spirits of the infants they have delivered, or of the environments in which they will grow up. Like all of us, they trust. Many of us fare well. Others do not.

———————

Children attend schools each day where they and their parents believe they are being prepared for life's challenges. Some have books and heat in their classrooms. Others do not. Some understand what is being taught. Others are so hungry or cold, they cannot. Little boys join scout troops, serve at the altar, and go to various sports team practices, trusting that they are safe from harm. They have neither the cognitive development nor the emotional wherewithal to navigate any breach of trust visited upon them by those they look up to. Little girls trust that their fathers, brothers, uncles, and teachers, will protect them from the world's hidden dangers so they will not become defenseless prey. In many instances they discover that their trust was woefully misplaced.

Young men often congregate on the street corners of towns and cities in every state to share tales of who they are and hope to be. They trust that their robust youth and bravado as well as the volume of their testosterone-laden speech will reassure their mamas not to worry about them and will also give notice to those who are up to no good that they are a presence to be reckoned with. Yet far too often, their reckoning, the calculation of their life's value, comes from the weapons of those entrusted to keep their corners safe. Enforcers of the law see them and, perhaps fear them, even when they don't know them; trusting the worst of their thoughts about them, they become self-appointed judge and jury, rendering justice blind.

Young women leave home for New York, Chicago, and Los Angeles with high hopes and big dreams, believing that their talent and dedication will yield a great harvest of success and fulfillment. They trust that if they do the right things, in the right ways, with the right people, they will one day be able to call home with good news. Some live long enough to make those calls. Others do not. Some make it back home physically broken and emotionally battered. Others show up with just the baby and no ring, trusting that if they just keep going, everything will be okay. Many times it is. But navigating the space between where they are and where they long to be can take forever—especially when there's no trust map available.

The pain of broken trusts gets our attention. And the deeper and greater the pain, the more apt we are to listen, to feel, and to seek healing. In our culture, most of us are generally so anesthetized that we can deal with a slight headache. We can even handle a throbbing aggravation. But when our pain escalates to an unbearable migraine and no prescribed painkiller can offer relief—then we start to pay attention and prepare to take action.

Today the pain from our individual and collective trust violations has reached the excruciating migraine level! We are at migraine-level pain mentally, economically, socially, politically, and spiritually, and we're puking all over ourselves. We want the pain to stop, but it doesn't do so just because we've reached out for relief. Relieving pain, like building trust, is an inside job. It is only when you have been broken down mentally, emotionally, or spiritually and choose to stand up and keep moving that you can know the true meaning and value of trust. Trust is a function of choice. Trust grows in hearts that have often been broken open by pain. Trust can unfold in response to devastation, disappointment, and, more often than not, a depth of dysfunction that threatens the human soul. But we avoid, as if our lives depended on it, the very thing that we most need to do to relieve our pain. And be assured, our lives *do* depend on it.

We've got to learn how to trust ourselves and dare to acknowledge what we really feel. We've got to learn how to trust that God is in the mix and that we are a part of God. We've got to learn how to trust each other to do the right thing because it's the right thing. We've got to learn how to trust in the process of life and surrender our inflated human egos. Because we have refused to pay attention to the pain caused by our individual and collective broken trusts, we all suffer. What you resist really does persist!

Trust is not some neat, one-size-fits-all, self-help formula with a tidy beginning, middle, and end. No. Not at all. If anyone offers you a guaranteed 7, 14, or 21-day plan to master trust, run as fast and as far as you can. Why? Because there are no trust shortcuts.

No matter where or how we live in the world, trust is an essential requirement for human life. Without trust there can be no peace of mind. The four essential trusts—*Trust in Self, Trust in God, Trust in Others,* and *Trust in Life*—are like oxygen; we can't live without them. Yet as we survey life in the 21st-century global village, we are confronted by a terrible truth: Many folks are not *truly* living. Too many of us go through life as if we're on portable oxygen tanks, praying that when we exhale here on our desecrated planet, there will be enough time and air for us to inhale once again.

———

President Barack Obama spoke about our rancor, complacency, and fear of one another at the funeral of state senator Clementa Pinckney, the pastor who was murdered during the Charleston massacre. When the Emanuel African Methodist Episcopal congregants attended their Wednesday Bible study class that night, they trusted the Lord's commandments to love thy neighbor as thy self. They welcomed the stranger who joined them, hoping he would return for Sunday morning service. The senseless murder of these innocents not only challenges our ability to trust ourselves, it also ignites mistrust of one another and our institutions.

In a world where our trust in God seems to take too long or is somehow naive, it's easier to abandon trust altogether and live in the coma of not knowing who we are in God's eyes. It's easier to be driven by the negative ego, toxic emotions, and societal dogma that render us completely unable to trust ourselves or anyone else.

As a result, we have become masters of self-betrayal. We lie to ourselves about ourselves and then become highly offended when others impose their lies on us. We violate our most basic instincts and in doing so invite others to do the same. We put our faith in everything that can go wrong, and when it does, we feign shock. We trust that we can't trust, and in doing so, we deplete our oxygen supply of love, joy, peace, truth, and forgiveness.

Learning to trust is so simple, and yet it is the hardest thing we must learn to do in this life. For me, it begins with knowing that my thoughts and feelings are valuable.

When I trust what I think and feel, then I am empowered to take actions that are self-supportive, self-respectful, and self-nurturing. I can do this now because I have done my work, cleaning up my past, forgiving my own transgressions, and taking complete responsibility for what I think, do, and say—moment by moment. These, I believe, are the seeds of self-trust.

I can trust myself because I have developed and cultivated an intimate relationship with God—the God of *my* understanding, not the masculine God that was passed down to me. I can trust myself because I trust God in both masculine and feminine forms. I trust God because I have cultivated the awareness that life is a process of growing and knowing and having a deeper understanding of His/ Her role in the process of life. I now believe and trust that God gives us life as an expression of love and that the purpose of life is to grow in love.

Contributing to our living a purposeful life is where other people come into the trust picture. God has given us life and other people as the mediums through which we learn about love: what love is and what love is not. Our interactions with others—from our parents to our soul mates to our children—are the mini-classrooms we enter to learn big love lessons. In the process of learning how to love, we must rely on trust. In the process of trusting, we learn about betrayal and disappointment and all sorts of stuff we would rather avoid or deny. In the end, it all boils down to trusting that we can find and experience and express love, because God lives in us and that is what being a manifestation of God requires of us.

Over the decades, I have worked with many, many people, all of whom were at various stages of experiencing a trust breakdown or breakthrough: The mother who did not have the courage to tell her daughter she did not know who her father was; the transgender woman whose father was a minister and could not accept her lifestyle; the reality star married to a pro athlete who was abusive and cheated on her; the man who fathered 34 children; the NFL player who lost his sense of self when he lost his career; the minister who fathered a child with one of his congregants then ignored the child in the pews every Sunday morning; the 600-pound woman who did not leave her home for seven years, her bed for five years.

Many of these individuals never learned that they could trust themselves. Some placed their trust in others, only to be abandoned, rejected, or exploited; others forgot that trust builds character and spiritual power. Each person represents a microcosm of the world in which we live—where anger and fear, confusion and isolation, lack of faith and a wanton disregard for the divine process of life causes people to act against their true nature. Since our true nature is to be trusting, every small violation of individual trust creates a ripple effect that ultimately impacts the entire world in which we live. That's how important we are as individuals, and that's how powerful trust is in our lives.

We take our first breath outside of the womb because something within us trusts that the next breath will come with grace and ease. Many of us lose that natural instinct as a reaction to our day-to-day personal experiences with the people closest to us. They hurt us, betray us, and violate the trust we place in them. We grow up in a world where our trust can be easily manipulated. We are lured into buying things that we are told will help us or make us happy—they do not. We read things believing they are true, only to discover that what we accepted as truth is incomplete or totally false. Until and unless we develop and sustain trust within ourselves, we cannot trust the process of life, and we will not trust the power that gives us life. So what's a human being to do?

> TRUST IN THE LORD WITH ALL YOUR HEART
> AND LEAN NOT ON YOUR OWN UNDERSTANDING;
> IN ALL YOUR WAYS SUBMIT TO HIM,
> AND HE WILL MAKE YOUR PATHS STRAIGHT.
>
> *Proverbs 3:5–6 (New International Version)*

When I consider the challenges faced by Barack Obama, the 44th President of the United States, the nation's first African American president, I can only marvel at a human being's capacity to trust. Faced with unprecedented and vicious political attacks and opposition, the President continues to rise each day to advance the interests of our nation. Why? How? I believe, at his core, this man trusts in the process of life. As he has said, "If people cannot trust their government to do the job for which it exists—to protect them and to promote their common welfare—all else is lost."

President Obama understands that no matter what he does, certain people are not going to like him or his policies. Yet no matter where one stands politically, the President is a fascinating example of the four essential trusts—*Trust in Self, Trust in God, Trust in Others,* and *Trust in Life*—in action, and he demonstrates the freedom that belief in these principles can bestow. Just ask the 16.4 million Americans who now have health insurance.

I am similarly inspired by another contemporary leader, Pope Francis, whom *Time* magazine honored as its 2013 Person of the Year. The former Archbishop of Buenos Aires, known as the People's Pope, is a spirited septuagenarian who has embraced the ministry of Jesus and has used his power and platform to advocate for the poor, promote social justice, and protect our fragile planet.

As the celebrated yet humble pontiff affirms, "I prefer a church which is bruised, hurting, and dirty because it has been out on the streets, rather than a church which is unhealthy from being confined and from clinging to its own security." The Holy Father's ability to walk his God talk reflects an unshakable self-possession, anchored in his profound trust. As he wrote, "Although the life of a person is in a land full of thorns and weeds, there is always a space in which the good seed can grow. You have to trust God."

If we believe that God is in each of us and our job is to demonstrate more of God every day, we can see how the four essential trusts can be cultivated and manifested in our lives. When we are able to trust in ourselves, we recognize the interconnectedness of all life. When we trust God, we find the strength, courage, and clarity needed to move beyond the people and situations that challenge what we know to be true and right in our hearts. When we trust that people, in spite of their bad intentions or behavior, are actually doing the best they can, we are not dissuaded by public opinion or attack. Like President Obama and Pope Francis, we can trust that although our fruits of the spirit may not be gathered in the places that we sowed our seeds, our harvest is absolutely assured.

Learning to trust is a huge mountain that we are all required to climb, whether we want to or not. Some of us don't like heights; others are tired or lazy or simply resistant when it comes to doing the hard work required to move through the challenges of life. Doesn't matter! At some point, you will face the mountain; you will be required to trust someone or something in order to get where you are going. You don't start mountain climbing by scaling Mount Everest without equipment. So start where you are. Start with the anthill in your own backyard. Build your trust muscles by considering the following questions.

- Do you trust your own voice?

- Do you trust that you can hear the voice of God?

- Do you trust yourself to see and hear what others are really saying and doing?

- Do you trust (no matter how hard it may be) that there are no mistakes in life?

Because trust is a process that develops and deepens with experience and practice, these questions are a good starting point for the development of the four essential trusts. What you will find is that, with honesty and commitment, your responses to these questions will support you in knowing when it is safe and appropriate for you to trust others.

You need not bring everything and everyone into your process right away. Start small, and use the four essential trusts as your building blocks. If you do, what's going on around you won't matter; what unfolds within you will get you to where you need to be.

———————

Although the words *In God We Trust* are stamped on the U.S. currency, most of us trust in God only when it's convenient, and we resist doing the real work necessary to ensure that trust becomes "a state of mind and a state of being." And that's what this book is about. For me, trust is a way of thinking, being, and living that grows from experience, desire, and choice. It is a demonstration of hope, courage, and perseverance that moves the mind, heart, and body beyond what is known into the realm of what is possible.

Mastering the four essential trusts doesn't mean that we won't worry in the future. It doesn't mean that we will never again experience an upset or a disappointment. It doesn't mean that the person who betrayed us or violated us will be struck by lightning. Those are the signs of false trust anchored in the deceptive intelligence of the negative ego. It is a game of trust that too many folks play. We trust something when we can control it. We trust when we see a partial payoff or think we glimpse a guarantee that what we *want* to happen is what's *going* to happen. But establishing the level of genuine intimacy required to determine if we ourselves, and the people and situations we are involved with, are trustworthy requires hard, uphill work. And most often it is this work that we don't want to do. It's much easier to play the victim.

The purpose of offering this exploration of trust is to dispel the pervasive victim consciousness that permeates our society today and to support you in developing an inward rather than an outward focus. Everything you need to make it through the most painful, difficult, and challenging issues of your life exists within you. Do *not* under any circumstances doubt your power! It is real! You have not lost it, nor can it ever be destroyed. What disrupts and disturbs your belief in and reliance on your inner power, your authentic identity, and the inherent divinity that you were born with are the experiences that you face in life without knowing that you will be okay. Mastering the four essential trusts is your "blessed assurance" that you will be okay.

As you move through the pages of this work, your understanding of how your power became corrupted will expand. Once it was corrupted you were led to uphold the mistaken belief that you are a powerless victim of the circumstances of your life. You may have also come to believe that you have no power over what happens to you at the hands of other people. Growing from these two false beliefs is the absolute distortion that you cannot or should not trust yourself, God, other people, or the process of life. For some, these distortions have given rise to a belief that most, if not all, of what you have endured in life was either avoidable, unnecessary, or your fault—meaning that either there is something about you—or possibly some choice you made that subjected you to the painful and challenging experiences you have endured.

By the time you reach the last page of this book, I trust that you will know that nor is it what you did or did not do, it is not who you are or who you are not, that has contributed to any pain or trauma you have experienced. The only thing you may have done to contribute to the challenging issues you have encountered is to have lost connection with your power: your natural, innate capacity and ability to trust. Believe me when I tell you that you had lots of help in reaching these false conclusions.

The bottom line intention of *Trust* is this: You must commit to building your trust muscles on a daily basis through spiritual practice. Because trust is an inner process, the development and deepening of trust can happen only within you. That is why a consistent spiritual practice is so critical. It is the means by which you can reach the point within yourself where you know and accept that no matter what happens, you will be okay. You may not like what happens—it may be painful or difficult to endure, it may be the total opposite of what you want and expect for yourself—but until you can stand tall in the fun house of mistrust and distrust while knowing that whatever happens you will be just fine, you cannot and will not trust yourself.

———

Finally, I must confess: I am on a mission. My mission is to facilitate and support the evolution of human consciousness from a posture of victimization to one of conscious connection and choice. From woe is me, poor me, and why me to *I am Source, I am one with the Source, I am as God created me to be, and all things I see and experience reflect the ideas I create in my mind.*

The statements in the preceding paragraph are lessons I have learned from my 25-year study of *A Course in Miracles*, a book that offers steps for creating a shift in how we see the world and ourselves. I have undertaken this mission as my life assignment because I have encountered way too many powerful, creative, brilliant people who have suffered and grown to mistrust everyone and everything because they lack knowledge of themselves and their inherent divinity. For the majority of my life, I was among the many who suffered needlessly. I have also undertaken this mission because, when I finally took the time and gave myself permission to really know myself, this was the inner guidance and assignment that I received.

My initial response was, *Who me? Surely this must be a joke! I have nothing to say that anyone wants to hear.* My experience taught me that until I did what I was being instructed to do, in spite of what I had come to believe about myself, I would have no peace, no joy, and no purpose. The day came when I chose to listen to and trust that voice. *Everything prior to that moment in time has become my story, a tool I use to create my life moment by moment rather than the excuse I could use to remain a victim of my history.*

I will be the first to admit that mastering trust ain't easy, and that at times it may seem almost impossible. I will hang my hat on the *almost*, because I know it *can* be done. By exploring the mistrust-in-the-trenches stories presented in this book and what they can teach us, it is my hope that your understanding of what trust is will be expanded and that your ability to trust yourself will be restored. By contrasting these stories to your own life experiences, you will be empowered to create your own unique trust tool kit. Doing so is critical, because mastering trust is not a one-size-fits-all effort. Even in the information age, trust is not a mass commodity that can be acquired; it must be handcrafted in your soul.

My prayer is that you will recognize the absolute necessity of trusting yourself as a prelude to and foundation for trusting everyone and everything else. There is a process and a practice to trust. Life gives you the process through your experiences. People provide you with the opportunity to practice. You will also find it easier to trust if you understand that what you put out will come back to you. Trusting life is easy, but it requires that you understand and embrace the laws of life. Cause and effect, correspondence, vibration, attraction, love, and forgiveness are all concrete laws that govern the movement and unfolding of life. It is unfortunate that we are not taught these laws in school. It is even more unfortunate that we do not pay attention to how we do what we do, because that is how the laws are made practical and personal for us.

If I could offer the world a mantra, an affirmation for successful living, it would be, *Trust yourself, Trust God, Trust others,* and *Trust in life.* These four essential tools must be understood, embraced, and mastered. Without these tools, you will eventually become disillusioned, frustrated, embittered, or stuck. With them, you will be guided, protected, enlightened, and fulfilled. Without these essential ingredients, your mind will be confused, conflicted, clouded, and prone to giving the negative ego dominion over your consciousness. With them, your mind will remain open, flexible, and teachable.

Until and unless you master these four levels of trust, your heart will be at risk. It will become brittle, broken, hardened, and embattled. It will be prone to attack you and everyone else. When you do what is required to develop and deepen your trust in these four areas, *openhearted, lighthearted,* and *clear-hearted* are the words that will describe the fruits of your labor.

I wish I could tell you differently, but I cannot. What I have learned and now live is that you will be able to master these four essentials *only* when you are willing to be vulnerable, when you have successfully subdued the negative ego, and when you agree to accept total and compete responsibility for every choice you have made and the consequences of those choices in your life. Otherwise, you will simply continue to chase peace and joy. Learning to trust yourself, God, others, and the process of life is not an option. It is as essential as the air you breathe. So take a deep breath, beloved, as a reminder that you can do this!

What I have discovered is that the laws of life create the flow of life, and once you are in harmony with the law, your trust will always pay off with high dividends. When, on the other hand, you are ignorant of the way life works and flows, you'll just be out there, on your own, trying to figure out the things that have already been established. It is easy to trust the process when you understand that there *is* a process. When you are void of this understanding, things are not going to turn out well for you.

During my own trust journey, I read something that inspired me to keep going, no matter how difficult it became to believe I was worthy of my own time, energy, and attention. It was titled "Everything I Need to Know About Life, I Learned from Noah's Ark." Although I could never uncover the author, the spirit of it came to me as a divine revelation. For many years I have embraced and utilized the essence of the Noah's Ark story to motivate myself when I feel doubtful about my ability to come out okay. I invite you to do the same and visit Noah's Ark throughout our journey.

Here are the 11 empowering trust lessons that Noah's story embodies.

1. Don't miss the boat.

2. Remember that we are all in the same boat.

3. Plan ahead. It wasn't raining when Noah built the ark.

4. Stay fit. When you're 600 years old, someone may ask you to do something really big.

5. Don't listen to critics; just get on with the job that needs to be done.

6. Build your future on high ground, which may not be ground you are familiar with.

7. For safety's sake, travel in pairs.

8. Speed isn't always an advantage. The snails were on board with the cheetahs.

9. When you're stressed, float awhile.

10. Remember, the ark was built by amateurs; the *Titanic* was built by professionals.

11. No matter how bad the storm is, when you are with God, there's always a rainbow waiting.

Are you ready to begin your trust trek? If you are, consider this: Whether you are walking, running, flying in a plane, or cruising on a boat, trust is operating somewhere in your consciousness. From the time you get out of bed in the morning until the time you fall asleep at night, you are functioning, operating, and depending on something or someone you trust. For some strange reason we have come to believe that trust is something that we can do or not do. The truth is that trust as a state of being and a state of mind develops and unfolds in response to our willingness to be alive. That's right! Just staying alive is an act of trust. If you don't believe me, exhale and try not to inhale . . . If you allowed your body to take that next breath, you were trusting that it would happen, that you could do it, and that everything would be fine until you were ready to do it again. My encouragement to you is to live the rest of your life just like that: consciously exhaling, inhaling, trusting. I promise you, it really is possible. Don't believe me? Just watch.

MASTERING THE 4 ESSENTIAL TRUSTS

Trust in Self

Trust in God

Trust in Others

Trust in Life

Chapter 1

TRUST:
IT'S COMPLICATED

> ABOVE ALL,
> TRUST IN THE SLOW WORK OF GOD.
>
> —*Pierre Teilhard de Chardin*

Trusting in what I did not know was easy when I was a child. It required only that I did what I was told and accept whatever happened as what was supposed to happen. Growing up in my grandmother's Pentecostal church gave me a healthy respect for God and the tenets of my faith. Yet as I advanced in age and mental agility, there were some things that simply no longer made sense to me.

I grew up in a New York City tenement apartment that had pictures of Jesus prominently displayed in almost every room. Yet the consistent presence of a real, live father was conspicuously absent. What I learned from this reality was that someone I did not know and could not touch was supposed to take care of me, while someone I did know and could touch (when he was around) would not. In other words, I learned early on to trust the unknown rather than what could be seen and heard. This should have been a powerful lesson that could have yielded a great harvest in my life. Unfortunately, there were many seemingly unattainable conditions attached to being cared for by the unknown blond patriarch who governed my grandmother's household. You had to be unquestioning, totally obedient, and completely dependent on the Lord if you wanted to receive His blessings. You had to be good at following the rules of faith as they were interpreted and enforced by others. If you fell short . . . well, then, you should not expect to be blessed, and you should definitely expect to be punished by someone or something.

Trusting God was among the many things that I found confusing. Growing up in my grandmother's church gave me a healthy respect for God as *the Father* of all and for the tenets of my faith. It was learning to trust God to provide for me when I couldn't and didn't trust *my father* to do so that threw me for a loop.

Watching my grandmother work two or three domestic jobs at a time while my father gambled and hung out at the bar didn't do much to grow me up in my faith. It seemed to me that the harder my grandma worked, the poorer we became; the more she encouraged me to pray for my father, the less often he came home. Not only did this lead me deeper into confusion, it made me less and less trusting of God, my grandma, and my father. And in response to losing trust in them, I lost trust in myself. I believed there had to be something I could do to make them better and, hopefully, treat me better. As things seemed to stay the same or even get worse, my trust and faith in myself became weak and fragile. One day, they simply disappeared.

I learned a few other mystifying things about trusting myself as I grew up with a frustrated, hardworking grandmother; an absentee father; and a deceased mother. Grandma—like the Lord she taught me about—needed me to be obedient, to follow her instructions to the letter, and to limit my questions for her to one or none. Unfortunately, I was not that kind of kid. I was creative, which meant I always had to add my special twist to things. I could often see another, better way of making things look and feel good, which took me off of the path of following her clear instructions. I was active, which meant being still and quiet just didn't work for me. I loved to dance and make noise. None of this worked for my grandmother.

More important, and very vexing to everyone involved, I had a deep need and desire to know how and why things worked the way they did. This meant that, unlike my brother, I questioned everyone and everything. From the number of times I was punished, beaten, and denied dinner or my favorite TV show, I learned that who I was, as I was, equaled a problem in my home; as my grandma said on many occasions, "Ain't nobody gonna put up with your mess in this world!" This statement was more often than not followed with the caveat, "And the Lord is watching everything you do, 'cause He don't like disobedience either."

While I am sure it was not conscious or intentional on her part, my grandmother taught me that most of what I did was wrong, and that the best of what I did always fell short of the instructions I had been given. My grandmother wasn't a perfectionist; she was simply a woman raised in a time when toeing the line was the key to survival. Growing up half black, half Native American, she had learned that your best hope for avoiding death was to do exactly as you were told, with no thought about yourself, your desires, or your own needs. She impressed upon me as a life requirement the need to do everything the *right way*, which was, more often than not, determined by the person who was telling you what to do.

Doing something wrong meant that I had not pleased the person or people in charge. It also meant that what I thought, what I felt, and what I needed or desired was of little or no consequence. As I grew older, more creative, and increasingly independent, there were many situations when I acted out in unmistakable defiance of the authority figures in my life. In each and every instance when I attempted to assert my thoughts or my voice, I was corrected, punished, or both. Grandma always made it clear that her job was to make sure that I got "in line" and stayed there in order for us all to be blessed by God. The underlying message of her efforts was that I could not trust my own instincts because to do so might lead to a fate far worse than the punishment I had received. It also communicated to me that my behavior could, and often did, cause problems for other people.

5

Believing, or being taught to believe, that *what you do* is wrong is one thing. Learning, or being told, that *who you are* is wrong opens up a much deeper wound that has a direct impact on your ability to trust yourself.

In life, we eventually learn there is nothing wrong with making a mistake. Although we hate to admit that something we have done was the wrong thing to do, making mistakes can become great learning opportunities. *Doing* the wrong thing can be corrected. *Being wrong*, on the other hand, is a fatal flaw. When being who we are—our essence—is deemed wrong, everything we touch becomes contaminated. Our innate wrongness becomes the filter through which we see the world and measure our worth, value, and deservedness.

There is another distinction that must be made: the difference between *having* something wrong with you and your *being* wrong. There was something wrong with my brother: He was a chronic asthmatic, which limited his capacity to do certain things. Grandma said, "You know what's wrong with him! He can't do that . . . bless his heart."

Likewise, my grandmother, with all of her desire to be perfect in the Lord, could barely read. Everyone in the family knew it, but only a few people were allowed to acknowledge it and help her when she wanted to read the newspaper or needed to sign something. Behind her back, people would say, "Don't say that! You know she can't help it." In both cases it was made very clear to me that these so-called wrongs or deficiencies were acceptable and could be overcome. In my case, the wrongness I carried was some sort of curse that I had somehow inflicted upon myself and would surely follow me throughout my life. The curse of wrongness also meant that I was bad. It is very hard to learn to trust yourself when you are taught that you are bad, wrong, and cursed—and that you did all of it to yourself.

How We Learn to Trust and Distrust

From conception to age six, children learn critical things about themselves that become the foundation on which they create their lives. While most of us believe that we learn to trust others and ourselves in response to our later life experiences, many psychologists think that our basic sense of our own trustworthiness is established within the first year of life, and that what we learn about the essential trustworthiness of others develops in response to the care we receive as infants.

Trust versus mistrust is the first stage of Erik Erikson's theory of psychosocial development. He believes that this primary developmental stage occurs from conception/birth to one year. During the first year of life, we are dependent on others to provide all of our basic needs: food, clothing, warmth, protection, and affection. It is during this period that we are able to trust our parents and/or caregivers blindly, because we know nothing else. If our needs are met consistently and responsively, we develop an attachment to our parents and not only do we learn to trust their ability to provide for us but we learn to trust our environment as well. If, for any reason, our basic needs are not met consistently and affectionately, we learn and develop a sense of mistrust toward people and even toward ourselves for having needs that were not or could not be met.

Trust is the first task of our human ego. It grows from the need to be safe, to belong, and to survive. Learning to trust others and ourselves is something the ego continues to struggle with for our entire lifetime. Being well cared for, nourished, and nurtured as an infant is a good first step, but it does not seal the deal. If or when we learn that we cannot trust that our needs will be met, anxiety, frustration, suspicion, anger, and a lack of confidence often result.

When we are children—dependent and innocent—we do not understand why our cries are not heard. If we live among abrupt noises and angry voices, even when they are not directed toward us, we begin to perceive people and the world as dangerous. For preverbal children, this results in the sense or feeling that our survival is at risk and that those responsible for our care cannot be trusted.

Trust is an essential soul need. The psychological injuries and emotional wounds we experience as children affect our soul. When the soul does not develop within the experience of trust, there remains within us a child who is in a constant search for attention, understanding, love, respect, and possibly justice for her abuse or neglect. These needs, when left unmet and unaddressed, will fester and grow into disruptive and/or dysfunctional behavior patterns that will impact every aspect of our lives.

As children we are psychologically and emotionally hardwired to seek the attention, approval, and protection of the big people who take care of us. When our needs are met by those entrusted with our care, we experience feelings of safety, security, and satisfaction. Unfortunately, this process supports the establishment of emotional and behavior patterns that make us dependent on others. This level of dependency is absolutely essential for children's survival. The challenge comes if and when we do not have a smooth transition from dependence to independence, with the approval and support of the big people we once relied on.

When we were children, in order to get what we needed, we learned what to do and how to feel to keep the big people happy. As we become adults, this people-pleasing behavior can become frustrating, debilitating, exhausting, and disappointing. Discovering that adults are not as willing or able to meet our needs as they were when we were children often leads to blame, resentment, stress, and the experience of helplessness and rejection. When we learn to trust and rely on someone or something outside of ourselves to keep us safe, secure, and nourished—and are rewarded for that behavior—trusting ourselves becomes impossible.

When our parents are successful in meeting our needs, we will grow through this period of life learning that to trust people is safe and that, as a result, life can be trusted. This also gives us a basic sense of confidence in what is to come and our ability to handle it. If our parents do not fare well and we are constantly frustrated because our needs are not met, we can end up with a conscious or unconscious sense of worthlessness, helplessness, and a mistrust of people and the world in general.

In some cases, wounded children internalize the seen, sensed, and verbalized wounds of their parents. When this happens, children will use excuses and denial to justify how they were treated. In the process of surviving in an environment that is void of trust, children also learn to deny themselves and their wounds in order to protect the image and needs of the big people in the environment.

It is this inner child, or inner victim—who has been denied and often forgotten, the aspect of the self who has endured a thousand hurts—who will emerge later in the life of the adult. This inner child, who was buried alive deep within in order to be protected from further injury, shame, guilt, or humiliation, is the part of the consciousness that holds the key to our authentic identity and capacity to trust.

In order to reconnect with and heal this aspect of our identity and learn to trust ourselves again, we must acknowledge that we feel angry, sad, and injured, even if we do not understand why. Redeeming this inner child and reestablishing trust within ourselves also means learning how to love, care for, and nourish ourselves in the way we longed for as children. As we learn to heal the inner child and reconnect with the innocence and trusting nature of this authentic self, learning to trust others becomes a conscious act in response to experience rather than an unconscious reaction to unhealed wounds.

CHILDREN DO WHAT THEY SEE

I began to numb out my feelings at age five because it was clear that the "big people" in my life didn't seem to care how I felt or what I felt. I was simply too young to process the feelings of guilt and shame that were constantly being imposed on me. By age ten, I became a junior overachiever. I washed dishes better than anyone else in my household. I could iron for hours without stopping to eat or pee. In school, I sat straighter than anyone, got more compliments from the teacher than anyone, never missed a homework assignment, and always added two extra pages to my book reports. School was the place where I felt acknowledged, prized, and valued. Unfortunately, no one at home noticed that I was a good student. By age 12, I had become a master of criticizing myself, expertly anticipating my own mistakes and beating myself up in advance for anything and everything before anyone else had the chance to do so.

Even before my grandmother could beat or punish me for one thing or another, before my father could sit me down to lecture me about my defiant disobedience, I was already hemorrhaging internally from dragging myself through my own mental and emotional bloodbath. Years of beatings and lectures and punishments had taught me not only that was I untrustworthy but also that I should not and could not trust my own instincts. I carried those thoughts and feelings—a sense of myself as shameful, guilty, and wrong—well into adulthood. In the process, I gave others way too much space and authority to define me and determine my choices, because what I wanted didn't matter and I could not trust myself to make good choices.

I was 14 when I first began to understand how the badness, wrongness, and curse of my life would get me into more trouble than I knew how to handle—just like my grandma had warned me. The *Reader's Digest* version of the story is that I went somewhere I was told not to go, with someone I was instructed not to associate with, and did something I knew I should not do. And I ended up pregnant.

When you are pregnant at 14, shame and guilt are the least of your worries. Living through my brother's embarrassment, my father's rejection, and my grandmother's "I told you so's"—as well as the decisions that were made for me and about me, without my input—became the minefield through which I had to navigate. I had done the wrong thing, and it had had a bad outcome, because there was something about me that needed to be fixed, changed, and healed. It was all my fault, or so I was told.

At age 15, I buried my first child, who had died of SIDS. I traveled to her funeral on the New York City subway and attended the service alone. By age 21, I had married, divorced, given birth to three children by three different men, and was living in a physically abusive relationship with the father of my youngest child. It took me nine years, three cracked ribs, and a broken jaw to muster up the courage to say, "Enough!" After a horrific night of arguing that erupted into fighting, a stabbing (his not mine), and police intervention, I packed up my children and left that home. It was then that I began to believe that I had made so many mistakes and poor choices that I could only *hope* to find a way out.

I had three children, a high school diploma, and a distorted self-image—sleeping in my girlfriend's living room was about as much as I could expect to accomplish at the time. But where there is hope, trust is not far behind. In whom and what could I trust? And did I have enough hope, faith, and trust to turn my ship around? In that moment, I did not. As time passed, though, I found all that I needed by learning to trust myself in spite of the mess I found myself in at any given moment.

SELF-TRUST

Like every other spiritual lesson you must learn in life, there is a meaning, purpose, and value in *trust*. Self-trust is the development and mastery of an unwavering, unquestionable inward conviction about your own value, worth, and ability to be, to create, and to enjoy all that you desire in the process of living and learning more about yourself. This requires an inner belief that you *can* rely on your own character, abilities, strength, and capacity to know the truth and act upon that knowledge in a self-supportive manner.

In other words, trusting yourself means having the confidence in yourself to do what is best for you, moment by moment. And if the choices and decisions you make do not work out for your highest good, you know and believe that you will still be okay. The biggest lesson and challenge in the development and practice of trusting yourself is giving yourself permission to make a mistake.

My father did teach me that flaws are not fatal and mistakes are not mountains that cannot be crossed. He was very good at applying that wisdom to himself . . . not so good, though, when it came to my brother and me.

Self-trust has nothing to do with passively expecting that you can or will have and receive everything you want, when you want it, just like you want it. Self-trust is about having an inner voice, being connected to that inner voice, learning how to hear and follow that voice, and doing the personal healing work required to make sure that the voice you hear brings your best interests to the forefront of your mind.

Connecting to your inner voice is where things can start to be a bit challenging. Most of us have several voices playing in our heads and hearts at the same time: There is the voice of your parents or of the adult authorities who raised you. Then there are the voices of your siblings and extended family members, friends and acquaintances, co-workers and bosses, religious leaders, and members of society at large. There is also your ego, the part of you that wants to survive and look good in the process, as well as your negative ego, the part of you that reminds you of all the reasons why you won't survive and how stupid you will look rolling down the hill to self-destruction.

THE NEGATIVE EGO

Everyone has an ego. It is the aspect of the mind through which we view the outer world and decipher our experiences in the world. The *negative ego* is the aspect of the mind that is created in response to fear. It is the part of us that sees fear instead of love in response to any and every difficult or challenging experience. Think of it this way: the ego is the part of you that knows it is important and necessary to brush your teeth every day so that you do not offend others and you get to feel good about your pretty teeth. The negative ego reminds you that if you don't brush your teeth, they will fall out of your mouth, and you will be scorned and cast off by the rest of the world. While this may sound a bit dramatic, this is exactly how the fear-based, worry-magnet negative ego works. It amps up every thought and feeling by focusing on what could possibly go wrong and leading you to believe that it *will* go wrong and you will suffer as a result.

The negative ego reminds you of every slight, every hurt, and every mistake, as well as of the insufficiency of your responses in order to install and maintain a fear-based reality. When people speak of the devil, I often think of the negative ego. This, I believe, is the lowest possible level of consciousness, the seat of all wretchedness and the aspect of our own mind that absolutely believes we are not, have never been, nor will we ever be connected to or worthy of God's love, protection, and support.

One might ask, "Why in the world would I need this in my life?" or "Why would I create this experience within myself?" The answer is simple and difficult at the same time. The negative ego began the first time you experienced fear or hate. Fear is the normal response to the belief that love is not present or that your survival is at stake. The mind conjures up images of being "out there" on your own. Since God is love, any belief that love is absent results in an experience of separation. When you are separate from God and separate from others, it gives rise to fear and establishes a firm belief in lack. The negative ego thrives on lack. When you are out there on your own—alone—you are basically just a human, lacking and deficient, left to your human devices and struggling to survive. Anything that appears to threaten your survival becomes a larger-than-life menace to be feared and ultimately hated because, as you are reminded by the negative ego, you lack what is required to overcome or overpower what threatens you.

A healthy sense of fear is one thing. Fear keeps you alert, and it can and often does makes you mindful or cautious. Hate is a totally different animal. Hate requires that you eliminate, by any means necessary, the thing or things that you believe threaten your survival. Hate is a dark, heavy energy that motivates you to behave in ways that not only harm others but also harm you. Hate will harm your spirit. Since the negative ego is tied to your humanness, what you lack, and the physical world, it makes fear and survival so predominant in your psyche that you forget about your spirit, and your connection to Source, God. Since few of us are even aware of the presence of the negative ego, it is often difficult to let go of the thoughts and beliefs that fuel it and keep us stuck in its unconscious choices. Unfortunately, the more time we give our unconscious identification with negative ego and the things we fear and hate, the stronger the negative ego becomes.

The longer we believe what the negative ego feeds us and the longer we see ourselves as human and separate, the more challenging it is to dissolve. The negative ego hates change because it engenders fears. Consequently, as you begin to change your thoughts, beliefs, and reactions to the physical world, the negative ego will fight you. It is the aspect of you that does not want to heal. It does not want to change, and it is certainly not willing to trust anything or anyone, including you! Why? Because it knows that any changes you make for the better will cause its death.

The truth is that you cannot change the negative ego into a positive ego. The negative ego must be dissolved through deep, spiritually grounded work. This means an aspect of who you are and who you have believed yourself to be must die. This can be very, very frightening. The more understanding and awareness you have about spiritual principles and the more you trust yourself to survive the death of this aspect of yourself, the faster the dissolution can be carried out. As the negative ego dies, your natural, authentic self will expand and take dominion in your consciousness. As this process unfolds within you, trusting what you know, what you feel, and what you believe will become a natural state of being.

SELF-TRUST IS SOUL WORK

Does trusting yourself mean that you must be willing to *hear voices?* Absolutely! However, it must be the one true and authentic voice that comes through your spirit self that is connected to your Source, Creator, or God—however you choose to define it. I am speaking here about the voice of your Highest Most Divine self, your soul's voice. We all have one, and your soul's voice is the archenemy of the negative ego. This voice is connected to your heart, not your intellect, where the ego owns the majority of the real estate. This is the voice that gives credence to the age-old wisdom, "Trust your gut!"

Because developing and mastering self-trust is *soul work*, its purpose is tied to a very high calling. The purpose of self-trust is to provide us with the divine, God-given, and God-driven opportunity to learn and master how to make ourselves available to the intangible, invisible, ever available support that the universe offers us on our journey. Self-trust is an act of knowing and an act of reliance that requires deep vulnerability as we master the art of becoming inwardly, rather than outwardly, focused.

As human beings we are taught, programmed, and conditioned to trust only what we can see, hear, touch, taste, and smell. Consider how many times you have gone to a restaurant, looked at a picture on the menu or heard a description of the special, and then ordered your meal in response to those external stimuli. Consider also the number of times you have been disappointed by the taste or smell—or both—of the meal you were served. We live in a world that is so externally focused and sensory driven that we are almost expected to ignore, deny, or dismiss what we feel in our hearts. In addition, more often than not, we are taught to trust what we can see or hear and therefore control, rather than giving ourselves over to the still, small voice that knows more than the senses can ever reveal.

Then, there is the issue of the V-word—*vulnerability*—another archenemy of the negative ego. Somehow, somewhere, we have learned or been taught that to be vulnerable means to be weak and/or stupid. When you are weak, you can expect at best to be hurt, and at worst to be totally eliminated. Now remember, we learn about trust early in life when we are vulnerable and our survival is at stake, so when it comes to self-trust, safety and survival will continue to be an issue. When we have unresolved childhood issues related to trust or even when we don't, being vulnerable raises all sorts of red flags in our head that are difficult for the heart to overcome. This is where soul work and the purpose of trust come into play.

One of the most self-loving, self-supportive acts we can undertake is to do all that is required to ensure that the voice of the heart is louder and stronger than the voice of the negative ego. For some, this may mean meditation; for others, it may mean prayer; and for those who are less spiritually inclined, it may mean simply refusing to falter, fall, or fail. Whatever it means for you, the bottom line is that you must grow within yourself a voice, a muscle, a level of consciousness that knows and believes—without a doubt—that you are safe. This aspect of you must be steadfast in the knowledge that no matter what happens, you will be just fine. You see, the soul already knows you are always safe and survival is not your issue. It is your Creator's issue.

Finally, let us consider the value of self-trust. When you see, know, and own yourself as being valuable, worthy, confident, and capable as you move from one life experience to the next; when you trust that there is a force and power greater than you that always, and in all ways, has your best interests in store; and when you really understand and believe that all things and all people come into your life at the request of your soul, the value of self-trust becomes clear. It is simply another tool in your tool kit that you can use to move yourself into and out of any experience you face. Self-trust is an invaluable learning device as you move through the curriculum of your life to heal what you need to heal, learn what you need to learn, and grow in the direction your soul is pulling you.

The value of self-trust is that it takes the guesswork out of living, eliminating the negative ego's drone of "Why me?" or "Why not me?" Instead, when you trust yourself, you come to recognize that your outer world is at all times a reflection of your internal landscape and that anything that challenges you is a high calling to "clean up your act" within so that you will have a better experience without.

THE DIVINE SETUP

One of my favorite teachings from *A Course in Miracles* is this one: "All things are lessons that God would have us learn." (W-pI.193.1:1) It took me years to really understand what this meant for me and to me. Coming from a childhood filled with mental, physical, verbal, emotional, and sexual abuse, my negative ego kept reminding me of how bad, wrong, lowly, and despicable I was, according to the big people.

When I was first introduced to *A Course in Miracles*, I could not see what God would want me to learn from all that I had experienced as a child. What kind of God would want me to learn a lesson by being raped? What kind of lesson should I glean from the experiences of physical and emotional abandonment? Was there really no other way to teach me about life and the beauty of it other than to have adults constantly belittle and berate the creative, inquisitive nature of my child mind? This is where my second favorite lesson from *A Course in Miracles* comes into play: "Truth will correct all errors in my mind." (W-pI.107.1:1)

The truth for me, as it is for everyone else, is that I had to learn about my own value, worth, capacity to love, authentic identity, and ability to forgive. The truth is, my soul knew and chose the exact time, place, conditions, and circumstances of my birth that would provide me with every experience I would need to become the person that my Creator ordained me to be in this life. Everything I experienced in life was a divine setup orchestrated by my soul to grow me into the consciousness required to fulfill my purpose in life.

The truth is, I had to find my sense of self, my authentic identity, my voice, and my center beyond the restrictions, limitations, and definitions that anyone else taught me, imposed upon me, or expected of me. My parents, my grandmother, and all of my childhood caregivers were the supportive cast in the production of my life. The truth is, I needed to recognize that I was the screenwriter, the director, and the producer. I determined how the supporting cast would play out their roles in my life's drama. I had to grow into the understanding that I was the only one with the power and the inherent right to *choose* when cast members would enter a scene and how they would depart from the stage of my life experiences.

The bottom-line truth is that I needed to learn how to be grateful to myself for figuring out how to survive, how to be grateful to my supporting cast for showing up exactly the way they did, and how to forgive myself and everyone else for the things "we" did to hurt, harm, and endanger me.

Now, granted, these were very difficult lessons to learn with the negative ego constantly reminding me of every wrong I had committed and endured. In addition, I was an extremely resistant learner. It was so much easier to allow my negative ego to lay blame and fault at the feet of others. It was so tempting and much less painful to make them wrong and to hold myself out as an innocent victim. I mean, after all, most of the damage to my psyche took place when I was a helpless and dependent child. On the one hand, it is a given that childhood experiences can and do cause imbalances and damage to our psyche. On the other hand, there comes a time when we must realize that our time becoming and living as adults—armed with the power to choose—is much longer than the time we spend as dependent, helpless children.

Still, I could never quite justify why I should accept responsibility for what they had done and said to me. In fact, it was easier to blame God, holding Him responsible for allowing these seeming lunatics to have free destructive rein in the shaping of my mind and heart. What kind of God expected children to accept responsibility for the adults in their lives? This is where a few of my favorite scriptures from the Bible came to my rescue. I remembered what I had learned in Proverbs 4: 23–27 (New Living Translation):

> *Guard your heart above all else,*
> *for it determines the course of your life.*
> *Avoid all perverse talk;*
> *stay away from corrupt speech.*
> *Look straight ahead,*

and fix your eyes on what lies before you.
Mark out a straight path for your feet;
stay on the safe path.
Don't get sidetracked;
keep your feet from following evil.

"FIND THE GOOD AND PRAISE IT"

When I realized that it was my grandmother who had taught me about the Bible, I knew that I needed to be grateful. Even though she had often broken God's commandments in her dealings with me, she had also taught me that it was wrong and evil to speak ill of others even when they did not treat you well. The fact that she used her understanding of the Bible to abuse and demean me was not my business. It was her business and God's business. Once I was removed from her authority, my heart became my business.

If that wasn't enough to convince me to resist the indictments of my negative ego, there was the Gospel of Matthew 5: 14–16 (NLT):

> *You are the light of the world—like a city on a hilltop that cannot be hidden. No one lights a lamp and then puts it under a basket. Instead, a lamp is placed on a stand, where it gives light to everyone in the house. In the same way, let your good deeds shine out for all to see, so that everyone will praise your heavenly Father.*

This was a hard one for me to accept or acknowledge about myself. Me? A light? No way! One of the major steps toward developing self-trust is the willingness to release the belief that you should have or could have done something to stop or prevent the painful experiences. Self-trust becomes an extremely difficult challenge to overcome when you blame or beat yourself up about what you could have and should have done. One way to overcome this hurdle is *to seize every opportunity to remember and celebrate the good that you have done and experienced.* I did remember the family road trips to Philadelphia, Washington, D.C., and Virginia. I still have good memories about the hot summer night we spent on the boardwalk at Coney Island.

I had to force myself to remember the number of times I sat with my brother, nurtured him, and cared for him after he had an asthma attack. Even my grandma had to admit that I was the only one who could make him smile, even though she considered my antics annoying. I gave myself permission to remember and embrace the fact that I had been a good student all the way through school and that I had graduated from college at the age of 30, summa cum laude, as the valedictorian and president of my class, *after* leaving an abusive marriage with three children.

I finally understood that it was not prideful or bragging to remind myself of the number of people I had helped or supported through difficult times, even if none of them were speaking to me now. It wasn't me; it was the light that they had needed. That light was God's light within me.

Chapter 2

THE WAY IN IS
THE ONLY WAY OUT

> I DO NOT WORRY ABOUT
> THE PAST, PRESENT OR THE FUTURE
> FOR I HAVE PLACED MY TRUST IN GOD.
>
> —*Daily Word, May 14, 1991*

I did not expect my journey of self-trust to be paved with milk and honey, warm bread and roses. The work of listening within, weeding out the distortions you may hear, finding your true and authentic voice, and learning to trust and follow the voice of your soul as you battle with the inner demons of the negative ego is postdoctoral spiritual work. And it is worth every moment of your effort. If you remain consistent, focused, and disciplined, and if you are blessed with grace, you may end up with a Noble Prize in self-mastery.

With my first several attempts at learning to trust myself, I failed miserably. I had not practiced enough forgiveness of enough people for enough of what I blamed them for. I made some pretty valiant attempts, but each time I was called to go deeper within myself, I became resistant and fell prey to my negative ego. In my case, there were a few things I continued to miss or skip over, and they became my biggest roadblocks. The first major hurdle was that I was afraid to challenge and discard what my grandma had told me about myself. There was a little girl within me who was terrified of challenging her grandma's word and running the risk of being punished or beaten. All of those feelings I had numbed myself to as a child were locked up inside of me, and I couldn't find the key. Instead, I said the words and did the things to try to convince myself that I was no longer bad or wrong or cursed. But the truth was, I still believed I was those things because my grandma, the "biggest person" in my matrix, was still in control.

YOU ARE "THE ONE"

It was not until I had seen *The Matrix* for the fifth time that everything Morpheus said to Neo made sense. That understanding finally transformed the events of my life from useless, unnecessary, and painful issues into purposeful possibilities and healing opportunities.

Morpheus explained to Neo that in the 21st century, humans were engaged in a war against the *intelligence machines* that they had created. Morpheus was the leader of a group of rebellious humans who had taken on the task of unplugging enslaved humans from the intelligence matrix so that they would no longer be controlled or endangered. It was Morpheus's belief that Neo was "the one" who would free all humans from the matrix of their own intellect. Neo just needed to trust that he was "the one" and behave accordingly. In my mind, this analogy meant that I was still plugged into the distorted programming and dysfunctional energy of my childhood, and I was allowing it, rather than the truth, to control my mind, choices, and possibilities.

It was three or four viewings later when I realized that everything Neo was experiencing was taking place *in his mind*. In every action scene he was immobilized in a chair with some kind of contraption strapped to his head. From fighting against Agent Smith, who challenged his sense of self and power at every turn to his visit to the Oracle and how he interpreted her information and his love for Trinity—these were figments of his imagination. It was not until the third installment of the *Matrix* saga, after Neo had been physically blinded, that he developed enough trust in what he knew and what he had gone through to save the human race.

Most of us can point to one reason or another as to why we cannot and should not trust our instincts, yet at the same time we come to realize that we are the only ones who can figure the way out of the matrix of our lives. There is no requirement that we be perfect at it. There is no requirement that we do everything the right way the first time. If you are familiar with the Matrix series, you know that just when it looked as if Neo was going to be captured or killed, something or someone came along to help him. I was like Neo. Many of us are all like Neo. We must all learn to trust ourselves and to remember that the purpose of self-trust is *to learn and master how to make ourselves available to the intangible, invisible, ever available support that the universe of life offers us on our journey.*

It all begins in the mind. We must fill our minds with the grander, deeper truth than the one we may have learned during childhood. We must fill our minds with a truth loud enough to drown out the incessant defeatist voice of the negative ego. Studying the Word is one way to learn how to do this. I must once again thank my mean ole grandmother, who took me to Sunday school and Bible study, where I learned Philippians 4: 6–9 (NLT):

> *Don't worry about anything; instead, pray about everything. Tell God what you need, and thank him for all he has done. Then you will experience God's peace, which exceeds anything we can understand. His peace will guard your hearts and minds as you live . . .*

> *And now, dear brothers and sisters, one final thing. Fix your thoughts on what is true, and honorable, and right, and pure, and lovely, and admirable. Think about things that are excellent and worthy of praise. Keep putting into practice all you learned and received from me—everything you heard from me and saw me doing. Then the God of peace will be with you.*

When it comes to self-trust, there is a powerful choice we must all make. As human beings we often seem primed to remember who and what hurt us rather than focusing on how we made it through the pain.

Some of us have lived through some horrific experiences as children and adults. At some point, however, if we ever want to trust who we are and the power we have, we must choose to remember that we can in fact rely on ourselves to handle difficult situations, circumstances, and people. In order to learn to trust ourselves and to make self-honoring, self-supportive choices, we must be willing to surrender and forgive those who may have caused us hurt or harm or who threatened our mental, emotional, or physical survival. We must recognize that the emotional center of the brain is a primary decision maker and that the negative ego feeds on and is fueled by negative, toxic emotions. Difficult, traumatic, and painful emotional experiences can and will create a filter in our minds that will grow into negative self-judgments, judgments of others, and habitual beliefs. When such emotional wreckage is left unhealed, it will taint and cloud our choices about who we are and the world in which we live.

Learning to trust yourself means focusing on the good you are, the good you have, and the good you desire so that the truth can heal all error thought and allow you to see the blessing hidden in all that you have been through, gone through, and grown through.

———

Following my daughter Gemmia's death, six months of severe depression, a divorce, and two years of unemployment, I was counseled by my long-time accountant to file for bankruptcy. The changes in my living arrangements and the loss of a major publishing contract meant I was living beyond my means. While I didn't have any credit card debt, I had outstanding loans and other encumbrances that would, according to my accountant, take me a lifetime to pay off. Certain debts could be released through bankruptcy, thus giving me a clean slate and the opportunity to start over. The thought of not paying someone something that I owed was both overwhelming and humiliating. At the same time, my well-intentioned efforts to pay what I owed and stay up to date were just not working.

After much prayer, many tears, and endless conversations with financial experts, I finally surrendered to the reality that filing bankruptcy was my only hope for re-creating and rebuilding my life. After a series of profound losses and a period of major transition and uncertainty, I felt defeated, ashamed, and totally wrong about what I had done, although I wasn't sure exactly what that was at the time. I also felt crippled and guilty about what I was about to do, that is, relieving myself from debts I had created in pursuit of my dreams and goals.

As a part of the bankruptcy process, it was necessary for an appraiser to come into my home and assess the value of my possessions. I thought watching a stranger dig through and count my belongings would be the worst part of the process—I was wrong. What came after the appraisal was the low blow that caused my knees to buckle.

The appraiser was a very mild-mannered man who arrived accompanied by a Realtor and a court-appointed trustee. His job was to photograph and appraise all of my china, silver, diamonds, furs, art, automobiles, and designer clothing. My china had been a wedding present, and I had no idea of its value. Neither did he. I did not own any silver, diamonds, or furs, and I drove a Honda. Very notable African American artists with whom the appraiser was totally unfamiliar had created the artwork I owned. The most expensive item in my closet was a five-year-old pair of Yves Saint Laurent shoes that I had worn many times. He assessed they were worth about $50. I didn't own a boat, and I had no vacation property.

The only thing I owned of any value at that time was my home, which the Realtor, the trustee, and the appraiser all agreed was "lovely," just before they informed me that it would need to be sold to satisfy my secured debts. Then they asked me if I could be out of the property within 30 days. When I informed them that I had nowhere to go, they let me know that they would be putting a lockbox on the door and that the Realtor would always give me one hour's notice before she arrived to show my lovely home to interested buyers.

During this period, anytime I attempted to get involved with something good for me, such as a project I felt good about doing, something inside of me would rise up and sabotage my efforts and energy. This would result in my pulling out and abandoning the work, or my getting thrown out because of my bad behavior. I was always late, my contributions were always incomplete, and I always insisted on having the last inappropriate or unnecessary word. In the end, I felt victimized, angry, and always self-righteous. The filter of bad, wrong, and cursed was in full operation in the matrix of my mind. I continued to make poor choices that ultimately reinforced the hidden belief that I was untrustworthy and that I could not—under any circumstances—trust myself or my thoughts and feelings.

Another stumbling block for me was that I had not yet allowed myself to know, acknowledge, or accept the complete, radical truth about my feelings. It was not until the day I was standing in my bedroom watching the appraiser count my costume jewelry that I realized the truth I had been hiding from myself: my home was not, and had never been, a happy place for me. As a child, I had been shamed in my home, made to feel guilty in my home, abused and violated in my home, and eventually taken out of my home to be placed in the care of some "big people" who never let me forget that I had no home.

As an adult, I worked feverishly to purchase and maintain a house I thought would make everything right in my world, only to come home to a husband who made it clear that he did not like me. In the process of navigating his judgments and displeasure and my own fear that I had made yet another terrible mistake, I lost my voice, my authentic self, and my sense of purpose in the world.

When I purchased my first home, I told myself it would be my legacy to my children. The truth is, there was a part of me, the hurt-little-girl part of me, still trying to prove to my grandma that I could be more than she told me I would ever be. I had forgotten about my own childhood promise to myself that I would someday own my own home. I had forgotten to celebrate myself for keeping that promise. Instead, I used my energy and money trying to prove something to someone else.

———

On the journey to self-trust, trying to prove something never works. Either you know, believe, and trust that you can do a thing and you do it, or you don't believe you can do it, force yourself to work on getting it done, and then sabotage it. I fell into the latter category. There was no way I could have held on to my first home because buying it had not been a self-supportive, self-honoring, or self-loving act. It was fruit of a poisonous tree. It was an act of defiance and rebellion to prove that the messages I had received about myself as a child weren't true.

Yet some part of me still believed those messages. I knew it, and I hated myself for holding on to and embodying those beliefs in every area of my life. I did not trust that I was worth my own efforts or that I deserved to live a good and happy life at home and beyond. I frequently terrorized myself with thoughts of failure. I brutalized myself by spending far more time working than I spent resting or nurturing myself. I dishonored myself time and time again by giving in to what others wanted from me and expected of me rather than standing up for what I knew, what I felt, or what I wanted. It was not until I found myself homeless, unemployed, and alone that I remembered another lesson from *A Course in Miracles:* "This need not be!" (T-4.V.2:2)

When I turned the keys of my home over to the Realtor, I rented a small house nestled on 30 acres of sacred land and got busy creating a home in which I could experience pure joy. Home had to become a happy place for me, which also meant that I had to explore, examine, and heal the feelings about home that made me unhappy. This also meant I had to be willing to feel bad yet still trust that I would recover. I had to recognize that no matter what happened, I would be all right—just like the woman in the Book of Revelation.

THE BOOK OF REVELATION

During my study to become an ordained minister, I learned to read the Bible from an allegorical and metaphysical perspective in addition to the literal interpretation ascribed to by certain faiths. Each of these methods of reading and understanding the Bible led me to discover the hidden meanings behind the words that allow us to apply scriptures to our real-life experiences.

Today, I am still an avid student of the Bible and study it almost daily. My two favorite books of the Bible are the Gospel of John and the Book of Revelation. I love the Gospel of John because it is topical and speaks to the humanity of Christ. This gospel speaks to all people, regardless of their chosen faith, as it reveals the seven miracles Christ performed and seven "I Am" statements he made as he walked his very human journey. Metaphysically, John's gospel is also known as the gospel of love.

The Book of Revelation, which scholars often refer to as the Apocalypse of John, is believed to have been written by John of Patmos. For me, the Book of Revelation represents the passages in the Bible where the truth of what is required of us in life is unveiled and revealed. A revelation is more than mere understanding. It is a process and tool of total and complete transformation. A revelation is a profound realization of truth, and when recognized and embraced, it forever changes who you are and how you live your life. On my journey to self-trust, I had a personal revelation after reading "The Woman and the Dragon" in Revelation 12: 1–2 (NLT), which reads as follows:

> *Then I witnessed in heaven an event of great significance. I saw a woman clothed with the sun, with the moon beneath*

her feet, and a crown of twelve stars on her head. She was pregnant, and she cried out because of her labor pains and the agony of giving birth.

These two verses when read as an allegory and interpreted metaphysically speak specifically to the journey of self-trust. Woman represents the feminine, the heart, or our emotional nature—the aspect of our being that feels or experiences emotion. Proverbs 4:23 (King James Version) instructs us: *"Keep thy heart with all diligence; for out of it are the issues of life."*

"A woman clothed with the sun": Who you are within your heart is brilliant, as represented by the sun, which is considered to be a masculine, life-sustaining source of power. Just as the sun provides nourishment and power in life (i.e., solar energy), what we hold in our hearts (i.e., lunar energy) determines how we move through life.

"With the moon beneath her feet": In metaphysics, the moon represents spiritual intelligence, that which we know intuitively. According to the *Metaphysical Bible Dictionary*, the moon symbolizes "an inner conviction of our ability to accomplish whatever we undertake and calls forth the very best in us that helps us to succeed."

In the allegorical sense, the moon refers to the clarity, wisdom, and light that resides within the darkness, or the unseen places of the spirit housed within us. In our physical-world reality, the moon comes out at night, when it is dark, and it determines the movement of the oceans' tides, which make up 96 percent of the water that covers the Earth. Mother moon is one of nature's most powerful feminine forces.

The first verse of the scripture underscores that the moon—the symbol of spiritual intelligence and power—was "beneath" the woman's feet. In other words, she was standing *on* her power rather than *in* it. Isn't that indicative of what we so often do in life—put down the very thing we need when we need it. In this case the woman placed "spiritual intelligence" beneath her.

"And a crown of twelve stars on her head": Since stars are recognized as another source of light, something high above us that can provide both light and guidance, there is a powerful point to this reference. The woman, just like us, had all that she needed in her mind and in her heart. The trick was to get them working together for her benefit.

The woman, however, has a serious issue: *"She was pregnant, and she cried out because of her labor pains and the agony of giving birth."* As an allegory, to be pregnant means to be filled with life and the possibilities of life. To be in labor represents the work we must do and what we must all go through in order to create anything new in our lives. Whether you are writing a book, opening a business, pursuing a career, or getting established in a new location, work is involved. Sometimes that work is painful, meaning it's unpleasant. Pain doesn't always refer to a physical hurt. Often it means that what you are being called to do or what you are choosing to do is laborious, uncomfortable, and downright inconvenient. The aspect of labor that I would encourage you to be mindful of is that, when you are in labor, you are vulnerable, a condition most of us go to great lengths to avoid.

To keep us on track, let's consider why I believe these two verses of scripture are so closely related to the journey of learning to trust yourself. Trust is an individual experience and the practice of reaching into yourself and pulling up and out what you need in any given situation. It requires that you have a pretty good sense of who you are and what inner resources you have at your disposal. The condition and conditioning of your heart and mind are key factors as you learn to trust yourself. What you learned about yourself during childhood and what you have experienced as an adult will come rushing to the surface in every situation where you are required to make a major life choice. New decisions reveal a host of unknowns. This is where you are most vulnerable. As human beings, we want guarantees.

We all have a deep desire to know that we are doing the right thing, in the right way, to get the right result. More often than not, we are more afraid of doing the wrong thing than we are committed to doing the right thing. It's in those moments when self-doubt and indecision join with the absence of guarantees that the labor of creating something new or desired begins.

Until or unless you can draw on or tap into "the stars in your crown" during your labor, you will be left to your limited human resources. That is when things can really get tricky and even more painful, as the woman discovered in Revelation 12: 3–4 (NLT):

> *Then I witnessed in heaven another significant event. I saw a large red dragon with seven heads and ten horns, with seven crowns on his heads. His tail swept away one-third of the stars in the sky, and he threw them to the earth. He stood in front of the woman as she was about to give birth, ready to devour her baby as soon as it was born.*

The metaphysical meaning of the color red is survival, security, and safety. The dragon, therefore, represents those things that threaten our sense of safety. Can you imagine being in the throes of labor, the pain and discomfort of giving birth, only to be confronted by a dragon? It's hard even to imagine surviving such an experience.

Here, I believe, the dragon describes the negative ego. The part of us that misinterprets and misunderstands can become a huge obstacle in the development of self-trust. It is this hidden aspect of our consciousness that questions and doubts our ability to survive life's experiences, while simultaneously demanding that we look good in the process of crashing to the ground. The dragon's seven heads represent our seven physical senses or abilities: what we can see, hear, touch, taste, smell, sense/perceive, and think. We are programmed early in life to rely on physical things, depending least of all on our inner perceptions. The physical senses are the aspects of our experience that we crown and hold in highest regard. They also constitute what forces us to default to automatic pilot when we face life-altering decisions.

The way the dragon uses its tail demonstrates how the negative ego operates to block the divine power present in the mind and heart. Some animals use their tails to support themselves and to maintain balance as they swing from branches. The tails of others are used to help them swim, navigate direction, or gather food. Animals like horses and cows use their tails for their own comfort, to swat away annoying insects that attempt to bite them. While the tail of a scorpion or lizard can be used as a defense mechanism, a rattlesnake uses its tail as a warning signal. Suffice it to say there are some very specialized tails in the animal kingdom. However, look at how the dragon used its tail in our story: to destroy the pregnant woman's source of light, connection, and guidance in the midst of her most difficult time.

Snatching the stars from the sky and throwing them to the ground is a very apt description of what happens to us when we rely on the demands of the negative ego rather than drawing down on the gifts that the Creator has bestowed on us—our capacity to think and our ability to feel.

Now please, do not get it twisted. Your thinking and feeling, on their own, mean nothing; they cannot and will not help you fight the dragon. It is thinking with your higher mind, the divine gifts and fruits, that you must master. It means keeping your heart clear of the toxic emotions that often accompany negative, ego-based thinking that keeps your crown on your head. These two things—a willingness to think far beyond what is revealed to you by the physical senses and a diligently kept, kind, caring, open, and loving heart available to yourself and others—are the foundational pillars of self-trust. If you do not learn to think rightly and keep your heart toxin-free, the negative ego, like the dragon, will devour good ideas, relationships, experiences, and possibilities; and it will use your own mind to do it.

Oh! But there is more! Let's take a look at Revelation 12: 5–6 (NLT).

She gave birth to a son who was to rule all nations with an
iron rod. And her child was snatched away from the dragon

and was caught up to God and to his throne. And the woman fled into the wilderness, where God had prepared a place to care for her for 1,260 days.

These two verses teach us the power of trust, faith, and grace. No doubt the woman reached the point where she simply had to stop worrying about the dragon and lie down to have her baby, which rendered her completely vulnerable again and susceptible to all sorts of hurts, harms, and dangers. This is when God stepped in on her behalf.

Now take notice that it does not say the woman prayed or meditated. These things are absolutely essential to the development of a crown, yet they were not required when she was most vulnerable. In addition, I believe that she had established a deep relationship with her Creator by praying, meditating, and developing a good character before, when she was *not* in a vulnerable position.

Notice that there didn't seem to be another living soul around to help this woman. There was no one to hold her hand or to give her advice. There was no one present or available to shield her, cover her, or distract the dragon. At some point this woman had to stop worrying about what the dragon could or might do and focus on what *she* had to do. In other words, she had to trust herself to bring forth a new life, and she had to trust the benevolence of life to protect her while she did it.

As the woman focused her thoughts and attention on the task at hand, God protected her and the child she brought into the world from the thing that threatened them both. Now, whether you consider God to be a presence or state of mind within yourself or outside of yourself, the point is, the woman and her child were saved by something the woman could not see, hear, feel, taste, or touch.

Then, without showing any signs of fear, anger, resentment, or bitterness about what she had just experienced, she kept it moving. The woman fled to the next stage of her growing, healing, and learning, and, as you can see, that place had been prepared for her. She did not ask for it nor did she question it. She moved into that place—out of harm's way—because she trusted herself and trusted something greater than herself to make it happen. Later verses tell us that the dragon was really pissed and continued to pursue the woman. Everything he threw in her direction was waylaid by another act of grace.

LIVING FROM THE INSIDE OUT

This story, for me, serves as an accurate description of the greatest foe of self-trust, the negative ego. The negative ego is a dragon in the mind that feeds on and feeds us the most negative interpretation of every experience that we have faced in life. From my own experience, I know that when I respond to life with fear or anger or hatred or guilt or unworthiness, the negative ego will and does eat every good thing I have or desire to have.

This is why the first and only necessary step to developing, deepening, and reaping the rewards of self-trust is to develop, deepen, and build a trusting relationship with your Source, that which we call God. Think of it this way; if you are simply a human being, lacking that which is essential and required for survival, struggling through life to make it on your own, you should expect yourself to fall, fail, and be eaten alive by the dragon. When, however, you can see, hold, or imagine yourself to be a divine expression of all that is powerful and good, when you know that you are connected to and protected by the One who created the universe of life, it is probable and possible to trust that you can be who you need to be and have what you need when you need it.

What if we are all learning to live from the inside out? What if every experience, no matter how devastating in the physical world, is simply a divine setup to grow us up in spirit? What if, should we encounter something that frightens us, we can retreat within ourselves to find the strength and courage we need? What if there is nothing wrong about anything we have encountered, and all we need to do is trust that someday it will all make sense? What if trust is the only lesson we have all come here to learn? What if it is just that simple? What if?

Chapter 3	# CAN YOU TRUST YOURSELF?

> IF YOU CAN TRUST YOURSELF WHEN ALL
> MEN DOUBT YOU / BUT MAKE ALLOWANCE
> FOR THEIR DOUBTING TOO . . .
>
> —*Rudyard Kipling*

A s human beings, we are often taught to discount, fear, and avoid the still, small voice within. We are rarely taught that self-awareness, self-confidence, and self-trust can only grow from our connection to and reliance on our inner voice, which is at all times connected to our higher and most holy self. Our relative ignorance and inner disconnection is what makes trust such a difficult concept to master, because trust is an individual experience that grows both from your relationship with yourself as well as your belief in and experience with something greater than yourself.

Carol, an extraordinary musical talent, nearly lost her life's biggest dream because of her inability to trust herself.

The Good Hope Church was the first audience to encourage Carol's abundant gifts when she sang her first solo at age six. By the time she was nine, Carol was winning contests and talent searches across her city and state. After many knock-down, drag-out arguments, her mother finally conceded that she was good. While she had allowed Carol to participate in numerous competitions,

Mama herself had attended only two, the two in which Carol had placed second. It was after the second "loss" that Carol's mom told her that if she wanted to sing for a living, she could not do so until after she graduated from high school. Carol sang the musical selection at her graduation and got a rousing standing ovation. Mama was not at all impressed. She told Carol that singing was not going to get her far in life and that she needed to continue her education. At the end of that summer Carol left her hometown for college in New York City—on a full scholarship—to purse her love of music and singing.

Carol was a sophomore when she got her first big break; she was contracted to sing a jingle for a commercial. When Carol called home to tell her mother, the reception was lukewarm and the warnings were issued nonstop: "There are lots of people who try and fail . . ." "You need an education to get ahead in life . . ." "Make sure they are paying you enough . . ." "You'd better not fail your classes while you're messin' around with those music people . . ." Carol did not fail. In fact, not only did she pass all of her classes, but the producer of the commercial hired her for enough gigs to keep her busy throughout her sophomore and junior years of college; then he introduced her to another producer who wanted to sign her to a label.

Everything Carol had ever wanted was about to happen; her dreams were about to become reality. But she was also plagued with doubt: What if her mama was right? Carol had an attorney review the contract and was about to sign when the fear overwhelmed her. Maybe she really wasn't as good as she thought she was. Maybe this wasn't the right label. What if she was being taken advantage of? She had a long conversation with the producer, who told her, "Just trust yourself and do what feels right to you. You are really good, and you can only get better with time." But with her mother's warnings swimming in her head, Carol did not sign the first contract offered to her.

After she finished her senior year of college, Carol stayed in New York and accepted jobs in small clubs. Her next big break came as a backup singer for a pretty big name in the New York jazz community. From there the offers poured in, at least two a week for the next five years. Carol's mom was happy for her, but now she wanted to know when Carol was coming back home, to settle down and get married. Carol thought about it and decided that she was now ready to sign with a label. Unfortunately, her reputation as a backup singer was so good that people paid her very well to stay in the background. One night her producer friend met her as she was leaving the club. He wanted to know why she was still singing backup and had not ventured out on her own. Carol said she needed some support to begin moving in that direction. As always, he was willing and ready to help her. His only concern was her lack of confidence. He told Carol that all of the deals in the world would not take her anywhere if she did not trust herself and have confidence in her ability. She knew exactly what he was talking about. Unfortunately, she did not know what to do about it.

Carol suffered from something that plagues many people when they do not receive the support and affirmation they need and want from those closest to them: She valued *her mother's* opinion of her more than she valued *her own* opinion. When external validation has greater meaning than self-affirmation, self-trust is forever out of reach. Another interesting twist in Carol's story is that what she wanted came so easily. She had witnessed how other talented singers had waited for their break, been disappointed, been taken advantage of, and ultimately ended up desperate. Yet the moment it seemed as if Carol would have exactly want she wanted, fear and doubt kicked in to undermine her self-trust.

Comparing herself to others sent Carol's ability to trust herself—her instinct to do what felt right—into a downward spiral. Self-trust begins with *self*. It may or may not be supported by others. It may or may not look exactly like what's going on with someone else. If you don't trust you, it doesn't matter what anyone else says or does, you will not be able to move beyond the level of the confidence you have in yourself. When you don't trust yourself, nothing will sound or feel or look right, because you will be waiting for a guarantee that will never show up. And even if it were to show up, chances are you wouldn't trust it anyway.

So the good news is that trust can grow as a result of what you are taught about yourself by other people. Unfortunately, this is also the *bad* news. As we know, children too often believe what other people tell them; they don't conduct their own independent investigation and assessment of whether or not the information they're getting from others is true and accurate. Then they grow into adults, still believing the same, potentially faulty information. As a result, a huge part of your journey to self-trust will be learning how to deprogram yourself from all of the misinformation that has hijacked your mind since childhood.

Once you have identified and separated *your* truth from all the misinformation that you believe about yourself, you'll understand that you—*just as you are*—are fully equipped to navigate through all the challenging people and circumstances in your life and come out on the other side intact. Always remember that this power is within you, it will guide and protect you, and you will be okay.

SELF-TRUST IS AN ENERGETIC EXPERIENCE

Self-trust is an internal, energetic experience that fuels and enhances desire, confidence, and courage. But when you don't acknowledge and trust the energy that you see and feel, you are rendered deaf, mute, and blind.

Mary recounted a story to our prayer circle that everyone could relate to. "I knew the guy was a crook. I wish I could tell you how I knew, but I can't," Mary began. "There was just something about the way Pete tried to convince me that what he was saying was true that did not land peacefully in my body or spirit. My daughter kept telling me it would be okay, but I knew it wouldn't. What I did not know was how to say, 'You are a crook and I don't trust you!'"

"We were hiring Pete to do renovations on a building we were renting. He wanted $4,000 to do the work. He was asking for a $2,000 deposit, then $1,000 for labor and $1,000 for supplies.

I told him I didn't have that much but would give him $1,000 that day and the balance at the end of the week. He resisted, but since a mutual friend had referred us, he finally agreed. I wrote a check that Pete promptly cashed, and then we never heard from him again. Our friend was shocked. She tried to reach him and couldn't. On the one hand, if I had trusted myself fully, I would have saved myself a $1,000 loss. On the other hand, because I trusted myself, I saved myself a $3,000 burn. My challenge was not understanding and honoring what I was feeling, and also not knowing how to communicate it."

The greatest impediments to the development and experience of self-trust are the stories you tell yourself and the voices to which you grant permission to run wild in your own mind. When you allow horror stories to ricochet throughout your brain, or when you have the tapes of various unidentified and abusive voices playing on repeat, not only will it be difficult to trust yourself, more often than not you will sabotage your deepest desires and greatest efforts.

My friend Ruth Carlos *lost* her life because she didn't trust herself, while I trusted myself and *saved* my children's lives. Ruth was my daughter Gemmia's godmother. When I was going through a major transition in my life, Ruth was always there, willing to watch all of my children because it gave her more time to spoil Gemmia.

Ruth had been dating a man whom she wasn't 100 percent sure of, but he was good to her. She suspected that he had a sordid past and maintained some dangerous alliances, but she liked bad boys. On one occasion, Ruth told me about a guy her man had brought to her house who had given her the creeps. Later, the guy came around looking for her boyfriend and tried to force his way into her house. She kept him out and told her boyfriend about the incident, and he said that he'd take care of it. A few weeks later the creepy guy came back once more, and again Ruth refused to let him in. As a result of that threatening visit, Ruth would not open her door to anyone unless they called in advance to tell her they were coming.

It was a Saturday morning when I asked Ruth if she would keep my children for the day. I had some things to do and knew I'd be able to move faster without the kids. I told her I would be there by 1 p.m. On the way to Ruth's house, I felt compelled to make two stops, knowing that doing so would delay my arrival. I thought to myself, "She's not going anywhere—she'll wait for me." I was going to call her, but something told me it would be okay. When I arrived at Ruth's house at 3:40 p.m., I rang the bell and got no answer. This was very unlike her. I went to the corner and called her from the pay phone. Still no answer. At first, I thought she was mad and was teaching me a lesson. So I went back to her house and called up to her window. Totally ghetto, I know! Still nothing. It was hot, and the children were tired and were starting to whine. I promised them that we could go for pizza and that we would come back to Auntie Ruth's house the next day. We left to finish my errands.

It was 9 p.m. when Connie, Ruth's sister, called to tell me that Ruth and her neighbor had been murdered in Ruth's apartment. Based on witness statements, the police suspected the crime had occurred around 2:30 that afternoon. I explained to Connie that I was supposed to meet Ruth at 1 p.m. For years I carried the guilt of not telling Ruth about my change in plans. I was able to forestall my self-reproach only when I acknowledged to myself that by trusting my gut, my children—who would have been in Ruth's house—had been spared.

SELF-SABOTAGE

Someone once referred to a prestigious university environment as "the hallowed halls of learning." But when it comes to learning to trust yourself, the greatest and the most challenging hallowed halls exist between your two ears. This is where your history, present, and future intersect to create what you use as the blueprint for your life. In this case, "hallowed" describes something that is respected and admired, usually because it is old or important, or has a good reputation.

When you are not taught that you can and should respect, admire, and trust your own thoughts and experiences, you begin to question and doubt yourself. This leaves you vulnerable to feelings of inadequacy and inferiority. These feelings fuel the negative ego and unleash its tirade about your unworthiness and inability to survive. Such thoughts and feelings then become the seeds of self-sabotage.

Self-sabotage is a common response to forcing ourselves to do something we do not believe we can do or should be doing. Rather than run the risk of finding success or meeting with failure, we pull out, abandon, or mess up before we can even complete the task. Another common self-sabotaging behavior is procrastination. When self-trust is low or lacking, we will put things off by making the unimportant, important. We will do all those things we tell ourselves must be done before we can begin something that's new, or frightening, or less pleasurable. We also use the need to prepare, the need to know, or the need to have something we do not yet have before we begin something we do not trust ourselves to do. Fear, shame, past guilt, and lack of forgiveness will also fuel procrastination. When these feelings are present in our consciousness, we will manufacture excuses not to do what we need to do because we don't believe or feel that we can or should do it. Self-sabotage is an internal response to—as well as an attempt to save us from—the energy generated by our disowned negative feelings.

Often we are clueless about our own instances of self-sabotage. My friend Mike grew up in the foster care system. From the ages of 5 through 13, he lived in 12 different homes, each one with a different set of rules and standards. In one home he was physically abused, and that resulted in his being moved into a group home. Although it was good that he was moved, the subsequent drama left him feeling as if the abuse had been his fault and he had gotten the foster parents "in trouble." In another home Mike was sexually violated. Rather than risking the possibility of being moved again, he vowed to remain silent. The violations continued until someone else discovered the abuse and reported it to the authorities. At that point Mike felt doubly violated, and somewhat persecuted, because he had not spoken out. In the aftermath of this trauma, he felt damned if he did and damned if he didn't speak up about his experiences.

As an adult, Mike had a very difficult time making decisions and rarely, if ever, did he allow himself to feel good without expecting it to unleash some unforeseen or hidden catastrophe. Mike always oversolicited opinions and input from several people before making any decision; he was always waiting for the other shoe to drop because of his childhood trauma. After years of watching this pattern and even participating in it, I shared my observation that he really didn't trust himself.

Mike explained that trusting himself was something he had never learned how to do. How could he? Mike's instincts and feelings were always invalidated. So it became safer and, in fact, often a matter of survival to give people what they wanted—no matter what the price. Listening to Mike, it became clear to me that what was true for him was true for many, if not most, of the people whom I knew. I began to understand that there was no blueprint or training available to help Mike and other folks unpack their "trust issues." And I count myself among those "other folks."

PEOPLE WHO UNDERMINE YOUR SELF-TRUST

There are some people and experiences that can and do undermine your sense of self-trust and self-confidence. Don't take it personally! Misery loves company! These are more often than not the same people who don't trust themselves. They do not want you to do what they believe they cannot do. As a result, they will project their limitations, cautions, and fears onto you in an effort to assure that you do not surpass them or exercise your personal autonomy.

As children, none of us had control over the negative people in our lives. As adults, we do have control, and hopefully we learn to establish clear boundaries. Boundaries—the invisible line that dictates where you end and another person begins—keep us safe and prevent intruders from crossing into certain off-limits areas, both physically and emotionally. This means it is up to you to surround yourself with people who can recognize and support boundaries. Internal and external supports are necessary ingredients in the development of confidence and self-trust. Be mindful, however, that the same people who support you will inevitably want to give you advice. You should expect to hear various suggestions and opinions—some helpful and inspiring, some not so much. It's up to you to pick and choose from what is offered. Learning what advice to accept and what to ignore is a critical step on your journey to self-trust. If what you hear doesn't feel right to you, trust your gut and don't act on it.

OWNING YOURSELF

Once we understand that the voices in our heads have a significant impact on our ability to trust ourselves, it is important to set up a positive voice as your personal default. This means you must develop the habit of speaking kindly to yourself about yourself. We all know someone who consistently, perhaps even unconsciously, puts herself down. You can recognize these people as those who begin speaking with a disclaimer. Phrases like: "I know I'm going to say this wrong, but . . ." or, "I know you probably won't believe me, but . . ." Then there's the classic: "I don't really know how to explain myself, but . . ." When a person begins her communication by making a disclaimer about who she is or what she is about to say, that's a pretty clear sign that self-trust is an issue for her. Disowning yourself is a learned or unconscious habit that must be changed if you are to develop a healthy sense of self-trust.

Most of the things we do that remind us that we should not, cannot, and do not trust ourselves are unconscious habits. They grow from hidden, unhealed feelings and unconscious thoughts. They may also mimic some form of what has been said to us or about us by someone we trusted. A major step toward developing self-trust is to become vigilant and conscious about whether or not the things you think and say to yourself are really accurate rather than simply what you have heard about yourself.

If you are a person with the habit of offering a disclaimer, a put-down, or a criticism before you speak, it is important to ask yourself, "Whose voice was that?" Identifying from whom you first heard it can be a major step toward forgiving and releasing the experience, the person, and the voice. When you cannot connect what you say about yourself to an earlier experience, you can still cancel the words as soon as you recognize them by saying, either quietly to yourself or out loud, "Delete. Delete." This releases the energy of the thoughts and the spoken words. It is also a good idea to follow up on the deleted words by replacing them with a positive spoken affirmation that will eventually override the negative programming.

I loved how the character Aibileen, in the motion picture *The Help*, coached Skeeter, the little girl whom she cared for, into learning to trust herself. The film is set in the Deep South in the early 1960s, among privileged white women who busied themselves by competing with one another for social status. Skeeter's mother, one such privileged lady, was a pretty nasty character who had very few nice things to say about anyone, including her daughter. In 1960s Mississippi, women were raised, programmed, and conditioned to believe that their attractiveness would secure them a husband who would provide for them. Based on Skeeter's looks, even at a young age, her mother determined that her chances of being socially acceptable and finding a husband were slim to none. In response, she kept the child hidden and took every opportunity to voice her negative opinions to and about her child.

Aibileen was a black maid who taught Skeeter, a little white girl, to affirm, "You is kind. You is smart. You is important." I believe Aibileen was actually talking to herself and using Skeeter to do it. Although Aibileen's grammar was a bit off, the powerful intention behind the words had a profound impact on Skeeter. Whenever she caught wind of her mother's disapproving words or glances, Skeeter would repeat that affirmation. It was, in fact, Aibileen's counsel and courage that inspired Skeeter to break with the tradition of her plantation owner family and Junior League peers and go rogue, denying the rules of white privilege and daring to tell the stories of the invisible black women who served as maids to the white status quo in Jackson, Mississippi. Aibileen reminds us that it is vital to remind yourself always of good things that you can accept and believe to be true about yourself. Once you commit to believing that you can trust yourself, your positive internal voice will eventually become louder than the negative external voices. Trusting what you hear—whether or not those around you agree with you—is a powerful and important step toward trusting yourself.

FEELINGS ARE THE MATTER

When we grow up in an atmosphere of negligence, constant criticism, or aggressive correction, it's possible that we'll learn to fear being happy and feeling good about ourselves. Such experiences are unfamiliar. As a result, when we start to feel the energy of joy or happiness, we can't trust it or allow ourselves to feel it fully. This is sometimes evident with people who cannot accept compliments or who disaffirm compliments by pointing out something negative to deflate the offering. Good feelings give us a sense of safety and security that can and do inspire us when we make choices and decisions. When we do not trust our good feelings, we cannot trust ourselves.

Not only do our feelings matter, they are at the core of whatever we believe is *the matter* with us. Feelings are a fundamental means of communication that arise from our internal landscape. Feelings cannot be faked. They are critical landmarks on your journey toward building self-confidence and self-trust. Thought patterns, emotional responses, and habitual behaviors all have their roots buried in a feeling, whether from the past or present. It is, therefore, up to us to identify and ferret out the feelings that fuel the negative ego and keep us stuck in a vicious cycle of feeling victimized by life and other people.

For example, if your first reaction to someone is anger, chances are that something has triggered your negative ego. *A Course in*

Miracles reminds us: "We are never angry for the reason we think." From this perspective, ANGER becomes an acronym for that spitfire of emotion we feel: **A**nother **N**egatively **G**enerated **E**motional **R**esponse. When the negative ego is active, it will reference the past and trigger an old memory in the present. When this happens, we cannot actually discern what is being said now. Instead, toxic emotions we have been holding in our mind or body rush to the surface, canceling out everything else. When anger is your first response, take a breath! Ask your companion to repeat what he just said—there's a good chance you did not actually hear it and so don't know what he meant. If the angry response is related to an experience, ask yourself, "What is the upset here?" Give yourself a moment to regroup, then become present to what is happening now, rather than reacting to that flood of emotions from the past.

Feelings carry energy, and all feelings are registered somewhere in the body. Once a feeling is registered, the energy of it becomes fuel that will either motivate us or prohibit us from moving in a productive manner through our life experiences. Hurt, betrayal, disappointment, abandonment, rejection, sadness, loneliness, ugliness, unworthiness, neglect, inadequacy, shame, guilt, and fear are all feelings we experience as children and throughout our lives. Whether we are aware of it or not, the energy of these feelings really exists and can never be destroyed—but it can be transformed. This means once you experience a negative or toxic feeling, you must be consciously proactive about altering its impact on how you do what you do.

Let's say, for example, that throughout your childhood, people negated your feelings. You may have been told to be quiet or to stop crying when you were sad, or you may have been threatened or punished for feeling and expressing anger or upset. If you became overly excited or expressive, your good feelings may have been deemed unacceptable. Many children have experienced having their emotional expressions be stifled or considered problematic.

For adults, it is much easier to control information than it is to deal with expressed emotions. They would rather have a quiet and miserable child than one who is freaking out in the supermarket. Emotions can be *terribly inconvenient!* As loving and well-meaning as parents may be, they often stifle their children's emotional expressions and undermine their ability to trust themselves and what they feel. These children grow into adults who either are afraid to have a full emotional experience or do not know how to have one. As soon as they begin to feel an emotion, they deny it or cut it off. It is hard, if not impossible, to learn how to trust yourself when you cannot give yourself permission to feel what is going on inside of you. Learning how to trust what you feel is one thing. Learning how to express what you feel is a completely different issue. Many of us resist the first part because we have not mastered the second.

Your feelings give you information so that you can make necessary adjustments in your behaviors and your environment. On a physical level, if you feel cold, your body is telling you to do something: to take the necessary steps to get warm so you can protect the organism. Likewise, if we have an emotional experience, the mind and body are sending you a message. There is something you need to do, or stop doing, some action you need to take or bring to an end, in order to protect, nurture, and take care of yourself. If no one is home, meaning if you are not in touch with or cannot identify your feelings, you either will not make the appropriate adjustment or you will be driven by external stimuli that is often misperceived or judged through past experiences.

Feelings are the language through which your life speaks to you. It is important to trust what your life is trying to communicate. If you have a limited emotional vocabulary, meaning you cannot name what you feel, or a sparse emotional library, meaning you have little to draw from, you will spend a great deal of time chasing things that will not truly fulfill your needs. This is how self-trust breaks down. When you are unwilling or afraid to feel your feelings, when you don't want to cry or say the wrong thing, you can get stuck in thinking about what you should feel rather than acknowledging what you actually do feel. When you are not in touch with your feelings, when you cannot name them or do not give yourself space and permission to feel them, you are left with needs that do not go away and that you are unable to fulfill. This leads you to believe that you are not safe in the world, that you make bad choices, that you cannot have what you desire, and that your best efforts will never be good enough. You spend so much time gathering facts externally that you miss the information you receive internally through your feelings, and this is how you miss the boat outfitted to deliver you into self-trust.

When you are just a doughy blob on the planet, a baby—before you have muscle control or language or information or even an idea about yourself or anyone else—everything you need to know comes through your feelings. If you have a need, you make it known through crying, an emotional expression. In fact, you cry about everything you feel, because that is the only language babies have that expresses what they feel. Babies do not think or talk themselves out of their needs; babies do not believe their needs are wrong. They hold fast, trusting that if they keep on crying, their needs will be met.

But as adults, we think or talk ourselves out of what we feel. We convince ourselves that working is more important than eating, or that watching television, doing the laundry, or finishing an assignment for work is more important than sleeping. We tune out our feelings, essentially committing a form of self-abuse and neglect. In doing so we reinforce the false belief that what we need or want doesn't matter. With this mind-set in place, with abusive behaviors active in our consciousness, we have difficulty identifying, trusting, or expressing what we feel.

When we shy away from our feelings, whether good or bad, a filter covers our mind that determines how we see and evaluate people and the world. When we do not trust or pay attention to our feelings, we rely on habitual patterns of thought and action grounded in what happened before and what we already expect to happen. *In life, we always get what we expect.* When we expect to be judged, criticized, or put down—no matter how much we may try to avoid it—we will get exactly what we expect. These experiences serve to fuel the negative ego and prove just how right we were about how wrong we are in the world. When we believe we are wrong or bad and expect to mess up and be criticized for what we do, we cannot trust ourselves.

Celebrity gossip columns are filled with stories of people who seem to have it all yet behave badly in public and blow their lives to pieces, largely because of their disowned, unprocessed feelings. Brian Williams, Josh Duggar, Chris Brown, Justin Bieber, Alec Baldwin, and Lindsay Lohan are contemporary examples of celebrity self-sabotage that could very well stem from disowned feelings and self-trust conflicts. Each of these individuals accomplished a level of wealth, fame, and success that most people would sell their souls for, and yet they very publicly, somewhat systematically, engaged in actions that led to a fall from grace. While we may never know the most intimate details of their childhood stories, or the how's and why's of the secret feelings they hold about themselves, we can make a few fair assumptions. Whether you're a celebrity or not, often the root of such self-destructive behavior is a hidden feeling, a disowned belief, or an unshakable sense that you do not deserve all that you have. And if you don't feel that you deserve it, you can't trust yourself to keep it. That's why it feels easier to throw it away, rather than risk having it taken away.

The Dark Side of Trust

It takes a great deal of energy to doubt yourself constantly, and even more to beat yourself up—or down—even if it's only in your own mind. While you are engaged in mental or emotional battery, you are bound to feel exhausted. In the midst of mental or emotional exhaustion, the negative ego can and will trick you into believing that you now have a valid justification for why you should not, cannot, and do not trust yourself. This is what I call "the dark side of trust," the internal experience of questioning and doubting yourself, your desires, and your ability to hold your own.

When you wander over to the dark side of trust, it is quite normal for the negative ego to dredge up evidence to prove what it believes is going on both inside of you and outside of you. This is when you will remember every poor choice, bad decision, mess-up, failure—and the potential for more of the same. It is absolutely essential that once you realize that you are, in fact, in a dark place, you make every effort to free yourself. The way to do this is to recognize and acknowledge that you have created this experience for yourself, within yourself. It has nothing to do with what you want to do, should do, or should not do. Activating the dark side of trust—self-mistrust—is a tool that the negative ego uses to pull you deeper into the pit of self-doubt, proving once again why you must never trust yourself.

Keep in mind that the number one reason we do not trust ourselves is because we were taught that we were not *really* feeling what we were feeling, or that what we were feeling was unacceptable. Typically, people who were afraid to feel their own feelings taught us this. Remember hearing this line: "You better stop that crying *right now* . . . You don't have anything to cry about . . ."

Another detriment to self-trust is comparing what we feel inside to what other people are thinking, needing, wanting, doing, and expressing. We look at the "happy" family walking in the park—the mom, the dad, the three children, and the dog—and we imagine that our life should look like theirs. But in reality we have no way of knowing that she is a filthy pig, or that he beats her, or that they haven't actually spoken to each other in 15 days. In other words, we compare our lives to the fantasy lives we assign to other people.

The third reason we don't trust ourselves is a response to our need to know we are in control. We want to control everything and everyone. We want a guaranteed outcome, and we want that outcome to be exactly as we picture it. Whenever there is a possibility of not being in control, we find it difficult to trust ourselves or anyone else.

How you treat yourself on a daily basis can provide some critical feedback about your current level of self-trust. Compare your level of agreement with the statements in the list below to reveal the thoughts and beliefs still present in your consciousness that may be undermining your ability to trust yourself fully—*give yourself permission to stay in touch with your feelings and tell the absolute truth*.

21 SIGNS THAT YOU MAY NOT TRUST YOURSELF

1. I have a hard time recognizing, understanding, or believing in my innate value and worth.

2. I accept the negative, self-rejecting messages that I received in childhood.

3. I think that I could have done something to change or stop the childhood abuse, neglect, or abandonment that I experienced.

4. I do things to prove myself and my value to others.

5. I try to control everything around me so I can feel safe.

6. I compare the choices I've made to those made by others.

7. I minimize or deny my own needs.

8. It's sometimes difficult to recognize or tell the truth.

9. I am unable to find, or value, my own voice.

10. I'm unable or unwilling to recognize or challenge my self-sabotaging or self-destructive thoughts, beliefs, and behavior patterns.

11. I'm prone to catastrophizing—i.e., I'm filled with the constant expectation of failure, disappointment, or betrayal.

12. I mentally relive or rehash past traumas or adverse events.

13. I engage in negative and harmful self-talk, and my negative ego takes control.

14. I participate in self-sabotaging or compulsive repetitive behaviors that create shame, guilt, or self-punishment.

15. I break the promises that I've made to myself.

16. I fail to keep the commitments and/or agreements that I've made with others.

17. I find it difficult to finish what I start.

18. I hold in anger, resentment, or ill will toward—or I speak negatively about—those who I feel have hurt or harmed me.

19. I deny or minimize my power of choice.

20. I defer to others—allowing them to make choices and decisions for me.

21. I rely heavily on my physical senses to make decisions and am often disconnected from my instincts, intuition, and inner guidance.

For a long time, I did not trust myself because I thought I had made too many mistakes and poor choices. I also realized that I was, in many respects, a liar. I lied to myself about myself. I lied to make myself look and feel good. I also lied to others when I was afraid. It is hard to trust a fool who repeatedly makes poor choices. It is even harder to trust someone you know is prone to lying. What turned everything around for me was the day I realized that I was teaching my children to lie. It was a very simple lie—I told my son to tell someone I wasn't home. When he looked at me and said, "Where are you, Mommy?" I knew I was in trouble. There are many things I did that were acceptable for me but not acceptable for my children. Teaching my children to lie and to be afraid were among those highly unacceptable things. It took me a good minute, but I eventually figured out that the things I did and said that I was not proud of were the result of my not trusting myself. Eventually, through the process of compassionate self-forgiveness and a commitment to building and strengthening my character, I discovered that self-trust was my life preserver and my only hope.

Chapter 4

DARE
TO TELL
THE TRUTH

> TO BE TRUSTED
> IS A GREATER COMPLIMENT
> THAN BEING LOVED.
>
> —*George MacDonald*

Trust is not something that can be bestowed upon you by the benevolent forces of the universe. Trust is an internal experience that is supported and enhanced by thought, choice, belief, and behavior. So, it is imperative that our actions are aligned with principles and practices that support the transformation of our thinking. If we can shift our beliefs and change our behavior, we can learn how to trust ourselves.

The fundamental principle of trust is *Be-Do-Have*. *Be* trustworthy to yourself, within yourself. *Do* what is trustworthy for yourself and for everyone else. *Have* a greater experience of trust in your life because what you attract is a function of who you are in the world. The *Be* part is internal. The *Do* part is external. The *Have* part is your behavior, that is, the marriage of your being and doing.

Because trust is a function of your being and doing—trust must be practiced. Practice! Practice! Practice! Practice is the only way to build your *Be-Do-Have* muscles. You must be willing to acknowledge your tendencies toward bad behavior and do something about them. In order to know that you can trust yourself, you will be required to live in the now and make conscious choices moment by moment rather than defaulting to doing what you have always done or what you believe has been done to you.

If you are serious about teaching yourself that you really can trust yourself and that you are worthy of the trust of others, you will need to program, condition, and teach yourself to practice conscious behaviors that override the default reactions of the fear-based, smack-talking negative ego.

THE BEST WAY

Andrea and Paul were all-around partners. They had been married for 12 years and were owners of the Best Way Event Planning Inc. Andrea was the people person who trusted her instincts. Paul was the bottom-line guy who trusted high profit margins. Their different perspectives sometimes caused friction in their business because Andrea preferred to hire smaller subcontractors who paid close attention to details and offered unique customer service. Paul always went for the bigger firms, who handled lots of clients at once and who got the job done fast and, if necessary, with a little dirt around the edges.

Andrea believed that the Best Way would grow and thrive if they maintained a high standard of excellence and integrity, always delivering more than they promised without sacrificing quality or jeopardizing the business bottom line. Paul believed that customers were entitled only to what they paid for, and if corners needed to be cut to maintain a profit—so be it. The gospel according to Paul was that people were out to get whatever they could, for as little as they could, and that the more you gave people, the more they wanted.

On paper it looked like a simple outdoor wedding. Outdoor events always involved lots of details and weather contingencies. Paul was to handle the tents, valet parking, sound, and lighting. Andrea took on the food, flowers, decorations, and gifts for the guests.

Andrea spent what Paul felt were too many hours talking to the bride and her mother. Paul's position was "It's a wedding! Jesus! Twenty minutes and then it's over. After that the people will be too drunk or having too much fun to recognize or appreciate the details." He thought Andrea was wasting too much time on this one event instead of bringing in new business.

Excellence. Integrity. Personal care. These were Andrea's mottos, so she ignored Paul's rants. The wedding went off without a hitch. The bride and groom were extremely pleased. In fact, the company acquired four new clients within 48 hours because the guests were so impressed. However, what really turned Paul around was the letter that came from the bride's mother about three weeks after the event.

Dear Andrea and Paul:

I just wanted to thank you again for the care and excellence you put into the planning and execution of my daughter's wedding. She carried the joy of every little detail with her as she departed from this life. You see, my daughter had a rare form of leukemia. We all knew that she had very little time left. She and her husband decided that her last wish, to have a dream wedding, would be the memory she would take with her and leave with us. Because of your attentive care to every little detail, my daughter's life ended on a very high note. You will never know how much it means to us that without having this information you treated us and our daughter's wedding like the grand event we wanted it to be. We can never thank you enough. We will forever refer our family, friends, and anyone we know to do their events with the Best Way.

Enclosed in the letter was an unexpected gratuity—a check in the amount of $20,000.

BOUNDARIES

As a life coach, I recognize that having clear boundaries and honoring them is such a critical element in developing a foundation for self-trust that I am pausing to offer a definition so that we will literally be on the same page.

As the Oxford dictionary describes it, a boundary is: "a line that marks the limits of an area; a dividing line; a limit of a subject or sphere of activity."

Here is my working definition of a boundary: "a mental construct, expectation, request, or system that you put in place within yourself to define, prescribe, limit, or exclude behavior, people, experiences, and internal or external intrusions." A boundary makes and keeps us aware of how far we can go, how much we can do, and what we can expect and will accept from others.

For the purpose of cultivating self-trust, the boundary line is the one you create for yourself, within yourself, and around yourself in order to keep yourself safe. For example, this is one boundary I grew up with: I did not have permission or the privilege to call people 10 or more years older than me by their first name. Such people were considered elders, and I was expected to show them respect. It is a boundary I never crossed.

Now that I am an elder of sorts, it is still difficult for me to address people with gray hair by their first name. In addition, because of the work I do and the places people permit me to enter in their minds and hearts, I always want to demonstrate respect. Today, I call anyone I am working with *Ms.* or *Mr.* so that they will know that no matter how close I step into their world or face, I am offering them my respect.

In a world where some children call their parents by their first names, where young people swear at elders without batting an eye, and where social media posts hang virtual scarlet letters with impunity, we have become insensitive to slurs, insults, and rampant disrespect. Degrading and dishonorable titles and references to each other have become common slang. Parents have become "baby mommas" or "baby daddies." Men have become the N-word. Women have become the B-word and the W-word. My old-school sensibilities find it hard to accept that the more profoundly you embrace a derogatory title, the more you will be elevated and celebrated.

What is most disheartening and sad for me is that our children not only hear these verbal assaults, they embrace them and take them on as acceptable identities: the thing to be, do, and say. We now have names for them: They are bastards and MFs and pains in the MFin' a——.

Now clearly, most people do not speak this way, nor do they find it acceptable. Yet at the same time, we hear these words and allow them to exist in our environment, forgetting that *words create energy*. Energy cannot be destroyed. It can be altered, but it can never be destroyed. That's why boundaries are necessary. Boundaries create and alter energy. They are an announcement to yourself that you are willing to honor and take care of yourself. They are an announcement to other people of your requirements and expectations. They create a structure and parameter for what is and is not accepted, permitted, accommodated, and tolerated in your presence and space.

A boundary is a demonstration of self-respect and respect for others. When you know what is expected of you, you have the power to choose whether or not you want to participate or be in relationship with people. Boundaries related to privacy, confidentiality, time requirements, personal space or property, and commitment expectations serve to create, facilitate, and enhance the quality and integrity of any relationship. The purpose of having boundaries is to protect the physical, mental, and emotional self from unwanted intrusions. You need to be able to tell other people when they are being or behaving in ways that are unacceptable or frightening to you.

A major step toward self-trust is understanding that you have a right to protect and defend yourself when you feel it is necessary. In addition, not only do you have the right, it is your duty to take responsibility for how you expect and allow others to treat you. I have discovered through many years of ruthless self-examination that one way I participated in the ongoing erosion of my self-confidence and capacity to trust myself was by allowing other people to "behave badly" in my life. I allowed my boundaries to be overstepped, and sometimes I allowed them to collapse altogether. When I did have the courage to draw a line in the sand, and someone crossed that line, I would go back and draw another one.

When there is a breakdown of trust within you or between you and other people, it is, more often than not, the result of what I refer to as "bad behavior." Underneath bad behaviors there are often whirlpools of believing the worst about people, expecting that the worst will always happen, and experiencing a lack of self-trust. At its core, bad behavior results from mental and emotional programming, social conditioning, personal experiences, and the incessant demands of the negative ego. Bad behavior leads to poor choices, and a negation of the soul's needs—all of which can destroy self-trust and the ability to trust God, others, and life.

Bad behaviors include:

- Making assumptions instead of asking questions

- Ignoring, dishonoring, or violating boundaries

- Betraying confidences

- Lying or withholding information

- Wishing harm on others or doing harmful things to prove a point

- Making preemptive strikes: doing to others what you think they are trying to do to you

- Behaving hypocritically: saying one thing while consciously doing another

Bad behavior can range from the trivial to the criminal, but learning to check bad behavior when it happens by enforcing your boundaries can serve as energetic jujitsu. Once, when I asked a friend not to refer to me or any other woman using the B-word, she thought I was being too sensitive. Even after I explained to her how that word and energy made me feel, she continued to use it without making any effort to correct or stop herself. I finally drew my boundary and explained that if she continued to call me by that name, I would be forced to end our communication, whether in person or by telephone. She thought I was joking. I was not. The next time she said, "B——, you know what I mean," I said, "No, actually I don't," and hung up.

It was not until I created and upheld clear boundaries for myself that I began to realize that when people care about you, they will respect what you request and expect. If and when they cannot, they will offer a compromise. Today in our technology-addicted culture, it's easy to feel ignored, dismissed, or unheard. So my technology boundary request to my partner and children was simple, "I am asking that you not bring your telephone to the dinner table, and if you must answer the phone when you are talking to me, please excuse yourself."

It took a few reminders, but eventually, everyone respected the newly defined boundary. The powerful thing about boundaries is that when you trust yourself and the people with whom you share your life, your boundaries can be flexible, and you will still feel safe. Boundaries are fixed limits, not walls. They are meant to keep you safe within them, not to prevent other people from coming in.

WALLS

Now that we've explored boundaries, I would like to present a few additional parameters I believe are important to acknowledge. There are boundaries. There are walls. There are comfort zones, and there are traps. We've already covered boundaries. Let's examine mental and emotional walls. In our exploration of self-trust, a wall can be defined as a mental, emotional, or a physical barrier held in place by an individual with serious trust issues that requires people to prove they can be trusted. The good news is that people who erect walls are doing the best they can to take care of themselves. The bad news is walls—more often than not—serve to keep people out, even when we want people to come in.

A wall can be a request, a requirement, a demand, or a prescribed behavior that is always a reaction to an unpleasant past experience that you are trying to avoid in the present. Say, for example, that when you were a child, your parents would always give you the third degree before responding to your requests. When you refused or avoided their questions, you were denied whatever it was that you had asked for. Not only did this make you feel that they did not trust you, it confused you.

As a result of your parents' behavior, you concluded that when people care about you, they want to know and have a right to ask every minute and intimate detail about you, your desires, and intentions. Consequently, today when you care about people, you ask way too many questions, and if there is any sign of resistance or challenge to your third degree, you may conclude that your companions don't care about you or that they are hiding something. The latter is what your parents often accused you of doing, which in some cases was accurate. The point is, requiring people to give you chapter and verse of their every thought, action, belief, and desire then accusing them of dishonesty when they challenge your requests creates a wall that most people are not willing to climb.

Walls keep people out in the same way a comfort zone keeps you in, stuck, and alone. Whether we know it or not and call them by their proper names, we all have boundaries. The caveat here is to know the difference between a boundary that keeps you safe and one that keeps you in a familiar and controllable comfort zone. Being safe and staying comfortable and in control are not the same.

COMFORT ZONES

Even when you have clear boundaries, you can expect to feel uncomfortable at times. Say, for example, when you meet someone new or you are having a new experience, just sharing your boundaries can make you uncomfortable. Until and unless you become willing to face your fear of the unknown, get comfortable with taking risks, become willing to be vulnerable, and perhaps look like a fool in the process, you will stay comfortable and stuck. A spiritual teacher once told me, "As long as you are comfortable, you are not growing." That was all I needed to hear to learn to trust myself enough to move out of what kept me comfortable and in control.

Most comfort zones will prevent you from trying or considering anything new. Until you are courageous enough to venture beyond what is known and familiar, a comfort zone can become what you impose on and require of others, not to keep you safe but, rather, to keep you in control. If you have never flown, taking a short trip may be frightening, but it will move you out of your comfort zone. If you have never tried ethnic food, just be open and willing instead of saying, "I don't like" to what you have never tried. While in some cases comfort zones may promote slow growth, and personal or spiritual development, others stunt your growth, create a false and limited perspective of reality, and rob you of the possibility of discovery and adventure.

The dangerous thing about many comfort zones is that they are created in response to fear and are actually smokescreens in disguise. One such comfort zone heist threatened to undermine a joyful celebration.

We were all delighted to be bridesmaids in the wedding of our friend Mavis, and the stylish bride chose strapless dresses for the wedding party. Our two very "substantial" friends were both concerned about wearing a strapless dress in fear that their "girls" would not have the support they needed unless they wore a bra. Sara, one of the bridesmaids, was scared but willing. Several of us went shopping with her to find just the right strapless bra that would give her the support she needed to be comfortable. Clara, the other bridesmaid, insisted that she needed to wear a shawl. When the bride objected, Clara started picking fights with everyone about everything. Eventually she and the bride had a big argument, and she excused herself from the wedding party. We all understood that the blowup was really about the dress and Clara's inability to risk trying something new, but she insisted that the bride was disrespectful and that we were all brownnosing just to be in a wedding in Hawaii, which she refused to do. Staying comfortable and forcing others to co-sign your requirements and demands can end up keeping you stuck and stunt the development of genuine self-trust.

TRAPS

Creating and having boundaries *is not* a sophisticated means of manipulation. But a trap is just that. Although some people will say they are honoring their boundaries when they make certain requests, have specific requirements, and make demands on others, the truth is that very often they are trying to manipulate or prove they are right about someone or something. The difference between setting a boundary in a healthy way and setting a trap to manipulate is that when we set a boundary, there's an open-ended conclusion. When we set a trap, we predict the outcome. While systems, walls, and comfort zones constitute boundaries, traps are straitjackets.

Let's say, for example, you know that people have done or said something that has upset you, violated a boundary, or betrayed your trust. Rather than confronting (or, as I like to call it, "care-fronting") them directly, you set up a trap to prove that you know what you know. The ensuing scenario outs their behavior. Or, if people care-front you about a troublesome offense, rather than dealing with the situation, you resurrect a transgression from their history or accuse them of being insensitive or find some way to make them wrong in order to avoid dealing with your own stuff. Just be clear that a trap is a trap, and this kind of diversion, distraction, or sneaky low-down way to avoid an issue has nothing to do with your dignity or safety.

ESTABLISHING AND MAINTAINING HEALTHY BOUNDARIES

It is impossible to have a healthy relationship with someone who has no boundaries because boundaries are essential steps in learning how to be a friend, even when you are learning to befriend and trust yourself. It is equally impossible to learn how to trust and become loving to yourself without owning yourself and your rights and responsibilities as a creator of your experiences.

Boundaries can be flexible, changing contours that can and will accommodate the shifts and growth in self and relationships.

Boundaries can also be inflexible, rigid, and overly controlling, thus making it impossible to accommodate growth or change in yourself or relationships.

On your journey to self-trust, I would encourage you to create the limits that serve you best. Even if you start with a less stringent comfort zone or a short wall, make it your intention to create boundaries that make both of these defenses unnecessary. Paul Ferrini, author of *Silence of the Heart: Reflections of the Christ Mind*, wrote this about boundaries: "Somewhere there is a decision that honors you and also honors others. Find that decision. Be committed to finding it."

Boundary Etiquette

Consider the following supportive tips when you are in the process of establishing or maintaining your boundaries:

1. Identify the parameters of your boundaries. Explain the "what and why" of your boundary.

    Example: "In my world, agreements and commitments are important. It's how we know that we can trust each other and that we respect each other's time. So it's important to me that when I make an agreement, I keep the agreement. It's also important to me that you keep your agreement. So let's agree that we will both show up on time."

2. Let others know that the boundary exists, and inform them if and when they have violated it.

    Example: "You know that I am a little crazy about punctuality, so I hope we can agree on a time to meet and that we will all honor our agreement to be on time."

3. Create a consistent means of broadcasting the presence of the boundaries.

    Example: "I'm counting on your support so I don't feel crazy. I want to remind us both that we have an agreement to be on time."

4. Announce to others as to how the boundary operates.
    Example: "You know what, if we want other people to respect us, I believe we have to learn to respect ourselves. We have to honor our word and keep our agreements, if not, people will think they can treat us any old way. Let's really make the effort to show up and start on time. That way we don't have to make excuses and we will be less likely to accept excuses when other people don't honor their word to us. Remember, what you give to yourself you can expect to receive from others."

5. Remain aware of the process/action required to maintain the boundaries.
    Example: "Hey, I am just calling to verify that we are going to meet at such and such time."

6. Inform others of the consequences of violating a boundary.
    Example: "Beloved, it does not make me feel good when I make the effort to honor our agreement to show up on time and you don't do the same. I know that things happen, but I want to offer an amendment to our agreement; after 15 minutes, neither one of us has to wait for the other."

7. Warn others when they have violated, or are about to violate, the lines of a boundary.
    Example: "I am glad you are here, but I remember that we had an agreement to be on time. Since I did not hear from you that you would be delayed, it doesn't feel good that you have either forgotten or ignored our agreement. I want to remind you that after 15 minutes, we need not wait for each other."

8. Immediately activate the consequences when a boundary has been violated.
    Example: Once 15 minutes have passed and your companion hasn't arrived, leave. By doing so you honor

your boundary and keep the agreement. It may be difficult at first, but in the long run it is better than waiting 25 minutes and complaining about it.

9. Be willing to forgive when a boundary is innocently or unknowingly violated.

    Example: There are those times when people forget or perhaps misunderstand the importance of the boundary. This can result in an innocent violation or breach. In these instances, explain the boundary again and be willing to forgive the violation. Trust that you will know when this is the case.

10. Be willing to surrender the relationship for repeated violations of the boundaries.

    Example: It is unfortunate but there are some people who cannot, do not, or will not honor boundaries—their own or those of anyone else. These people have no limits. As such you must be willing to surrender the relationship or risk the repeated heartache and heartbreak of being violated.

11. Determine through practical experience whether or not the boundaries serve the intention for which they were established.

    Example: If the boundary is intended to keep you safe physically or emotionally, you must be able to assess whether or not the request you make is yielding the result you desire. If not, be willing to relax or release the boundary and establish a new one. It is not helpful or productive to make a request or establish a boundary that is not getting the results you desire.

12. When establishing boundaries, always pause to make certain that your efforts are really about what you need to feel safe rather than what you need to maintain control.

Example: It is important to know the distinction between being safe and exercising control. If your boundary is designed simply to give you an upper hand and get people to do what you want, it is not a valid boundary. Since control is the number one human addiction, the caution here is to be mindful of your true motives and intentions.

Timing can be an especially tricky boundary. Some people have a distorted internal clock and have great difficulty arriving on time. Others are simply defiant and disrespectful of time. The key is to discern whether or not the relationship is important to you and whether the behavior being demonstrated actually challenges your personal safety. For example, in the food service industry, workers may be asked to wear a hairnet to protect the customers. It is a safety and sanitary precaution: a boundary with a clear intention. Doctors and nurses have a rigorous procedure they must adhere to before they execute a medical procedure. Clear boundary. Clear intention. It is important that we use boundaries in our lives with the same rigor and purpose. Clear boundaries create a permanent foundation for trust of self and others.

SPEAK FROM YOUR HEART, NOT YOUR HEAD

Your heart or emotional being is the core of your soul-self and the place where the truth of your being resides. Your head or intellect is addicted to the satisfaction of your physical senses—the place that holds all of the programming and conditioning of your childhood and adult experiences and is the throne of the negative ego. Speaking from the heart means sharing the truth of your being, as you know it in the moment. This may change as you acquire new information and experiences; however, not only will your truth set you free, but also it will liberate you from guilt, shame, and fear.

Speaking from your head means regurgitating the stories you have been told and have heard about yourself and your life. It means defaulting to people pleasing and childhood survival tactics that are no longer required or necessary. It also means that you are probably more focused on avoiding a problem with other people than you are with honoring or taking care of yourself. The latter is a function of bad behavior!

Speaking from your heart is a wildly bold and courageous act. In so doing, you run the risk of meeting with disagreement, subjecting yourself to criticism and judgment, and upsetting someone else's needs and expectations. This may not always be the case, yet the chances are more likely than not that these things can and will happen. Your job is to remember that *you will be okay* if people cannot see, cannot accept, or cannot agree with what is true for you. Speaking from your heart and sharing your truth is the way you take a stand for yourself, within yourself. This is a major step toward reminding you that you can be trusted with your own well-being.

There is one small caveat I feel obliged to share about speaking from your heart. It is what is called a psychological, spiritual, or heart bypass, i.e., the way to go around something rather than deal with it head-on. Using so-called personal development or spiritual principles to discount others or to avoid taking full responsibility for your behavior is a dishonest bypass.

Here is an example of how a bypass can play out in real life. Let's say your best friend shares with you that she had a negative experience about something you said or did and she wants you to make amends or a correction. Deep in your heart you see or understand her point, but the negative ego steps in and tells you she is criticizing and judging you. Rather than acknowledging the validity of what is being offered and sharing authentically and honestly how it makes you feel, you default to a sense of shame, guilt, or anger.

Rather than acknowledge what you are feeling, you dismiss or deny what your friend has said, become fixated on "the way" she said it, offer an excuse and perhaps lay blame on her or someone else, or attack her past actions or current behavior. All of the above are forms of bad behavior that have nothing to do with the truth. They are also all forms of a dishonest bypass, an attempt to save face because you got called out. This is clearly unnecessary and inappropriate behavior designed to minimize a blow to the negative ego, look good, and survive.

A first self-trust-building step would be to share from your heart (not your head!) how you feel about what your friend has offered and the way she offered it. The next self-trust-building step would be to acknowledge the validity of what she has offered and to share that while it may not be true for you and your intentions, you appreciate or understand how she feels. The final step would be to ask a simple question: How can I make it better now? The lessons in these three steps can propel you a long way down the path of developing self-trust. They are important steps, so please underline them.

Steps for Developing Self-Trust

Lesson #1: Standing in your truth. You must learn that you can stand in the face of judgment, criticism, correction, or rejection without falling apart. Learning to trust yourself means accepting that (a) You will make mistakes, and (b) When you do or even when you do not make a mistake, everyone is not going to agree with how you do what you do; and you will be okay.

Lesson #2: Speaking your truth. Speaking from your heart means telling the whole truth about everything, to everyone, about the experience that you have in the moment. Speaking your truth does not mean that someone else's truth must be negated if it is different. This is a good place to consider a "what if." What if you feel the other person is totally and completely off base? What if what she has said or experienced has absolutely nothing to do with you? *It matters not!* When you are learning to trust you, it is imperative that in the face of a challenge, you default to the belief that what someone is offering is the truth as she knows it or feels it in the moment—even when it makes no sense to you. Why? Because this is exactly what you are doing, sharing your truth.

Lesson #3: Being courageously vulnerable. Speaking from your heart means being willing to be vulnerable. We have already covered the importance of vulnerability on the journey toward developing self-trust. While the challenge to your speaking, actions, or intentions may make you feel vulnerable and bad, you can feel bad and recover if and when you tell the truth. If your desire is really to trust who you are when you are interacting with others, you simply must learn how to be vulnerable and be courageous enough to stand in your vulnerability.

SPEAK YOUR FEELINGS WITHOUT ATTACK

Very often when people share their experience of us, they do so in a way that feels cold, distant, or just plain old mean. It would be wonderful if we all knew how to share what we need to say layered with compassion and understanding. Often, however, this is not the case. Instead, when it comes to conveying what could be perceived as a negative message, most people will do one of two things: (1) They will not say anything out loud but will instead demonstrate through their behavior that you have somehow caused them displeasure, upset, or anger, or (2) They will blurt out their retribution for your perceived transgression in a way that pierces your heart.

The first example, "punishing silence," is actually an act of violence. It is violent to withhold information that is required to keep peace in any given situation. In response and in an attempt to restore peace, you will either question your friend, only to get no response, or you will overcompensate with new behaviors and dishonor yourself in the process. In the second scenario, when the information she is blurting out hits your energy field, you will feel you *must* defend yourself against her attack. This means you will respond to her attack with a counterattack such as name-calling, swearing, or digging into your history book and pulling out facts about her tarnished past, whether or not they relate to the issue at hand. Again, this is all bad behavior!

In both of the scenarios outlined above, you have a divine opportunity to build your self-trust muscle by sharing compassionately how you feel about what your friend is or is not doing and saying or not doing and saying. The lesson here is to do so without any expectation that she will change a single thing! This is your journey. You are learning to trust yourself, and it has nothing to do with how someone else chooses to respond or not respond. If you expect her to hear you and shift on a dime, you will fall headfirst into the belief that you were wrong to share what you were feeling. Sharing your feelings without attacking someone who is behaving badly requires that you take a deep breath and share information. That's it.

Consider the following scenario: You and some friends are planning a trip or an outing. As a result of the ongoing conversations, you begin to get the feeling that your friend Sybil doesn't really want to go or that she has an issue with the plans you are making. Rather than speak these feelings into the trip space, you continue on as if what you are feeling has no meaning or value.

Two days before your scheduled departure, you ask Sybil a simple question about the trip. Does she have the address of the spa? Or has she confirmed your car reservation? You ask some detail that you have no recollection of having asked her before.

In response to your concern, Sybil yells at you: "Why do you keep asking me that! I told you I have done everything to make your trip go well. Why don't you just take care of what you need to take care of and stop bugging me?" The harsh words send a dagger straight into the tenderest spot of your heart. Confused and hurt, you shoot back, "I was just asking! Why do you have an attitude? And, what do you mean 'my trip'? We planned this together. If you didn't want to go, you should have said something before now. I knew you didn't want to go, and now that I've spent all of this money, you're making me the bad guy when it's your passive aggressive mess . . . You always do this! That's why I hate to do anything with you!" Of course, you know how the rest of the conversation or nonconversation will go, and this exchange will guarantee a bad start for the trip, if you go at all.

The lesson here is that you did not recognize and share your feelings when you first felt them. Perhaps you did not want to know the truth. Perhaps you didn't trust your feelings and didn't want to project them onto Sybil. Or maybe you knew that your feeling was accurate and you wanted to go so badly you didn't care what Sybil really felt, so you pushed ahead, hoping for the best. In any case, when you first felt that something was off kilter, you failed to address it. As time passed, a simple inquiry escalated into an attack/counterattack scenario.

On the journey to self-trust, not only must you trust your feelings, you must share them as soon as you feel them, and you must do so without attacking the other person. In the midst of the planning, a conscious conversation would need to look something like this: "Sybil, let me share with you what I'm feeling right now, and I take full responsibility because I understand that it may have nothing to do with you. The more we talk about the trip, the more it feels to me that you're not really satisfied or committed to this vacation plan. Is that true?"

Notice that you're taking full responsibility for what you feel, and you're asking a question rather than making an assumption or attacking her behavior. If you're really feeling courageous and really trusting yourself, you might add: "I want this to be a good experience for both of us, so please let me know what feels right for you."

When you put the last piece of conversation on the table, remember you must be prepared for whatever comes up and be willing to share how you feel about it again, without attacking her. And, if no matter what you say or how you say it, you feel she is attacking you, share that observation and request a behavior change.

Sharing with people what they do and how you feel about it is of no value without a clear unmistakable "ask," that is, a request for a behavior change. Mothers and wives have a long history of complaining about clothes being left on the floor, dishes being left in the sink, and assorted items that make up a laundry list of other mindless behavior. Screaming and complaining about these annoyances has done little to change things over the years. The underbelly of mom's angry response could be how it makes her feel when she's trying to keep things neat and orderly and the people she lives with don't seem to care.

An alternative approach to the ones that leave everyone frustrated is to couple a request for a behavior change with a clear context. For example, "Brian, I know you don't see me as your maid or slave, so I am asking that you make every effort to pick up and clean up after yourself—that way our wires don't get crossed." Or possibly, "When you leave dishes in the sink or your clothes on the floor, it makes me feel like I'm losing the battle to keep our home comfortable and in order. I need your support and ask that you take ten minutes to clean up after yourself when you start or finish a new task." Learning to trust yourself also means knowing you can make requests and expect that they will be honored.

BE TRANSPARENT

Vagueness is one way to avoid unpleasant and frightening people, things, and situations. Withholding is an act of violence, manipulation, and control. You will not learn and cannot practice self-trust when you avoid what feels unpleasant, when you act violently, or when you attempt to manipulate and control situations and/or people. Each of these behaviors is potentially self-destructive and will eventually eat away at your personal integrity.

When you have an opportunity to be vague rather than to share the truth of your heart, know that the negative ego is leading you down a dangerous path. When you are tempted to withhold information to spare someone's feelings or to get what you want by manipulating him or controlling the situation, know that you are sabotaging yourself and putting your relationship in jeopardy.

In all situations, under all circumstances, with all people, the most trustworthy posture is to offer all pertinent information as a demonstration that you have nothing to hide. It's a step toward transparency. It establishes and maintains clarity. The more transparent you are, the easier it will be to sense and feel what you are dealing with. Being vague and withholding will only muddy the waters for everyone. When you cannot see and do not know what you are facing, then trusting yourself, the situation, or the individuals involved is hard. Full transparency means you cannot omit small and/or important details. This is simply another way of being vague or manipulating people and situations in order to maintain control.

If fear is an issue that motivates you to be vague, get it handled within yourself. Doing what is required to develop self-trust is a powerful, productive, and positive way to handle ongoing or nagging fears. In many instances, fear is simply a warning sign. It is a signal that you need to be mindful, tread lightly, and be clear about your intentions and the importance of what you are about to undertake. Most things we fear exist only in the mind.

TRUTH, HONESTY, AND TRUST

One way to challenge and dismantle fear is to announce it. In your quest to be transparent, to share information, and to know that you can be trusted, let people know: "I am afraid of X, but I am willing to walk through it. I am asking you to please be sensitive to where I am right now." You cannot be any more transparent than this on the journey to self-trust. This means you can share information and the details of that information in a way that supports you and gives others the opportunity to support you as well.

One reason it is important not to omit details is because it can become very difficult to keep up with the pieces you left out. When this happens, people can and will begin to recognize the contradictions in your stories and will begin to question your trustworthiness. They may even consider you to be a fraud or a liar. It is always best to tell the whole truth without omitting what you may consider to be small details. When you endeavor to tell people what they need and want to know, they will come to trust you because you offer reliable information. There is nothing more damaging to self-value, self-worth, self-esteem, self-confidence, personal integrity, and the development of self-trust than being dishonest.

Consider this example from my personal files. I went shopping to buy some socks because they were on sale. I didn't need the socks. I wanted the socks. This is important because often we do not tell the truth about what we need and want. When we don't tell the truth about what we need, chances are we don't get it. A disowned need drives and motivates behavior from a place of fear or deprivation. And in this state, when your sense of well-being is threatened, you will think, say, and do all manner of things to get what you think you need. This raises all sorts of survival instincts that in turn can lead to bad behavior.

In my case, I did not need the socks, I merely wanted them. But I did need my integrity. On the way to the store to purchase the infamous socks, I decided that I would return another item. This meant I was carrying a shopping bag. While looking for the socks, I bumped into the shelves and knocked a pair of socks into my shopping bag. When I saw what I had done, I told myself I would account for that pair in the number that I was purchasing and remove them from the bag when I got to the counter. I continued shop, picking up socks, panty hose, and even a lovely nightgown on sale.

After paying for my purchases, I went to another level of the store to return the item I had brought into the store in the shopping bag. It was then that I noticed the fallen pair of socks lying in the bottom of the bag. Much to my shock, I heard a voice in my head say, *It's okay, leave them there. Look how much you have already spent.* Before I could stop myself, I let out an ear-piercing scream that sent the cashier and several customers scrambling for cover. Without a word to them, I ran away from the counter, took the escalator steps two at a time, and ran back to the counter where I had purchased the socks and other stuff. I hate to say that I was literally screaming, *"No!"* the entire way.

The cashier and all of the customers heard me before they saw me. When I got to the counter, I explained that a pair of socks had fallen into my bag. People were gathering around the counter to stare at me, which confused the cashier. I had to repeat myself twice before she said, "How many pairs do you have?" I said, "Seven, but I paid for only six." Still dazed, she reviewed the receipt I had shoved into her face and she said, "How many pairs do you want?" Realizing that I was a very public person creating a very public scene, I took a deep breath and explained again what had occurred, telling her I wanted to pay for the extra pair. As the onlookers drifted away, we completed our transaction; I paid another $6.50 for the extra pair of socks, and the cashier thanked me for my honesty.

Why did I have such an intense reaction to this experience? As a child I learned to lie about everything to everyone. I lied about my feelings, my needs, and my wants. I lied about being okay with less than, and I lied about having more than I was expected to have. I lied about what I knew and what I did not know. I lied to stay safe, to belong, and to get ahead. As a child, being dishonest with myself and with others was the only way I could survive the craziment of my environment. While I am not proud of it, I am willing to admit that I carried the energy of self-deception, emotional dishonesty, and lying into my adult experience.

My reaction to seeing the socks in my bag was fear. When I heard those words in my head, I was afraid that the negative ego that I believed I had put to rest was coming alive again. My response? *Run for your life!* If after all of the praying, meditating, and rubbing of crystals on my head, that "enemy" would dare challenge me for a pair of socks, nothing and nobody was safe! In that moment, in a crowded department store, I had retriggered an old trauma that suddenly felt real. And I had to summon every fiber of my being to let myself know that I could be trusted!

When I began the life-transforming work required to heal and learn and grow—to reestablish my value, worth, and esteem—I had to teach myself the process of honesty. I learned that being honest was not the same as knowing and telling the truth. I had to learn the Creator's definition of honesty, and I had to teach myself the spiritual imperative of being honest with others and myself at all times, in all situations, under all circumstances.

Truth is a universal principle. It is based on your awareness that universal principles exist. Universal truth is ever present and consistent through the universe of life; however, you may not be, or in most cases cannot be, fully aware of the totality of all that is true. What you can do is share the truth as you know it to be: as a function of your awareness, belief, knowledge, and experience in any given moment. This does not alter the universal truth. What it does is it keeps you in alignment with what you know. Now here's the kicker: *You can know the truth and still be dishonest.*

Honesty is determined by your values, by what really matters to you, and by your willingness to stand for those values when no one is looking. Being honest about what you know, need, or feel does not mean you negate what is true to others. They have had a different experience. They may have developed different survival skills than you developed. Honesty is a different animal. Honesty is about *your* values, worth, and esteem. It unfolds in response to *your* level of awareness, *your* experience, and *your* willingness to honor that which you believe yourself to be, moment by moment. The great thing about honesty is that when you stand in it, you give other people permission to do the same in your presence.

If you are going to trust yourself, you must be honest and honorable at all times, in all situations, under all circumstances. No matter where you travel on the road of life, trust and truth are what you must learn. Trust and truth are what you must practice. Trust and truth are what you must do.

MASTERING THE 4 ESSENTIAL TRUSTS

Trust in Self

Trust in God

Trust in Others

Trust in Life

VILLA NOVA

When things go awry, terribly awry, in your life, rebuilding confidence and trust takes time. Figuring out how you have contributed to the experience you are having takes time, and realizing that God has not abandoned you and that you are not being punished also takes time. When hard times hit, trust and faith seem to be the first things to abandon ship. When you find yourself in a situation you never thought you would face, questioning God's purpose and presence can be the key that opens a new door or the dark, desperate place in which you can get stuck. This is a scenario I know well. It is the way I learned to trust in God with my entire mind, my heart, and my soul—right down to my pinkie toe.

Walking into the bankruptcy court to surrender everything I owned was a deeply dark and desperate day for me. It was also a most necessary action. I was too numb to feel any of the shame or embarrassment that was lurking beneath the surface of my well-put-together face. In fact, I was quite grateful that I was about to end my regular desperate pleas to the bank to wait for yet another late payment for my mortgage or car note. I was grateful that I would no longer need to dread another first-of-the-month avalanche of demands for payment. Now that I was divorced, unemployed, and struggling to determine the next appropriate steps for my life, I really didn't need the pressure of trying to avoid or hide from anyone, even the IRS. Yes, it would be a welcome relief to have my debts declared null and void. However, I still faced a very difficult challenge: I would have no place to live.

Throughout my life I've learned to trust that there will always be a sister woman on hand to help me when I really need it. I trust that experience because it has been a powerful reality in my life. Perhaps that's because I have been that friend for so many other women. Or perhaps it's because I really do understand and know that the universe is a very fair and just place. What you put out really does come back to you from known and unknown places.

Just three days before I was scheduled to turn over the keys to my house, that sister woman called. She had found me a place. When could I come to see it? It was small, much smaller than the house I was giving up. It was clean. Clean is a good thing. It was affordable, but of course, in my current state, that would be subject to interpretation. Numbness and relief blinded me to the details of the small house that was to become my new home. Good thing! Had I really been paying attention, my ego would have probably led me to reject it. As I sat counting what I had and what I needed to move in, working to control my panic, it never dawned on me to trust in God to provide. Considering where I had risen to in my life and where I was now sitting, trust was way down on the priorities list that day. Stress, worry, and fear were my fallback positions until I got the call.

"Hey, Mama." It was Almasi, my right-hand sister friend who had walked many a country mile of difficulty with me.

"Hey! How you is?" I could not let her know I was a hot worried mess. Almasi is my dear sister friend who worries when I worry and who feels what I feel. We went through our daily checklist of what needed to be done and how to get it done to keep our programs afloat. As we were ending the conversation, she casually updated me: "I have a check for you that I'm going to put in your account."

"A check from whom?"

"It's a tithe from someone, but they want to remain anonymous. Do you want it in your personal account?"

"Absolutely! How much is it?"

"Ten thousand dollars, and don't ask me who sent it."

After what seemed like an hour of silence, she spoke again: "Hello? Are you there?"

It is hard to describe what happens when you feel the presence of God take hold of you. It is both peaceful and jarring. It is both a relief and a shock. It makes you cold and warm. One thing is for sure, when you feel it, whether you can describe it or not, you know exactly what it is, and you are grateful. I thought I was whispering, but I must have been yelling. Or maybe I was whispering, because I heard Almasi say, "Are you okay? Where are you?"

I was trying desperately to tell her the story about the new house. I was trying to express the depth of my gratitude.

I thought I was saying, *"Thank you, God!"* I have no clue what was actually coming out of my mouth, nor did I care. A few days later I paid three months' rent and a month's security deposit. When I picked up the keys and saw the house for the first time, all I could say was, "Oh my God! What the hell was I thinking?" It was clear that the wisdom and presence of God had blinded me to the realities of my new home just to get me in it. What a blessing!

With the aid of a very skilled contractor, referred by another sister friend, a few weeks of hard work, and the willingness to begin again, I moved into a very lovely "cottage," the home that would be my safe haven for the next eight and a half years. I knew enough to recognize that when you are growing, healing, and learning to trust God at a deeper level, there are situations and circumstances that you must encounter and grow through.

When you are rebuilding your life while learning to trust yourself, you must build from the inside out. When you are healing your soul and learning to trust the lessons you are growing through, you must build from a place of contentment rather than need. When you are building or rebuilding trust in God, you must build from a place of desire rather than obligation or duty or fear. When your life falls apart, there are tiny fragments of debris that must be examined and understood. Within each of the fragments of debris there is a piece of you that must be healed and a piece of God that must be acknowledged. This process of healing, growing, learning, recognizing, and acknowledging cannot be rushed or underestimated. It is a necessary process that affords you an opportunity not just for self-recognition but also for God recognition. In learning to trust God, you must also learn to recognize the nature of God and how God works within you, as you, and on your behalf. I admit that eight years is a very long learning process; however, I now know that there was much that I still needed to learn about trusting God and myself.

I have always said that a major portion of my life took place when I was not "at home." Although I was in my body, I was not present with my thoughts, my feelings, or the places within my consciousness that were in shambles. Living in my cottage helped me to get in touch with those aspects of my life that I had neglected along the way of living. I learned how to do so much more with less and to have fun in the process. I learned the vital importance of a daily spiritual practice and the joy that comes from developing an intimate relationship with God. I learned that I really do love to cook, and that music had always been my healing balm. I learned that I could live simply without complaining, and that no matter what else was going on in my life, I could always do something good for someone else. I learned to listen within and hear without fear. I learned to speak up for myself without defending my position. Most of all, I learned that when we miss steps along the path of life, we will stumble, but stumbling doesn't always mean we will or must fall. At times, stumbling means we can move ahead a little bit faster.

In the middle of year six in the cottage, my life blew up again. This time, though, it was a very welcome blowing up. A call from

HARPO, a powerful reunion show with Oprah, several appearances on *Oprah's Lifeclass,* and the beginning of my new show on OWN *Iyanla: Fix My Life.* It never dawned on me that my house was too small for me to do the things that were being placed before me.

I never thought to ask if someone living the life that was unfolding before me should move into a more comfortable home. I never even considered that I could have more closets and more space. I was content. I was at peace . . . or so I thought. The truth that I came to recognize was that I had never fully resolved the shame and embarrassment of filing for bankruptcy. I had never resolved the "money stories" or the pathology of poverty I had inherited from my parents. Recognizing how these things were operating in my life unearthed a deeper, more disturbing truth: I did not believe I deserved more, I was unworthy of having more, and I could not accept my "bigness" in the world.

There is no greater battle in life than the battle between the parts of you that want to be healed and the parts of you that are comfortable and content remaining broken. This is a battle that takes you deeper than complacency into defiance of your God-given authentic identity. This is a battle between the self-made negative ego—the deceptive intelligence that is hell-bent on punishing you for every poor choice, bad decision, and stumble or fall that you have experienced in your life—and the divine and holy essence of who you are that engenders your freedom from the past. It is a holy war that rages between the habitual unnatural thinking that dares you not to trust yourself or God and the call of the Holy Spirit that reminds you that you must always trust where you are and what you are learning. To learn is to heal, and when you learn something, you know it. When you know something, it changes your behavior.

Not until we know we can trust God and the process of life will we recognize and change those aspects of our behavior that are grounded in shame, guilt, doubt, and fear. Not until we learn and know and believe wholeheartedly that God does not punish us for our mistakes can we reassess and change the behaviors that feel like the rewards and/or punishments for what we have done or not done. Only when we truly learn that God is trustworthy can we recognize that where we are and who we are serves our purpose and God's purposes for us.

Somewhere between my big toes and my pinkie toes, I still believed that I deserved to be punished. For what, I could not tell you. In my body, perhaps between my earlobe and my neck, there was a secret belief that I could never, would never, deserve to have more than I had. And since I had learned to live contently in the cottage, there was no need for me even to want more.

Deep in the pit of my belly, there was feeling and a belief that if I did even one thing to change the current status of my life, I would experience again the pain of betrayal and abandonment that I had encountered in the past. In addition, some part of me was holding on to the fear that if I were to have more, something horrible would happen and I would lose it all again. Rather than go through that, I was stuck in the pit of *not allowing myself* to want anything and of being content with where I was despite the inner voice that was telling me: "*It is time to move.*"

There is absolutely nothing wrong with living a simple life, as long as that life and the environment in which it exists fits your needs. Mine did not. There is no spiritual law or physical-world law that requires you to have a big house or a fancy car simply because you can afford it. In fact, many people with great means live humbly and simply because they choose to do so. That was not my case. I needed more closet space so I could find what I needed without a 15-minute search. I needed a larger kitchen if only to accommodate holiday dinners for the family. I needed more space for the activities that had become an integral part of my growing life. I simply did not trust that I deserved it after having filed for bankruptcy years before. Nor did I trust that God would *let me have it* because of the pathology of my family history. However, God doesn't *let us* have anything, nor does God keep us from having what we earnestly desire. We create our reality with our thoughts and subsequent behaviors as a reflection of what we believe and whether or not we trust.

Year seven in the cottage began with high ratings for *Fix My Life* and the incessant whisper: *"You have got to move!"*

But I loved my house and the land it was on. I loved the location. I loved the fact that my grandchildren could play in the backyard or on the front lawn safely.

"Yes, but it is time for you to move."

I can't afford to move.

"Yes, you can."

I am living comfortably. I am content.

"Is that true?"

It was true that I was content. It was not true that I was comfortable. I was very uncomfortable with the world's response to the bankruptcy notation on my credit report. I had had a long conversation with Suze Orman, and she had told me exactly what I needed to do to overcome the blemish on my credit report. Although I had followed her instructions to the letter, I was still uncomfortable with the unavoidable question: "How old is your bankruptcy?" That question had come up the last two times I had applied for an apartment. I did not want to leave the cottage for an apartment, yet I was convinced it was my only option. It wasn't until a Realtor suggested that I rent a house that I began to entertain a wider range of possibilities. When I did, it led me on a search that lasted for almost two years before I recognized that I was on the wrong path, chasing the wrong rabbit.

Once we make up our minds that something is true, it is difficult to convince ourselves that our thinking might not be accurate. We really do trust our negative thoughts and fight with ourselves to believe the more positive ones. This, again, is the work of the deceptive intelligence of the negative ego. This is another aspect of the internal battle of learning to trust yourself and God in the process of growing, healing, and learning. While your soul needs very little evidence that God is real and that life can be trusted, the ego is forever providing you with evidence that the opposite is as true or truer.

While "How old is your bankruptcy?" is a natural question for people who want to know if you can be trusted to pay them on time, my ego decided the bankruptcy was the reason I would not, could not, get an apartment. Perhaps the real reason I did not get the apartments I applied for, though, was because I didn't really want them. I wanted a house, but at the same time I did not trust I could have one. Or perhaps, I did not get an apartment and could not find a house to rent because God had a bigger idea for me than I had for myself. Perhaps my learning was changing and my blessings were about to unfold, and I simply did not believe it was possible. Of course, none of this even entered my conscious mind until the day I saw Villa Nova.

I had just seen yet another house that was in the right location but did not have everything I wanted and needed. If I was going to move into a house, it had to be the right house. I had everything outlined and pictured in my vision book, and I was not going to budge until I found exactly what I wanted at the right price. I am not sure how the listing came to me, but when I read three descriptions of houses that day, I felt a quickening in my spirit. I noticed that two of the houses were in my immediate neighborhood. One was a rental property; the other was a lease to purchase.

When I could not reach my Realtor, I wrote down the address of the lease property and decided to do a drive-by. Perhaps if I leased the property for a year, I could prove to the owners that I was trustworthy enough to make the purchase. I took my godson Michael with me for company and support. As we pulled into the driveway, I started to feel both nauseated and light-headed. I loved the neighborhood and what I could see of the backyard. As I stepped out of the car do to a further investigation, I knew I had come home. This was my house, and I would somehow buy, not rent it.

The house was tucked away on a one-way street, in a quiet little community; the front door was not visible from the main road. A family of five deer met me as I inched up the driveway to the three-car garage. From the edge of the driveway I held my breath as I looked out over the spacious, semi-sprawling backyard. *This is my house!* Mindful that I was not accompanied by a Realtor and cautious because I had no business being on the property, I walked up the steps to the wraparound deck. Clearly the people who lived here had forgotten that a deck, like a house, needed to be cared for and tended. As the family of deer galloped across the backyard, I became fixated on the double glass doors that led into the kitchen. Without thinking about it, I tugged on one of the doors. It was open! Like a thief, I peered over both shoulders to make sure no one was looking, not realizing that no one could see me over the trees and bushes. Still, I slammed the door shut and ran back to the car, where my godson was trying to open the middle garage door.

In a whisper I asked, "What are you doing?"

"It's empty. I wanted to see if the door would open."

"The doors on the deck are open. Come on."

My heart was racing now. We bumped into each other trying to run up the deck stairs. Without a moment's hesitation, Michael flung the glass doors open and stepped into the disheveled kitchen. I was peering over the deck, looking for deer and people but most of all for the police, when I heard him say, "Oh my God!"

Not sure if he was looking at a dead body, a scampering rat, or something spectacular, I followed his voice into the empty house. My immediate response was also, "Oh my God!" This was, in fact, my house; I knew it with every fiber of my being. This knowing took my heart from a mild racing to a full-on gallop.

With complete knowledge that I had no business doing it, I walked through every room of the house. In my mind's eye, I painted every wall and put furniture in every room. By the time we did our second walk-through, I knew exactly what needed to go and what needed to be changed. I called the Realtor as soon as we got back into the car. I told her that I wanted to lease the house and gave her the address.

"That house isn't for lease. It's a foreclosure, so it's for sale."

At first my heart sank as I thought to myself: *If I cannot rent an apartment, there is no way I can purchase a house—not yet. I'll need more time.* Then, as if my heart was speaking to me, I heard, *"Trust. Just trust."*

The Realtor continued: "If you want to prequalify for a loan, we need to put in the application soon, because there are already two offers on the property."

"What do I need to do to prequalify?"

"Just fill out the application. I'll e-mail it to you now."

My godson asked, "What are you going to do?"

"I am going to buy this house." I didn't say another word until we arrived back at the cottage.

God—Infinite Intelligence, your Higher Mind, your authentic Self—speaks to you, within you, in your own voice. In essence, trusting God means trusting the deeper essence of who you are. The challenge many of us face is that we are taught to worship an external God: an identity or being that exists somewhere outside of ourselves. God, as many of us have been are taught, is something that we cannot see or touch. In response to this teaching, most of us come to believe that we cannot hear God, and that those who do hear God are special people. *What I have discovered is that the more I trust myself, the more I hear God.* I know the feeling that the presence of God generates in my body. I know the stillness that comes over me when the voice of God is speaking. I know the peace and calm that I feel when I hear that voice. And I also know the results that come when I am obedient and act on what He/She tells me.

Within 24 hours I had prequalified for $200,000 more than I needed to purchase the house. The Realtor had managed to discover the exact amount of the two standing offers and told me how much I needed to offer to secure the deal. I offered that exact amount. After making the offer, I drove back to the house again, just to make sure that it was still there and that I still wanted it.

This time I took my son with me. We walked up onto the deck, just as I had done before. This time, however, the door would not open. It was locked. Peering through the window, I could see that everything looked the same. My son tried every door and window, but we could not gain access. Didn't matter. I knew this was my house. My fear was whether or not my faith would sustain me as I walked through the process of purchasing it.

Anyone who has purchased a home knows that it can be a mind-boggling, gut-wrenching experience. The number of questions you are asked, the amount of information you must provide, and the endless telephone calls come fast and furiously. At the same time, there is this dark cloud looming over whether or not your offer will be accepted, whether or not your credit score is good enough, whether or not you will get a loan with a good interest rate, whether or not this is actually the house you want. In my case, all of these thoughts and the associated emotions took a second seat to the guilt and shame I had about having already lost a home in bankruptcy court. "Trust, just trust," became my moment-by-moment mantra; it kept me focused on the outcome rather than the process. Then the telephone call came. It was my son Damon.

"Ma, I went by that house today, and there were some people in there."

"So?"

"Well, the door was open, so I went in and told them I was waiting for my Realtor. I looked around. It needs some work, but it's really nice."

"Yes, I know."

"But the people who were there had a contractor. He was telling them about all the things that needed to be done and was giving them prices. The lady was saying how horrible everything was and that she was going to report it to the seller."

Before I could panic, my heart spoke again: *"Trust in the Lord with all of your mind, all of your heart and all of your soul. Lean not to your own understanding."*

"It's okay, Damon. I don't care what anybody says; that is my house."

As I said it, I could feel the tremors of fear, shame, and guilt rising up from the souls of my feet. So you know what I did? I stomped my feet until they were numb.

The Realtor's voice message was short: "Congratulations. Your offer was accepted. Call me so we can begin the loan application process." My hands immediately started to tremble, and I could hear my heart pounding in my ears. I wanted to cry. I needed to pee. Instead, I drove back around to the house and stood in the front yard. Staring at the front door, I asked aloud, "Who are you?" I believe everything has a name. I also believe that when you call a thing by its name, it will respond to you. It was as if I were seeing the house for the first time. Walking through the yard, I could practically feel it breathing. It was a heavy, labored energy. By the time I found myself in the backyard, I spoke the words again: "Who are you?"

What I heard in response shocked me: "Hello, can I help you?"

It was the next-door neighbor. He had seen me on the property and came over to make sure I wasn't up to no good.

"Hello. I'm going to be your new neighbor. I just purchased this house." It was more an affirmation than a declaration of truth.

"Well, it's been empty a long time. Have you been inside?"

"Yes, and I know it needs a lot of work."

My new neighbor introduced himself and told me he had purchased his house about 15 months earlier. He had looked at my house but thought they were asking too much for it based on its condition. We chatted a bit longer about the neighborhood, the previous tenants, and everything he knew about the folks in the area. I thanked him and told him I probably wouldn't be moving in until the fall. He wished me good luck and continued on his way. I walked back to the front door as if I was about to enter the house, and that's when I heard the name: Villa Nova. A new vision.

My loan officer was an absolute angel. He was so calm and peaceful. Whenever he needed another piece of paper or verification of something, he would send me an e-mail that always began with, "Don't worry, everything is going smoothly. I just need you to . . ." Although his calm nature had only a minimal effect on my anxiety level, I really appreciated his manner. As we came closer to the closing date, and his requests became more frequent and my anxiety grew more severe, my thoughts became more negative and my greatest fear descended upon me. The house appraised at $95,000 less than the asking price. That should have been good news; however, the seller was refusing to lower the price. If I wanted the house, I would need to put up the cash to make up the difference, because I could not get a loan for more than the appraised value. Damn!

When you are learning to trust yourself and trust God, you must use spiritual tools to support yourself. Trust is not something you can convince yourself you have, nor is it an intellectual process. Trust is both a spiritual tool and a spiritual process, which means you must have a spiritual foundation and an approach to activate the energy of trust in your heart and mind. Unfortunately, when trust is challenged, much of what you believe and know about your spiritual foundation takes a backseat to the ruthlessness of the negative ego.

For hours, I could not hear myself think over the racing of my heart. I knew enough to keep my mouth shut, to refuse to voice even one word of doubt, but my mind was running amuck. *"Lean not on your own understanding. Trust, just trust. All things are working together for good."* None of what I tried to feed myself was helping, so I did what most normal human beings do when they hit the wall of their humanness. I cried, loud and long.

A good cry is a cleansing experience. It helps you think clearly and it washes away the seeds of doubt and fear. With a renewed sense of release and relief, I leaned into my spiritual practice; I prayed and then I listened. Two telephone calls later, I made a counteroffer to the seller. The response came in two days. They lowered the cash demand by $50,000, and they were willing to leave the house on the market for six months in the hopes that the appraisal price would rise. Two more telephone calls, and I had a plan to get the cash I would need to proceed to closing. The inspection revealed a budding termite problem. I took that back to the seller. There were also some issues with the heating system. Once again, back to the seller I went. There was a problem with the septic system. Oh, Mr. Seller!

For everything I put back in the seller's lap, they would take something else off the table. Gone was the $30,000 incentive to repair the kitchen. No more help with the closing costs. So much time passed since I submitted the original loan application, everything I had given to the loan officer had to be resubmitted. By the time he asked me for yet another bank statement, five months had passed, and I needed to put $60,000 cash on the table. Every day, I talked to Villa Nova. I told her to hang in there. I promised that I would take good care of her. I would thank God every morning that the deal was done. Then the loan officer asked me for a quarterly tax statement, and I all but lost my mind!

In his normal, gentle voice I could barely hear him when he said, "Iyanla, this deal is done. I promise this is the last thing you will need before Thursday."

"Thursday? What's Thursday?"

"You're closing on Thursday. I promise you, this is the last thing."

Somehow, in the process of faxing, e-mailing, praying, and checking my bank account to make sure the money was still there, I had missed the fact that I was actually scheduled to close on the house. I had also missed the fact that you do not receive a closing date until the loan has been approved.

Immediately after I left the closing with the keys in my hand, I called my team of prayer partners. All six of them would meet me at Villa Nova. First, I went in alone. Facing the winding stairway in the foyer I whispered over and over, "Thank you, God. Just thank you." As instructed, they waited 15 minutes before they rang the doorbell, and then I opened the front door of Villa Nova to receive her first guests. Together, we walked through every room and prayed, and then we screamed and laughed and wept. Now we would figure out how I would put together the money to do the renovations so that I could move in and live in my new vision.

Friends are good things to have when you have a new house that needs a great deal of work. Each of my really good friends committed to painting one of the 14 rooms in Villa Nova. One of those friends was a general contractor. His commitment was to bring a group of subcontractors in to give me an estimate for what would be required to bring the house up to standard. The day he was scheduled to come, I was scheduled to shoot a Christmas message for the OWN network. Along with the contractor and the six subcontractors, the film crew and a producer arrived at Villa Nova. Since the house was empty and in pretty dismal shape, I would stand in front of the stairway and give my brief Christmas message to all of the viewers of *Iyanla: Fix My Life*. I put a wreath on the front door, swept the aging carpet, and instructed the cameraperson not to shoot below my waist.

I was in the basement discussing the benefits of tile over hardwood when the producer told me I had a telephone call from OWN.

"Hello." I thought it was my executive producer giving me instructions about the holiday message. I was mistaken.

"Iyanla, it's Oprah."

"Oh my goodness. How are you?"

"Where are you? Are you at the new house?"

"Yeah. I'm picking paint and flooring and trying to figure out what I can do so I can move in."

"Well, you know they have been working on my house for two years, and I am not calling you about a Christmas message. I was thinking about you, and I know what you are going through. I know you will be fixing that house, room by room, for the next five years. So I thought, I want you to have a home that rises to meet you when you come back from doing the incredible work you do on *Fix My Life*.

"I want you to have a sanctuary to rest and enjoy yourself. So I spoke to Nate Burkus, and we are going to fix your house! Nate will be there in a few days, and we are going to do everything that needs to be done to make your home your sanctuary. Merry Christmas! Happy Birthday! Happy Easter, and Happy Groundhog's Day! *We are going to fix your house, Iyanla Vanzant!*"

My speechlessness is well documented because the cameras were rolling for a television special. I sat down on the stairs to avoid fainting. I took off my sweater because I started sweating. My mouth was dry, and my hands were once again trembling. I had done all that I could do and was willing to do more. Trust does not require doing. Trust requires that you simply believe. Trust had gotten me into the house, and now God's favor and grace would handle the renovations. There are moments when you simply do not know what God will do. If you walk through those moments, trusting yourself and God, you will discover what God *can* do.

| # GOD AND GRAVITY

> MAN SAYS . . .
> SHOW ME AND I'LL TRUST YOU.
>
> GOD SAYS . . .
> TRUST ME AND I'LL SHOW YOU.
>
> —*Anonymous*

A man was walking along a narrow path, not paying much attention to where he was going. Suddenly, he slipped over the edge of a cliff. As he was falling, he grabbed a branch growing from the side of the cliff and hung on for dear life. After several moments, he realized that he couldn't hang on for much longer so he cried out for help.

Man: Is anybody up there?

Voice: Yes, I'm here!

Man: Who's that?

Voice: It's God.

Man: God, help me!

Voice: Do you trust me?

Man: I trust you completely.

Voice: Good. Let go of the branch.

Man: What???

Voice: I said, let go of the branch.

Man: [After a long pause] Is anybody else up there?

If you are an average adult human being, I am sure you can relate to this story. How many times have you found yourself dangling on the edge or struggling in a situation where the guidance you receive scares you? How many times have you asked for help, yet when the help shows up, it's not what you expected, or what you wanted? How many times have you received clear instructions from a deep place within your being, from God or Your Higher Self, and failed to be obedient to that guidance in response to fear, doubt, or disbelief? These four human realities—fear, doubt, disbelief, and disobedience—are at the core of our ability or inability to trust God enough to follow the guidance we receive. How each of these dynamics plays out is a reflection of our ability to trust ourselves and a manifestation of our relationship with God.

ME AND GOD

I spent much of my youth being totally angry with God. The times when I wasn't angry, I was totally confused; and the times when I wasn't totally confused, I was afraid. Growing up in the church as I did, I came to know God as an amorphous, external entity. He was big, He was fierce, and He was waiting for me to mess up so that he could swoop down and get me. "Getting me" had to do with making me suffer and taking away anything that I loved. "Getting me" had to do with not approving of me or accepting me because of all the bad, inappropriate, or purely human things that I was prone to do. Somewhere in my life, I grew to understand that God was not too happy with me. That was just fine, because I wasn't too thrilled about Him, either!

My childhood perception of God—that He was everywhere and could see everything—followed me well into adulthood. He saw me steal the candy. He saw me kiss those boys. He knew that I had used four-letter words, had smoked, had drunk alcohol, and had been promiscuous. He knew that I had lied to my boss (killing off my grandmother and assorted other spare relatives), to my children, and to the IRS; and, of course, He knew that I had lied to my mother many, many times. He was really mad at me. For this, and for many other reasons, I was afraid of Him. His anger, I concluded, was evidenced by the ongoing drama and crisis in my life. He let me get pregnant at 14. He allowed me to marry a man who beat me, left me, came back to beat me some more, then cheat on me, only to leave me again. He let me be hungry and homeless. He refused to hire me for that job I really needed. Yes, God and I were rarely on speaking terms, and when we were, He always seemed to be punishing me for something I had done or not done—sometimes I couldn't figure out which.

If God was everywhere and had so much power, didn't he know I was already mad, confused, and afraid? And if He did, why didn't He "strike me dead" like my grandma believed was about to happen at any moment? If God was so lovingly concerned about me, why didn't He help me, stop me, and give me better guidance? Why did God allow bad things to happen to good people? And when bad people try to be good, why do they have to be punished? As a young woman, I wanted answers to these questions: What does it really mean to believe in God? What does it mean to trust God?

Many of us have adopted a concept of God based on what we were taught and what we heard about God as children. In this equation, the three common attributes of God were these: (1) God is male, (2) God lives in a place called heaven, and (3) God is powerful enough to hurt or destroy anyone, at any time. In my mind, God was most definitely a larger-than-life white man, although he looked and behaved like an ordinary person. I picked up most of my beliefs about God in church and from the way my grandmother spoke about Him. In the children's Sunday school, I was taught Bible stories that gave me small glimpses into God's capacity to make certain things happen for certain people.

I learned that good people got good things from God, while the not-so-good people got burned, scourged, punished, or destroyed. The good people were those who followed God's "law." The not-so-good people were those who broke God's law. To the mind of a child, not only was this frightening, it was difficult to understand. How is a child supposed to be "good" all of the time and to know what "good" really means to God when she cannot read or fully comprehend the Good Book? The only way to learn what to do and not to do was to rely on the adults, who obviously knew more and had a much better understanding of God.

My grandmother was my God liaison on earth. She seemed to know all there was to know about God because she used His name to punctuate almost every sentence she spoke: "I swear to God!" "God knows . . ." "Only God can . . ." "You better do this before God . . ." or "Stop that before God . . ."

Grandma continually told me that that God was everywhere; that He could do anything He wanted whenever He wanted; and, most importantly, that her God did not like me because *I* was bad.

Then there was my friend Delilah, who was Catholic. According to her, unless you covered your head in church and ate fish every Friday, you would go to hell. When I shared this information with my grandma, she told me that Delilah's God was not the same God we worshipped because Catholics do not read the Bible. "Catholics are like the Jews and do not consider the New Testament," Grandma intoned. "They got it all wrong." She said that all we could do was hope they got it right in the end so they could enter heaven. But for me, Delilah's God was better, kinder, and a bit more approachable than the God my grandma knew. The bottom line was, I came to believe that there was more than one God; some were nice, others weren't. I didn't get this confusion straight until well into my adult life.

Many children are taught to believe in a fickle God who likes or dislikes people based on the length and sincerity of their worship and the depth of their obedience. Few of us grew up with a genuine understanding of the nature of God or of the importance of having an honest relationship with our Creator. God was simply a remote and enigmatic being who was totally unreliable. Not only was God distant, he was external to our being and body. I was taught that our relationship with God was rooted completely in the externals, like our physical behavior, and not in the internals, like our inner consciousness or spiritual life.

Yet even my fire-and-brimstone God seemed better to me than those who were raised with no concept of God. Their parents or caregivers were not believers. They did not attend church. They did not read the Bible. They were never told that a relationship with God could be like a branch they could grab onto should they find themselves hanging off a cliff. These children were raised to believe that God was a man-made creation who controlled and manipulated people. Raised without an omnipotent savior, their key to advancement and success in life was the education, money, and power that you acquired or accumulated through hard work and intellectual prowess.

Because there are so many competing conceptions of God, knowing what to believe is often difficult. If God likes you, he gives you good things; if He doesn't, He will make your life miserable. These early impressions often have a staggering life span. They often leave little space to know God or to desire a healthy relationship with God. When human beings do not understand something, we will not, should not, and cannot trust it.

Much of what we know and don't know about God has rendered Him mysterious, unpredictable, and somewhat capricious. God is mysterious because we cannot see Him, and there is a great ongoing debate about the appearance of His most notable representative, Jesus. We judge God as inconsistent because bad things happen to good people all the time, and, conversely, bad people get away with doing bad things in His name—consider slavery, homophobia, and the many forms of discrimination. Because there are so many differing perceptions and understandings of Him, God can appear to be quite fickle in whom He chooses to bless and what He blesses them with as they journey through life.

When you want to begin a relationship with new acquaintances, you have a picture in your mind of who they are and who you desire them to be in your life.

So take a moment to ask yourself these questions:

- What is the nature or character of the God you were raised with?

- What is the picture of God that you received? Is that picture accurate? Or is it the picture that you simply accepted?

- Do you have any expectations of God? If so, what are they? If not, why not?

- What do you believe is required of you to get what you expect from God?

In today's world, more atheists and agonistics are demanding a voice in the public square. They are questioning who God is and whether He/She exists. There was a time when no one would question God aloud. Do you question God? Are your questions being answered? If not, what do you do with and about those unanswered questions? Those questions, whether answered or not, will influence your ability to be in an intimate relationship with God.

Accepting that God is the established authority of life—and that He/She influences the flow of life within and around every living thing—is the basis for learning to trust God. In this concept, God is not a person, nor does God behave like a person. For me, God is essence, energy, presence. God is not external. God is not mysterious. God is *all*, expressing in countless forms as life and vitality. I grew to understand, accept, and believe that the essence of what God is, *I am*. This essence is both internal and eternal. It flows through me as me, by virtue of the fact that I am alive. I now understand and believe that God is the relatable, reliable, active presence that grows more relatable, reliable, and active as I establish and sustain my relationship with the process of living.

This relationship is established in my mind as consciousness and in my heart as feeling experience, and the connection grows as I endeavor to be a true demonstration of the nature of God or life.

Life is an orderly process that unfolds along a natural path that is governed by a set of intricate principles. Birth, aging, and death are all a part of the flow of life. Success, failure, conflict, and resolution of conflict also emerge as we engage in the flow of life. How something comes into being, the very nature of its existence, and how and when it ceases to be are all governed by principles that support the law of life that I now believe to be God. For human beings, these principles are meant to govern our behavior as we live.

When, however, we do not know, understand, recognize, or adhere to this law of life, our existence can be viewed as a series of fortunate or unfortunate mishaps, unexplainable interactions, or a hodgepodge of experiences in which we can find no rhyme nor reason. God, as the ruling authority, the controlling influence of life, expands within us, as us, and through all that we do as a function of our willingness and capacity to align with the principles that govern the natural flow of life. When we understand and embrace the concept of God as law, like any other law, we want to obey and be in good relationship with it. However, when we hold the concept of God as a person with human traits and characteristics, we believe we can get away with the same "unlawful" behavior the way we do with other human beings. The catch is, because we do believe that God is powerful and that God can be vengeful, we believe that we must do everything in our power to protect ourselves from the potential of God's wrath.

CAN WE TRUST GOD?

Basically, I have found that people don't trust God for three primary reasons: (1) because of the things that they were taught about God, (2) because they don't understand God's nature, and/or (3) because they don't have a relationship with God.

For me, there's a simple bottom line—the creation always reflects its Creator. When we contemplate nature, we can see exactly who

God is because universal law exists everywhere—as above, so below. God exists in the four seasons and the four elements. And all of God's creations follow universal laws. Fire is hot; that's the law. Ice is cold; that's the law. You can't make fire "unhot" or ice "uncold" without changing its very nature.

We have been programmed to believe that God is either mean or nice. *No! God is both! God is all!* If you're in Alaska, God isn't punishing you with minus-25 degree temperatures and wall-to-wall ice. Likewise, neither are people in Phoenix being paid back when it's 115 degrees in the shade. The nature of God is present in its fullness at all times.

Once we really begin to understand and accept that we are made in God's image, and that all of the elements in the universe operate in our bodies 24/7, we begin to glimpse God's divine plan. Our lives are designed to bring to our awareness how these universal principles operate. When we understand how these principles operate and govern ourselves to live in harmony with them, we can trust the Creator who made them. This is why no peace can come from interpreting God's acts as good or bad—that's viewing Him/Her through a human lens, and it's too restrictive. Living from the distorted perspective that this lens offers would never allow us to trust God. How could you? Why would you?

Yet the irony is that we trust people when they're good and when they're bad. We trust people, but we don't give God that kind of break because of the way God has been introduced to us— punishing, harsh, and out to get us.

We believe we have free will, and yet we also believe that God will punish us if we use our will in the wrong way. Certain religious denominations believe that people go straight to hell for exerting their free will. Activities like drinking, polishing their fingernails, or going to the movies can deal them a losing hand for all eternity. So part of the key to learning to trust God is to stop trying to make God small and human.

We try to make God human because we know just how wretched we can be. We know we lie. We know we've done wicked, nasty things, and so because we humanize God, we say, "Well, if I can do this and create that, or if I can do this and behave in that manner, what makes me think that God wouldn't do the same?" So the humanization of God is really troublesome when it comes to trust.

When we think about Jesus on the cross, the human part of us identifies with God's abandoned son. "Where was God? How could God let that happen to Jesus?" People get stuck on the crucifixion and forget the resurrection. People get stuck in the pain of the moment because they don't understand that God's true nature completely transcends human nature.

GOD AND GRAVITY

Gravity is another good example of how natural laws operate and how we perceive them to be operating in our lives. We know and accept that there is a law of gravity. We don't question it, and we don't fear it. Gravity does what it does, and we don't even think about it. If we fall down, we don't get mad at gravity or think that we are being punished for some perceived violation. We fall, and we get up. We may even scold ourselves and demand that we be more careful next time. Or we may recognize that there was an obstruction in our way that we did not see in time. When it comes to our life with God, however, we often have a slightly more drastic view of our slips and falls.

As we mature and evolve through the process of life, if we do not watch our step—what we do and how we do it—we may end up falling into difficult experiences and situations. We are not being punished; we are simply functioning under the laws of life. Regardless, we often look to someone or something to blame and hold responsible, and God is often the most likely candidate.

When we do not know or understand the laws and principles that govern life, we have a tendency to make up a reason to explain away the challenges we face. We may point our fingers at other human beings. Yet when we are confronted by certain natural phenomena that we do not understand or do not find pleasant—such as illness, death, or the loss of what we hold near and dear—

we shift our pointed fingers in God's direction. We blame or get angry with God for what we believe we do not deserve and are not equipped to endure.

When we have a limited understanding of God and/or no relationship with God, trusting Him/Her is not even a consideration. It is hard to trust under those circumstances. And in the absence of an understanding or a relationship, you can come to perceive and believe that your falls, obstructions, and difficulties are just how God operates.

Another aspect of the law of gravity concerns how things fall and why they fall *on* you. According to the laws and principles of nature, when apples are ripe, you can pick them from the tree or gravity will cause them to fall from the tree. We know this and accept it without question.

We also know that all apples do not ripen at the same time. They ripen when they are ready. If you are sitting under the tree when a particular apple is ripe and ready, it will fall and bonk you on the head. If you don't understand the law of gravity, you might believe that the bonk on your head was a message from God. When you do not understand the laws governing life, you may be inclined to make something up about why something happened to you. One person might make up that the fallen apple is a revelation about something she needs to do or not do. Another person might make up that the fallen apple is an actual sign from God about something he has requested. Whether the apple is deemed a good or bad sign depends on what that person believes. Someone who skipped lunch might receive the bonk and the apple as a fortuitous snack, with no thought of God at all. The bottom line is, when you do not know the law, you will make up something that fits your perception, experience, understanding, and current needs.

We have seen and heard stories about the ancient days when people believed that it rained when God was displeased, or that a volcano erupted when the locals had not made the proper sacrifice. (They couldn't find a virgin!) Like many of us today, these people did not understand that these natural occurrences are simply what happens as the earth revolves and life unfolds. Instead, we look for someone or something to blame and/or we invent reasons why certain things happen the way they happen and to whom they happen.

I have often heard people lament their experiences with certain overreaching comments, like: "I don't understand why God let this happen to me." And the big one: "See, this is why I can't trust God, because . . ." We have a tendency to trust only what we like, what is comfortable, and what we know from experience.

Learning to trust God is a process of desire grounded in willingness and maturity. It grows from being in real relationship. And, we all know it's almost impossible to grow a relationship intellectually. Consequently, a relationship with the natural law of life—God—is not and cannot be an intellectual process. It is an evolutionary process that consists of expanding consciousness, emotional maturity, and the willingness to know God within yourself, for yourself. It is a process that requires trusting yourself enough to know that you can believe in something you cannot see or touch. That's fine until we remember how trusting other human beings can get us into a lot of trouble!

———

There is really only one thing you have to trust in when it comes to God: that everything is, at all times, just as it needs to be. You cannot trust in what is going to happen, what might happen, or what has happened in the past. These things are grounded in perception, speculation, and experience. What you can trust is that whatever happens is what is required for your growth and evolution, and that process is good, even if it hurts a little or a lot. When you trust God as the law of life, you know that no matter what shows up, you are protected and you will be okay. Without this level of relationship and trust, you spend your time, energy, and life force trying to be good enough or do good enough to prove that you are worthy of the protection from hurt, harm, and danger that you believe you need.

Trusting God also requires that we grow the muscle that recognizes that all things are working together to move life forward—*all* life, not just *your* life. When you understand, know, and recognize that life is an ever-moving, ever-growing, and ever-evolving process, you can trust that even when you can't see it and don't understand it, something better than what you now know is unfolding.

Sara learned this lesson when her husband of 23 years left her for her sister.

A PERFECTLY IMPERFECT LIFE

Sara and John lived what she thought was the perfect life. They raised their children, paid their bills on time, went to church almost every Sunday, and invested an adequate amount of time on date nights to keep their relationship alive and exciting. She had her friends and interests outside of the home, and John had the same. They had just begun to explore retirement and the possibilities of moving to a warm climate when all hell broke loose.

Sara and her sister, Liz, were fairly close. They spoke daily by telephone, shopped together, and alternated years of preparing holiday dinners for the family. Sara, the older sister, had a way of offering Liz unwanted advice that led to most of their upsets and knock-down, drag-out battles. They were known to go weeks without speaking to each other before one would give in, usually Sara, and then they would resume business as usual.

Liz, who had been single for about seven years, often commiserated with John about how nosy and controlling Sara could be and how she hated it. Sara, totally unsuspecting and trusting both her husband and her sister, often asked Liz to look in on John while she was away at a church function or doing something with or for her adult children. John often said that Sara's and Liz's cooking was neck and neck. In fact, he was not shy about admitting that he liked some things the way Liz prepared them better than the way his wife, Sara, prepared them. Sara never suspected a thing. In fact, sometimes she would ask Liz to prepare certain dishes for John while she was away. What started out as one sister supporting another ended up with that same sister betraying the other.

Sara left the church's annual women's retreat two days early because she wasn't feeling well. She tried to call John to tell him she was coming home early, but he did not pick up. She called Liz to ask if she had seen John but also got no response from her. Sara arrived home to an empty house. When John finally showed up, two days later, Sara asked him one question: "Who is she?" It was both a blessing and a disaster that John chose not to lie. "It's Liz, and neither one of us meant for it to happen. It just did." After several days of weeping and probing for details, Sara asked John to move out of the house. He did. He moved in with Liz, whom he had been having an affair with for more than three years.

Over the course of the next two years, Sara learned that Liz was not the only woman with whom John had had an affair. There was one at work; there was one at church; and there was another with whom he had fathered a child. That child was 14 years old when Sara discovered she existed. It did not seem possible that the man with whom she had spent most of her adult life—the man who brought her flowers, took her on trips, and provided so well for his family—could be such a scoundrel. As the details continued to emerge, Sara became more and more devastated. In fact, she stopped going to church, stopped communicating with her friends, and vowed never to speak to Liz for as long as she was alive.

Sara was angry. No, she was enraged. Not only was it difficult for her to believe this had happened, she could not understand why God had allowed it to happen to her. She was a good person who had lived her life in an honorable manner. By the time she came to me for coaching, four years had passed, and she was still a hot mess!

Like many women who divorce after the age of 40, Sara believed that her life was over and done. She felt lost. She could not shake the depth of the betrayal, and yet she knew that she needed to get her life back on track so she could start moving forward. She had always worked and continued to do so, which was a good thing because it gave her an outlet and a way to keep herself busy. She had sold the house she and John had lived in and split the money with him (he, by the way, stayed with Liz). When I saw Sara she was considering moving to another state and thought a life coach could help her create a vision and a plan.

After several meetings it became clear to me that Sara would be just fine, as soon as she gave herself permission to feel the hurt and devastation she had experienced. As we began to explore how that would be possible and if she would survive it, Sara revealed where and why she was stuck.

"What John and my sister did was one thing. It was hurtful and ugly. I certainly don't think I did anything to deserve it. But what has really taken my breath away is that God allowed this to go on right under my nose and never provided me with a hint or a clue that it was going on." Once she made that statement, Sara and I were able to begin to do the deep work required for her to reopen her heart to God and get her life back on track.

While creating a vision board to outline her next steps to move her life forward, Sara realized that she had observed several signs of John's infidelity along the way. She also recognized that she had dismissed and then negated her instincts, not just with John but in many aspects of her life. As we planned her move and career possibilities, Sara came to understand that she had seen, heard, and felt things that she now understood were, in fact, God's warning signs. But Sara, like so many of us, had an automatic program playing in her subconscious that would not allow her to acknowledge what she knew.

Sara grew up in a household with a mother who was clinically paranoid. Sara's father left the home when she was six because, as he said, he could not take her mother's accusations. Sara's mother escaped into religion and the Bible, embellishing those teachings and using what she made up as the foundation for raising her children. She taught Sara that God was like a crutch that would carry you through anything and everything if you simply showed up and relied on him. Sara told herself that if you did the things that were supposed to be pleasing to God, he would never let bad things happen to you. According to Sara's mother, God wanted you to pray, go to church, and stay away from people.

Sara never minded the praying or the going to church, but she vowed never to lock herself away in the house or peer from behind the curtains when people knocked on her door. Instead, her home would be a warm and inviting place, where everyone would be welcomed, even those people she did not particularly like.

While Sara and her siblings continued to have a good healthy relationship with their father after their parents' breakup, Sara vowed never to be paranoid and suspicious like her mother. Instead, she overcorrected, refusing to pay attention to the small inklings she received and ignoring her own intuition. That is how she missed her son's drinking problem until he crashed the family car. That was also how she pooh-poohed away her daughter's weight gain until the girl had a miscarriage at the age of 15. Through it all, she and John would talk things over until he came up with a plan for resolution.

Slowly, Sara realized that she had not been happy with John for several years. She had stayed in the marriage because she did not want her children to come from a broken home. She had stayed busy at church because she did not want to be alone with John. Our work together helped her to realize that her understanding of God and her relationship with God had been perfunctory, and not at all trusting. She did what she thought she needed to do to get from God what she thought she wanted. With that realization Sara broke down and cried for several hours. Six months later she moved to Florida and into a new job. Her vision was unfolding according to her intention. Within a year, Sara had met a really nice man at her new church, and they were getting serious. Last year, Sara and Liz spoke again for the first time. It was then that Sara learned that John had left Liz after rekindling a relationship with the mother of the other daughter he had fathered.

While Sara's story speaks volumes about trusting yourself and other people, for her, the real lesson came in recognizing the importance of having a relationship with God that goes beyond doing the things you think are pleasing to God. Sara was bargaining with God from the perspective of "if I do this, God will do that." She was also motivated by what she had been taught about God rather than what she actually knew and felt from personal experience. Trust in God must grow from your personal, internal experience rather than what you have been taught or told. It is unproductive to go into any relationship trying not to be something and relying on what someone else has told you. A healthy relationship is built on honest communication, interaction, and trusting what you learn and know from personal experience.

SEASONS: UNDERSTANDING GOD'S NATURE

Understanding and trusting God must begin with knowing the nature of God and how God's life essence flows in you, through you, and on your behalf. A teacher once told me that if I wanted to know anything about God, all I needed to do was observe nature. I began with the basics. Day brings light; night brings darkness. It ain't personal. It just is. We don't question why or how day and night happen, we simply accept that it is going to happen. We get to do more in the light than we do in the darkness. I happen to appreciate the light of day more than the darkness of night; however, equally important activities go on at night as go on during the daylight hours. Life is the same way. There are times when everything in our lives feels bright and sunny, then there are those times when it seems we are surrounded by and covered in darkness. And again, it ain't personal. It's a part of the process and flow. It is the law. God moves, flows, and is present in the darkness and in the light.

Then there are the seasons. Each season supports a purpose that advances life. When the world functioned as a primarily agricultural community, it was easy to recognize and embrace the primary purpose of each season. Now that the world is largely technologically driven, the seasons are more distinguishable by weather trends than by natural purpose and flow. This does not change the law; it just makes it more difficult to discern.

In the fall season, things that were once alive and blossoming change color, wither, and die. Fall signifies cooler temperatures, changes in form, and longer periods of darkness. It is a necessary process for the clearing, cleansing, and evolution of all life-forms. The lyrics of the song "Everything Must Change" is an appropriate affirmation about what happens to life and in life during the fall season. Yet when it comes to living out our personal experiences, we do not appreciate the value of change or death because we have not been taught to equate the laws of nature with the events of our lives. In fact, most of us hate change. We find change very uncomfortable; and when change is not to our liking, when it makes us uncomfortable, we look for something or someone to blame for it. The challenge: watching things die and learning how to be okay with it. God is present in all aspects of change as the very essence and natural flow of all life.

In the same way we trust and embrace that those things that die off in fall will be replaced in a new season, we must learn to trust that the people and things that leave our lives will be replaced by something fresh and new. The challenge we face is believing that those replacements will show up by a specific date on the calendar. Unfortunately, when it comes to human life and evolution, it just doesn't work like that. Remember, it ain't personal. It's the law.

I have come to equate winter with the time of life when I must slow down, rest, and get prepared for the spring. Things move slower in the winter season. Darkness lasts longer. We must cover and protect our physical selves more in the winter. Winter in some places is more severe than it is in others. The physical forces that confront us during this season can be life-threatening. And still, we accept this season as a part of life, knowing that, even in the cold darkness of winter, there will be bright days. Thanksgiving, Christmas, and New Year's Eve—the turning point of a new cycle, a new year, all occur in winter.

In winter, it is more difficult to get around and the limited amount of sunshine or warmth motivates me to stay close to home. I lost my daughter in the winter. My husband filed for divorce during another winter. Although it was July when I actually did it, filing for bankruptcy and turning the keys of my home back over to the bank signified to me that I was in a winter season; pieces of my life that were precious to me were ending. What I had to realize was that, according to the law in the natural flow of life, something was being born in the cold darkness of the winter that I would not see until the spring. The challenge—I simply didn't know when my next spring would begin. This is when I had to learn to trust God, because I couldn't see the good that was forming below the surface of my life.

When you don't know, cannot see, and have no knowledge of the law, it is like hanging off the side of a cliff. You are desperate. You are probably scared out of your wits. You know you need help, but you also want the kind of help you think you need. Your basic instincts will be simply to survive; however, the law doesn't work like that at all. The law of life is expansive, evolutionary, creative, and all encompassing. The law is concerned with past, present, and future, taking into consideration all of the circumstances, resources, options, and opportunities that will create a new life and a new way of being. So while you are hanging off the cliff, wanting desperately to survive, the law knows it may be time for you to fall, because the drop is only three feet. And you must learn to live beyond the fear of falling.

While you want to be saved from the fall off the cliff, the law wants you to realize how long you can hang on, building your muscles in the process. You see that law is about growth and evolution. It is concerned with your learning how to move beyond your fears and limitations. God is the law working within and throughout all of the situations and circumstances in which you find yourself preparing to get yourself off the side of the cliff. God teaches you how to look and work beneath the surface in order to germinate the seeds in your heart and mind that will yield a good crop or a bountiful garden when spring comes around.

Spring is the season of new growth when we start to see the results of the winter. Things blossom in the spring that we could not see in the winter. Once we see the new growth, we know the ground is fertile and receptive, so we plant our seeds. Spring also brings longer periods of daylight and warmer weather. As the weather turns, we begin to hear the birds and see the animals that were hibernating and hiding. There is an old saying that spring is for lovers; it brings people together again. And as people come together, their hearts and minds connect for a higher purpose.

Spring always gives us hope, signaling that we are halfway through another year. Spring reminds us that the winter does not last forever. Each new birth and the presence of new buds mean that our lives are still fertile and producing and hopeful. Spring births things on the surface that we may not have been aware were present. Spring is also a time for cleaning, making everything fresh and new. We open the windows to let fresh air in because we were shut in during the winter. We shake things out and blow the dust off because things became stagnant during the winter. In spring, we renew, revitalize, and recharge ourselves in the light of day and the warmth of the season. The challenge of spring is giving what you planted enough time to grow and knowing that if you haven't planted, you will not receive a harvest.

Graduations mark the onset of summer. Moving from one level to the next, one thing to the next, under the blazing heat of the sun. While it is a time of fun, rest, and celebration, certain things come to an end. School is out for the summer. Your favorite television program goes off or goes into reruns. The children go to camp or simply lounge around the house. We come together for family vacations and reunions. While we covered up in the winter, we expose ourselves in the summer. We are more vulnerable, more open. We engage the natural elements of life more in the summer, lounging on the beach, camping in the woods, and splashing in the pool.

While summer feels good to us because of what we can see, some of what we are looking at is preparing to wither and die. Make no mistake about it, the disintegration is already happening. We won't actually see it until the fall. The darkness of winter is already looming, we just won't feel it for a few more months. The challenge of summer is learning how to enjoy what is present while knowing that it will not last.

Because nature give us clues about how the natural law of life operates, it supports us in recognizing how God operates. If God is law, the seasons and the days are important elements that help us to understand the nature of God and develop a healthy relationship with Him/Her. We don't get mad at October because there are no strawberries available; nor do we blame May because we can't build a snowman. Why then do we blame, curse, and separate ourselves from our concepts of God when the seasons of our lives change? In most cases, it's because we have not developed a relationship with God and misunderstand His/Her very nature. Instead, we come to believe that we cannot trust God because we hate the winter and want the summer to last forever.

The seasons may not look the same everywhere, but all places, like all people, experience all four seasons. If we allow the duration or harshness of one season to break our trust in God, we are turning our back on the law of our life, fighting against the very thing that is in place to work on our behalf. Trusting God must begin with understanding we will pass through many seasons of life, and *it ain't personal!* It is the law. Once we understand that the law is always operating, that God is always present, the next step is to learn about the nature of God so that we will recognize God's presence as we live through all the seasons of our lives.

Chapter 7

BUILDING A RELATIONSHIP WITH GOD

> LET ME REMEMBER,
> I AM ONE WITH GOD.
>
> —A Course in Miracles, (W-pI.124.1:1)

I met my BFF Shaheerah over the telephone more than 30 years ago. She had heard a tape of a retreat lecture I did, and something in it spoke directly to her heart. She asked around, got my telephone number from someone, and called me to thank me for the lesson she had received. At the time, I did not think it was strange or inappropriate for a stranger to be calling me. There was something about her voice and her energy that made me feel comfortable with her. I did not question her motives or her background; I simply listened to her and shared my thoughts. As the weeks and months went by, we spoke almost every day, and in the process we learned so much about each other that it felt as if we had known each other all of our lives. Communication and sharing is an absolutely essential act for establishing a relationship.

How you are introduced to or first meet someone has a strong influence on the establishment and nature of your relationship. The same is true when it comes to creating, strengthening, and maintaining a relationship with God. Since most of us are introduced to God through the perceptions, understandings, and experiences of others, what we think about, know about, and believe about God may not feel real, true, or authentic in our own hearts. In the same way that we must create the opportunity or take the time to know a person, we must take the time to know God. This knowledge can and will change the nature and the energy of the relationship because it makes God relatable. In order to build trust in God, we must be able to relate to God. This takes time. It also requires the willingness and the desire and the discipline to put in the time, to have what is often referred to as a daily spiritual practice. Only by engaging in things of a spiritual nature can we come into the understanding of God as our own spiritual essence.

Because trusting God is a function of your understanding of God, it requires that you know and recognize the nature of God, not because of what you have been told but rather what you have experienced for yourself. Growing up in the Pentecostal church, I witnessed many things that I came to know were individual experiences of God. Crying, moaning, shouting, dancing, and running from one end of the sanctuary to the other were all considered personal experiences of God. Unfortunately, no one ever explained to me what was going on or why people were responding the way they did. Conversely, in my friend Delilah's Catholic church, none of those things happened, which for me was equally confusing. I was well into adulthood when I was able to make the distinction between what I call "churchianity" and the experience of God. One takes place externally, the other internally. I also discovered that it is the internal experience that supports the development of trust.

Trusting God is an internal response to the discoveries and awareness that come about during your independent investigation of God and His/Her nature. Human beings have so often humanized God—with gender classifications, personality traits, and expectations—that it can be difficult to know for yourself, within yourself, what God is. When, however, we understand God as law, as the presence and flow of energy and life, we can look for and expect a different experience. When we recognize God as life— the living, breathing energy that animates every living thing—we are less likely to put God in a box or narrow the capacity of God to the limitations of our humanness and our human understanding. When we become aware that God represents good and that good is often offset and amplified by the not so good, we have less of a tendency to blame God for the things we do not like, the things that make us uncomfortable.

Knowing the law of polarity is helpful in this instance. This law represents the universal reality that everything is dual, everything has a polar opposite, everything has a complementary expression. Opposites are identical in nature, but different in the degree of expression and experience. In other words, there are two sides to everything. Things that appear to be opposites are, in fact, extremes of the same thing. We may believe that heat and cold are different. They appear to be opposites when the truth is they are simply varying degrees of the same thing: the temperature. This reality applies to love and hate, peace and war, positive and negative, good and evil, yes and no, light and darkness, energy and matter. What transforms your experience or expression of anything or anyone is how you relate to it and what you understand about it.

Learning to fully understand and comprehend the law of polarity is a necessary step in learning to trust God. The law of polarity exists as a way for each of us to explore and experience life to the fullest. If what we perceive as bad did not exist, how would we recognize or understand when we are having a good experience? What we call "bad" is not the way God expresses displeasure. Like the conditions of winter or "bad" weather, it is a natural unfolding of the flow of life. Without the presence and experience of poverty, how would we know what it is like to experience wealth? Poverty is not the way God punishes certain people, any more than wealth is a means of God blessing certain other people. Each experience is an aspect of a continuum that individuals experience as a function of their personal history and ancestry.

If failure did not exist, how would we measure the experience of success? If there was no death or ending, we would not understand or fully enjoy and appreciate what it means to experience life or new beginnings. Since the nature of God is fullness and totality in all things, the presence and activity of the law of polarity as an aspect of the nature of God supports our understanding of the full spectrum of possibility—ranging from the extremely light or easy to the extremely dark and difficult, with any number of experiences in between.

By developing this level of understanding of God as law and learning to fully accept and surrender to whatever may show up in our lives as events, conditions, and circumstances, we find the basis upon which we can establish and maintain trust in God. As we learn to understand that all things—regardless of how they are perceived—work together for good, because God is good, even when we cannot see or imagine what shape that may really mean, we make progress in our given ability to achieve an authentic, trusting relationship with God. In this instance, learning to trust God is a function of unlearning or restructuring what we have been taught by other well-meaning adults based on their experience of God.

TRUSTING GOD IS A CHOICE

Trusting God is a choice. Often it is a hard choice. As human beings we are constantly bombarded with physical signs and evidence that what we want, feel, or know is impossible. We are forever being presented with hard-core physical facts and intellectual stimuli that entice us to accept and believe that what we see, what others say, and what seems logical and practical in the physical-world reality is what is and therefore must be accepted. Yet when it comes to trusting God, there may be no physical evidence, and what you are choosing may fly in the face of reason, logic, or practicality.

When I remember leaving an abusive marriage with three small children, no money, and nowhere to go, I had to make a choice. I could choose to continue to be afraid of my then husband, who was bigger, faster, and stronger than me, or I could choose to be obedient to the voice that woke me from a dead sleep with this message: "Leave now or he is going to kill you."

Trusting God may also mean that you dispel or dismiss everything being offered to you by the experts and the human beings you know and trust. When, however, you understand that God's nature is sacred, secret, silent, invisible, and intangible, you will have something solid to hold on to when it comes to making hard choices. *You must know God in order to trust God.* That knowing cannot and does not happen in the physical-world reality. It happens in the core and soul of your being.

Trusting God is a spiritual experience more than it is a religious act or an intellectual pursuit. This means it is an internal process rather than an external one. In order to have the kind of spiritual experience that allows you to understand God's nature in support of your ability to trust Him/Her, you must develop and deepen your daily spiritual practice of communicating with the God of your understanding. We live in a spiritual universe that is governed by, and operates in accordance to, spiritual laws and principles. It would serve us well to move away from considering these laws to be mysterious or mystical but rather understand them simply as the way the energy of life flows in and around us.

Just as day follows night and spring follows winter, there is an order to life; this order encompasses the full spectrum of all we can and have experienced. This order is the nature of God. Because God's nature is spiritual, intangible, and invisible, human beings cannot determine it, nor can they escape its influence or operation. Understanding the true nature of God and recognizing how it operates facilitates our understanding of Him/Her from a spiritual rather than religious or intellectual perspective. The key to learning and knowing that we can trust God is to recognize that there is a spirit within us that is connected to God. It is internal and eternal. It is God-given rather than something we can get or lose when we obey or disobey a commandment.

Trusting God means acknowledging that the essence of who you are is divine. But as long as you are shrouded in a veil of guilt, shame, unworthiness, and inadequacy, trusting God will be difficult, if not impossible. *A Course in Miracles* offers this teaching: "I am as God created me. My mind is one with God's mind. This makes me holy." (W-pI.94.1:1) These two premises indicate that our trust of God hinges on our ability to accept the idea that we are, at all times, one with God. Knowing and accepting this is a reflection of the spiritual intimacy that grows from our understanding of who God is and how God operates.

We cannot trust someone we don't know. That is the secret of learning to trust God. If someone were to say, "Trust me," chances are you would have one of two reactions. Either you would say, "Yes, I'll trust you," or you'd challenge, "Why should I?" Trusting God naturally follows when you recognize that you are divine because God exists within you. The bonus benefit of trusting God is that it facilitates, supports, and enhances your ability and willingness to trust yourself.

SPIRITUAL PRACTICE

Because trust is an intangible, invisible, inner process, the development and deepening of trust can happen only *within* you. And like the cultivation of any skill, inner mastery requires practice. Developing and sustaining a spiritual practice that can and will support you in learning to trust takes commitment, energy, and focus, which may sound too much like work. Yet we all work. Some of us work because we have to. Others work because we love to. After working to take care of all our necessary roles and daily tasks, we may be more interested in relaxing or playing than in pursuing a spiritual practice. In our hectic lives it has become easier and easier to focus on the external world, on working harder and harder to make things happen, to control things, to do more and have more. When a spiritual practice is considered to be just one more task, chances are we will avoid creating or sustaining it. If that's the case with you, I would encourage you to reflect on what's at stake when you *don't* make time for your inner life.

Benefits of a Spiritual Practice

- A consistent, focused spiritual practice supports you in developing and strengthening your inner essence, power, and authentic identity.

- A spiritual practice anchors, deepens, and expands your awareness of your connection to Source/Spirit/God/the Universe/a Higher Power.

- A spiritual practice establishes a foundation upon which you can gain a new perspective on your life and your experiences.

- A spiritual practice interrupts the habitual flow of thoughts and emotions that often lead to unproductive or distorted reactions.

- A spiritual practice reveals your addictive and judgmental nature and supports the discovery of the roots of your pain and suffering.

- A spiritual practice deepens your intuition and insight. It unfolds as an ability to recognize that true peace and joy can occur only when you are free from the grip of the negative ego, that is, repetitive toxic thoughts and emotional addictions/reactions.

- A spiritual practice creates committed and focused time for aligning your head, heart, and spirit with the indwelling divinity that is your authentic identity.

- A spiritual practice consists of activities and tools that build and maintain a sacred space and atmosphere.

As you can see, your spirit—like your mind and body—requires attention and dedication in order to become a meaningful power source in your life. If you are willing to invest the time and energy to develop a spiritual practice and to integrate those practices into your day-to-day existence, your understanding of who you are in life will grow into an experience of freedom and joy. Without a spiritual practice, it is more likely than not that your understanding of the process of life and your awareness of your true identity will remain shallow. As such, the experiences of pain and suffering will fill the space between the periods of peace and pleasure.

Barriers to Spiritual Practice

Lack of desire. The first barrier to developing a spiritual practice is lack of desire. Desire is one of the most powerful tools we have for accomplishing our highest priorities. It is a spiritual tool we can use to fulfill our intentions and realize the vision we hold for our life. When we strengthen our desire for spiritual growth, the motivation and energy to create and sustain a spiritual practice can only have positive results. There are many invaluable tools at our disposal: meditation, prayer, chanting, inspirational reading, devotional practice, and so on are all spiritual tools that you could spend a lifetime exploring. To overcome the barriers to developing a consistent spiritual practice, ignite your desire by working with the spiritual tool that feels right for you.

Lack of understanding. The second barrier to developing a spiritual practice is a lack of understanding of what a practice is and fear of what might or might not happen. If we consider our spiritual practice as just another task, but do not see the results we anticipate, chances are we will abandon the practice.

The Cornerstones of Spiritual Practice

1. No Expectations.
   Be open. Have no expectations.

2. Alignment.
   Practicing with faith and trust that your desire to be aligned and connected is all that is required. Release all preconceptions and judgments.

3. Commitment.
   Consider your practice to be an investment of time and

energy that takes you inside your own sanctuary and allows you to explore and discover your authentic self.

Self-inquiry, self-awareness, and self-acceptance are the roots and foundation of a spiritual practice. As you deepen your connection to your source, the essence of who you are will expand and grow. Over time, as the connection deepens and strengthens, your self-exploration will evolve into a spiritual perspective of who you are as a being of love, light, wisdom, compassion, and wholeness. You will gain clarity about your spiritual gifts and calling. With consistent focus, a spiritual practice contributes to your spiritual evolution as you begin to integrate the practices, tools, and insights into your life. The goal of a practice is not just to set aside a time for performing more tasks with an expected result. A spiritual practice supports you in discovering ways to make your daily routine and your spiritual practice one and the same.

Elements of a Productive Spiritual Practice

1. Getting Connected.
   The ability to focus your attention inward in a receptive mode. This connection can be attained and sustained with deep, conscious breathing.

2. Getting Out of the Way.
   The ability to remove distractions and focus attention inward is accomplished with guided meditation or inspired reading, followed by journal writing or reflection. This level of practice requires a commitment to maintaining your inner work despite any diversion, confusion, distraction, or perceived lack of progress.

3. Listening and Receiving.
   The ability to pray and listen, to focus within and identify the barriers/challenges/issues that come forward, and to suspend all judgments about what comes up in your process. As your practice deepens, prayer and meditation are tools you can incorporate to

clarify your desires; align your thoughts, beliefs, and actions; and follow the guidance you receive that will allow them to manifest.

Creating a Practice That Works for You

You may have to experiment with different spiritual practices to find what works for you. Based on your temperament, lifestyle, work habits, family situation, and available time you will need to determine:

1. When Will You Do Your Practice?
   Choose how often you will do your practice and whether it will be in the morning, in the evening, or during the day. You are encouraged to choose a consistent time and to schedule your practice into your activities.

2. Where Will You Do Your Practice?
   Create a sacred space where you do your spiritual practice and nothing else. Also consider that the space you choose should be free from distractions, interruptions, noise, and so on.

3. How Long You Will Spend on Your Practice?
   If you are new to a spiritual practice, it may be most beneficial to begin with 10 to 15 minutes and progress to 30 to 60 minutes. The elements of your practice will also determine the amount of time you will need. Consider that 5 to 10 minutes is better and more productive than no minutes.

4. What You Will Do During Your Practice?
   Breath, prayer, affirmation, meditation, inspirational reading, and silence are the basic elements of any spiritual practice. In determining the elements of your practice, choose what works for you and experiment with how you will combine the activities so that they are meaningful to your life.

"Because I Want to Live . . ."

Gladys was 31 years old when she called me to say she had been diagnosed with an aggressive form of cancer. In the moments of silence between her weeping and gasping for breath, I could sense that she was as angry as she was frightened. Her doctor recommended six weeks of aggressive chemotherapy. Radiation was not an option because of the location of the cancer. She talked for hours about why this had happened to her, what she could have possibly done to attract this experience into her life, and what was going to happen to her son if she didn't make it. I listened and reminded her to breathe, knowing that almost nothing I could say would make any sense or make her feel any better in that moment. What I also knew was that the fear she had expressed would be as damaging to her as the physical disease.

There are those moments when you simply need to be "with" someone, to listen and give her the opportunity to spin all of the chaos out of her mind before you speak or offer advice. When her weeping had subsided and her breathing was regulated, I wanted to support Gladys in moving into the only mind-set that would get her through what she was going through.

"Beloved, what do you want to happen?"

"I want this s—— out of my body."

"Why do you want it out?"

"What do you mean? I want it out because I don't want to die!"

Her anger gave her a passion for living.

"Do you believe the cancer will kill you?"

"It might. It can kill me."

"Do you believe it will kill you?"

"No, because I am not going to let it kill me."

"What do you mean when you say, 'I am not going to let it kill me'?"

127

"It means I am going to do whatever I have to do to get well."

"Great! Now, do you trust yourself to do that?"

"Yes, but I have no control over what the cancer will do."

"Right, you don't, but do you trust that you can do whatever is necessary to get to the other side of the diagnosis you have now?"

"I think so. I have to do it. I cannot leave my child here without his mother."

"So are you doing this for him, or are you doing this for you?"

"I am doing it for both of us. I don't want to die."

"Do you want to live?"

"Of course I want to live!"

"Do you trust that you can do whatever is required for you to live beyond the diagnosis?"

"I think so, I want to, but I don't know. I guess it is in God's hands."

"Do you trust God?"

"In this moment I have no other choice."

"Yes, you do. You have a choice to trust yourself to do what you can and trust that God will be with you while you do it. Is that something you are willing to do?"

"I guess so. I have no other choice."

Trusting yourself enough to trust God cannot be a choice of last resort; it must be a first choice based on your relationship with God. Gladys and I talked about her relationship with God and how it had developed. When her mother died, she was really mad at God and she told Him/Her so. She also prayed for peace and understanding. She remembered the day, almost three months after her mother had passed, when she heard the words: *"I am with you always. I do not need a body to love you.*" Gladys said she did not know if she had heard God speaking or the spirit of her mother speaking, but afterward she felt so peaceful that whose words they were didn't really matter. It was then that she knew, beyond a shadow of doubt, that God had answered her prayer and, more important, that God was real.

Gladys said after that day she still missed her mother, but she did not feel the pain of her absence. She also said that since then she would pray silently every morning, asking God for guidance. With that information, I asked Gladys, "What is your prayer now?" I realized that, like many of us, Gladys had learned to trust God during a difficult time rather than by building a strong long-term relationship. Ultimately, it doesn't matter how we get there, as long as we get there.

I walked with Gladys through two chemo treatments a week for six weeks. We prayed together before and after every treatment. We created a vision for her life beyond chemo. When fear stepped into her heart and mind, we talked about it, every aspect of it; then we prayed for peace and clarity. On some days, Gladys knew she was praying from a place of fear and desperation. Those were the days I prayed for her. On other days she prayed with gratitude that she looked good with a bald head and that she had such great medical coverage. When you really know and trust God, gratitude for everything unfolds as a normal way of being. The blood test results in the fifth week were so good that the doctors couldn't believe her progress. We kept praying for weeks after the chemo treatments ended.

It had been almost a year after treatments had ended when Gladys called to say that her blood work indicated that the cancer was back. This time there were no tears or upset. Gladys was in a very different place, ready and willing to do whatever she needed to do, trusting that this was a temporary setback and not a death sentence. She had been in treatment about three weeks when she had a total meltdown. I could barely understand a word she was saying until I heard her ask: "Am I going to die?"

"I really don't know. Do you want to live?"

"Yes, I do."

"Why do you want to live?"

"I want to live for my son. I want to live for my husband. I want to live because there are so many things I still want to do."

"What are you afraid will happen if you don't live?"

"If I am not here, my son won't have a mother, and he will be sad. I don't want that for him. I don't want him or my husband to be sad."

"I hear that, but what do you believe will happen to you if you don't live?"

"Well, I won't have to worry anymore. I won't have to take any more treatments. I won't get any older, and I guess I won't have cancer anymore. I guess I would also be at peace."

"And what do you believe serves God, your living or your not living?"

"I think it serves God for me to have what I want."

"Well, you are talking about life in terms of what you don't want for other people. How about seeing life in terms of what you and God want?"

"Wow! I didn't realize that I was doing that. God wants me to live because I want to live because my life serves God."

"And what do you believe will happen if you don't live?"

"Well, it's a little scary to think about, but in some way, I can still serve God because God will take care of my son and my husband."

"Does that frighten you?"

"No. I can trust God to do that for me and with me."

Eleven years later, Gladys sent me an invitation to her son's high school graduation. Today, she is doing what she loves, teaching graphic arts at a community college. She and her husband have been to Hawaii twice. When we talk about her experience, she says the one thing that she learned and continues to hold on to is that if you trust God, you know that, no matter what happens, you and everyone else will be okay.

TWO SIDES OF THE SAME COIN

Gladys's experience highlights a distinction that many of us need to make: the difference between placing faith in ourselves and our ability and trusting God. Most of us are familiar with the scripture that says, "Faith without works is dead." It means that when you have faith, you have to do something as a demonstration of it. Gladys was going to "do" chemotherapy as a demonstration of her faith that it would work. Her faith was not in God or in herself. She was putting her faith in the chemo drugs. She was "hoping" that God would permit the drugs to heal her of the cancer. Her faith was external, outside of herself, and actually not reliant on God. Faith, hope, and doing are not a complete or adequate demonstration of trust.

Another scripture speaks more fully to the issue of trust. In Proverbs 3: 5 (KJV), we are instructed to "Trust in the Lord with all thine heart." Trust is internal. It is a state of being, a way of thinking, and a level of knowing. When you trust, faith supports you. When you trust, there is no doubting or hoping or wondering. Trust is in your mind and heart, which are the places we connect to God. These are the places in which we must "know" God. If you don't have that inner knowing, if you don't have that place of total acceptance, awareness, and acknowledgment within yourself, you can do everything in the world, but you're still going to fall into doubt, and doubt is the kryptonite to trust. When you trust, faith is a natural outcome. In fact, I believe when you really trust yourself to trust God, you don't need faith. You will know what to do and what not to do as a demonstration of trust.

Gladys and I had this discussion one day when she said she needed to have more faith. I responded:

Baby, faith ain't the issue. Trust is the issue. You've got faith because you are looking at the facts. The fact that this could happen or that might happen or this may not happen, which means that will probably happen, are all based on facts. You are also speaking your faith into the possibility that everything you are doing, the work you are doing, may not be enough. You put lots of faith in what you don't know and what you don't want. You are doing what you think is required while still holding on to the possibility of a negative or undesired outcome.

When you trust, you know within yourself, and that knowing is unshakable. It is trust that grows into your ability to put your faith in doing what is required, knowing that regardless of the outcome you will be fine. Faith is unnecessary except to support you in what you're doing. When you know and trust, faith is a demonstration. Unfortunately, most of us try to convince ourselves that we have and can demonstrate faith by doing, when we really don't trust God or ourselves.

Understanding the nature of God as good and the presence of God as internal are key elements in developing trust, both within you and of God. Recognizing that God is not an external force means rethinking or perhaps unlearning all that you have been taught about God. God breathes life into us. The essence of who we are is God and is of God. When we know, believe, and understand that we are individual expressions of God, trusting ourselves and trusting God are the same. There is no separation.

When you don't trust yourself, you will place your trust in something or someone outside of yourself. You will make the assumption that it is your power that sustains your life. You may also delude yourself into believing that your ability, capacity, and personal power is greater than God's, which also means that you have seized control. If you screw something up, God cannot fix it.

The bottom line is that not trusting yourself reflects the belief that you are separate from God. When you are separate from God, you exist on your own. You must do things on your own. You must change, challenge, and fix things on your own, and when this is your belief system, fear, stress, and anxiety will naturally flow from you, through you, and to you.

There is only one trust. What you put it in doesn't really matter. Trusting God really depends on what you know about God and your relationship with that knowing. It really depends on your understanding and embracing the cyclical flow of life. We think of God in terms of doing rather than being, which means that when God does what we want, we trust that God is with us and for us. When, however, we must confront the unknown or face something that frightens us, we focus on what God will do rather than where God is and what God's nature is. More often than not, we base our trust on outcomes rather than the process.

Trust is an unfolding process based on experience. Many of us never have the trust conversation about God until we must deal with something we don't like. Then we wait to see what God will do. We wait, we hope, we doubt, we worry because we simply do not understand that the cycle of life experiences, like the seasons, flow in a natural order. Just because it snows for three days and leaves a deposit of 40 inches does not mean that spring will never come again. It always does, and when it does, we forget about the snow. This is not so when our lives do not turn out the way we want or expect.

SURRENDERING TO TRUST IN GOD

My best friend, Reverend Shaheerah Stephens, pastor of the Transforming Love Community, is my living, breathing, walking, and talking demonstration of what it means to trust God. Over the 30-plus years of our friendship, I have watched Shaheerah grow and deepen her trust and full reliance on the presence of God within her and in the management of her life. I once thought her trust was a result of her being a minister, but I came to recognize and understand that her trust was grounded in love and experience. I remember when Shaheerah was in ministerial school at Unity Village in Missouri. She left her home, her husband, and her life as she knew it to deepen her relationship with God in service to God. I was excited for her. We talked almost every day about what she was learning and how it was changing her outlook on life. When I went to visit her, I could see and feel her transformation. The only way I could describe it is as beautiful and peaceful. Watching her changed me, too.

Shaheerah was in her second year of study when her husband, Bobby, became seriously ill. He was hospitalized and faced a life-threatening surgery. The suddenness of it was disturbing. Shaheerah was torn. Did she go home to be with her husband? Or did she stay in school and continue her studies? What I have learned about being present with someone who is facing a difficult decision is that the best thing to do is listen and pray. Bobby told Shaheerah to stay in school, which made her want to go home even more. She wanted to be there. What if something happened to him? What if he didn't survive the surgery? She called me the morning she made her decision.

"I am going to stay here and pray."

"Okay. Are you okay with that?"

"Well, what the Holy Spirit said to me was that he could die with me sitting there holding his hand. My being there isn't going to change what is going to unfold. I am going to trust that God's got this, and me, and that everything is going to be as it needs to be."

"I am going to trust and agree that Bobby, and you, and everything else will be fine, whatever that is."

The surgery went well. Shaheerah finished school and went on to begin her ministry in Detroit.

When I talked to Shaheerah about what it means to trust God with your very life, what she told me was that it's dependent on your understanding of God. Shaheerah has learned that what you believe about God is a function of what you know and understand about who and what God is in your life. You cannot learn it from a book, nor can you rely on your intellect. Understanding God unfolds through your soul.

Shaheerah herself once faced a horrific health challenge, one that shook everything she knew, believed, and understood. She now calls it a healing opportunity, which she believes is the purpose of all disease. When several doctors told her that what she was facing was incurable, that they had never seen anyone recover from this particular disease, Shaheerah said she refused to accept that as her reality. After all of her years of study and the time she had spent teaching others about the omnipotence and omnipresence of God, she says she could not receive the finality of human judgment as the reality she would live. She believed and understood that God is everywhere, at all times, present and active. This led her to ask: "What could it be that God could not cure?" Her search for that answer led to her healing and complete recovery.

Shaheerah admits that the pain and suffering, which she experienced 24/7 for more than a year, took her to a place where she no longer knew what would happen. She says she got to a point where she actually did not know if she would survive, and that led her to the point where she didn't care if she did or not: she just wanted the pain to end. Shaheerah says there were moments when the pain was so intense that she thought about taking her own life. What stopped her was the embarrassment. She thought about her family, those who loved her, and those whom she had taught about God for so many years. She thought how embarrassing it would be for her to do what she had been taught only God can do: give life and reclaim life. She didn't want that for herself, for those she would leave behind, or for God.

That recognition, she believes, was her moment of surrender. Once she surrendered her wondering, and even her belief, that she would survive, living angels began to show up in her life. These angels brought her hope in the form of information and the motivation she needed to keep trusting and believing in God. Shaheerah says she was on a support call with people from all over the world who were experiencing the same disease when her hope was restored. One woman on the call said that just managing the disease for the rest of her life was unacceptable. She needed to be totally healed. Shaheerah found strength and hope in the woman's conviction of total healing as a possibility. Hope is utterly essential in the management of your life and the ability to trust God. Shaheerah's newfound hope led her to the teachings of Christian Science and Mary Baker Eddy. These teachings, although not new to her or different from the teachings she gained in the Unity Ministerial School, took her to a deeper, more expanded understanding of who she is and what God is in her life.

We are Spirit. The essential element that lives in every individual is Spirit, which is also the essence of God. While some believe that we are Spirit housed in a body, Christian Science teaches that the body is of little or no consequence beyond what it enables us to do on the physical plane of existence. Shaheerah learned to stop focusing on the symptoms present in her physical being and instead focused on Spirit, the essence of her being. This is what is called *devotion*.

Shaheerah said that, in order to make this shift, she had to shut her life down: no telephone, no television, no outside influences at all. She had to stay in the silence and contemplate the meaning of Spirit. This was the level of devotion that she committed herself to every day for many months. Now she knows that devotion is an absolute requirement in the process of learning to trust God. She read books, listened to lectures, and then reflected on what she had read and heard. She deepened her prayer life by not asking for anything. Instead, she affirmed her hope and what she believed and understood about God.

For years, literally years, Shaheerah lived in silence, focusing on the fact that Spirit had supremacy over every cell, tissue, and organ in her body. She says she simply "hung out" in the awareness that Spirit could and would change the chemical and molecular structure of her body. That was her turning point. She began to improve. The pain disappeared. She became stronger and stronger until one day, she says, she knew she had been healed. She came to understand that her body was like a car and that Spirit, as the mechanic of the car, knew how to restore the body to total working order. And it did.

When I asked Shaheerah why she believes it is so difficult for people to trust God, she said, "Because God is intangible and invisible, it is easier to believe what you been told about God than it is to learn about God through experience." As a minister, she knows that most people have been taught that God is punishing and vengeful. Thus, many people live in fear of God without the understanding that God loves them. God is love, and God sees us with love, regardless of what we believe.

Where are we taught that as human beings we are worthy of God's love? Where are we taught that God loves us and does not require us to prove ourselves worthy of His/Her love? Very few of us get this lesson in the development of our understanding of God. As a result, we also come to believe that we are not worthy of the things we seek from God. We believe we are not worthy of prosperity or health or even loving companionship because of who we are or what we have done. Instead, we wait to be punished for even asking for the things we desire. Our sense of unworthiness blocks our ability to receive what we desire. Then when it does not show up, we blame God and fall deeper into mistrust.

Trust in God is also a sign of spiritual maturity, which comes through experiences. If, however, you use your experiences as a sign that you cannot trust God or that God is punishing you for something, you will miss the learning present in every opportunity and remain spiritually immature. When you are spiritually mature, you understand and recognize that life is like a beautifully wrapped gift. You don't know what the gift is until you unfold the paper. As you unwrap the gift, there is a level of trust involved because you don't know what is in the box: You don't know if you'll find a snakeskin wallet or a live snake. Trust is about believing that, even if there's a snake in the box, it won't bite. Or, if the snake does bite you, someone will have the antidote. The distrustful, spiritually immature person will simply be upset that there was a snake in the box.

Trust is the master principle, and trusting God is required to master this principle. When you master trust in your mind, heart, and soul, you will have gained a hold on everything you will ever need in life.

When you trust in God you learn about flow and cycles, about acceptance and surrender. Without trust you will more often than not find yourself fighting to maintain control over things that you simply cannot control. When you believe, understand, and accept that God is in the flow of your life, you can surrender the outcome, knowing that it must be and will be perfect for everyone involved, even those whom you cannot see. When it comes to trusting God, the bottom line is this: *What have you got to lose?*

MASTERING THE 4 ESSENTIAL TRUSTS

Trust in Self

Trust in God

Trust in Others

Trust in Life

Chapter 8

TRUST OR CONSEQUENCES

> TRUST TAKES YEARS TO BUILD,
> SECONDS TO BREAK, AND
> FOREVER TO REPAIR.
>
> —*Unknown*

Wherever you are in this moment, stop, raise your hand, or nod if the following statement is or has been true for you: *"I have a difficult time trusting other people."* Most of us have entertained this thought or spoken these words with conviction at some point because we actually believe they are true. What I have discovered in my own life, as well as from years of working with other people, is that our issue is not really trusting other people, our core issue is trusting ourselves to get through the pain of the disappointment and betrayal we experience when people violate the trust we place in them.

Even when we have experienced such upsets time and time again, we cannot seem to figure out how to respond when someone we love and care about is inconsiderate to us, dishonest, or abandons us. And we long to know how to insulate ourselves from the possibility of being disrespected, rejected, or exploited by people we know or hardly know.

Trusting others is a difficult task and a powerful lesson we must all endure and move through, regardless of what happens. It means that we place our confidence in someone to be honest, to keep his promise, to honor her word, and to treat us with decency and respect at all times, no matter what. The point we all seem to miss is that trusting other people means that we have a realistic understanding and perspective about people and that we must prepare ourselves for their failures. It means knowing that people are sometimes broken and complex; that they will lie when they are afraid and sacrifice our feelings to keep themselves safe and comfortable. Trusting others means recognizing, acknowledging, and accepting that we all have a history, and in some instances that history is filled with hurt, pain, and wounds that can and do impede our best intentions, resulting in dysfunctional behaviors that can have a devastating impact on those we know or love and care about most. In essence, trusting others means knowing that at all times, under all circumstances, in every situation, and with all people, we must be willing to trust, forgive, and start all over again.

HIDDEN TRUST ISSUES

Reading books on relationships or researching trust-related issues might lead you to conclude that women have a monopoly on being disappointed, betrayed, and violated. That would be a false conclusion. Men have just as many trust experiences and issues as women do. The difference is, they aren't always able to identify the problem as a trust issue, and they are far less willing to talk about their experiences. More often than not, when it comes to men, their objectionable behavior looks like rejection, abandonment, fear of commitment, jealousy, or control, when the truth is: *They are afraid to trust.*

Men are lied to and cheated on; men have their boundaries violated; men are taken advantage of; men are disappointed, let down, and abandoned. While the process of developing trust in oneself and others is the same for everyone, men may actually have a more difficult time rebuilding trust once it has been broken, because it's more difficult for them to admit they were duped in the first place. It's also somewhat more challenging for men to forgive others, because they either don't see the need to or refuse to forgive themselves.

Kevin was a classic example of a man with serious trust issues who did not know it. He grew up under the iron fist of his very domineering mother, Anna. As a child, Kevin lost his voice, his ability to speak up for himself, and the capacity to express his personal needs, experiences, or desires. Anna had a bad habit of calling Kevin names and shutting him down whenever he tried to assert himself. Like a malevolent dictator, Anna decided what her son needed, wanted, and should be doing.

In an attempt to keep their sons in line, many mothers fail to recognize the distinction between discipline and emasculation. The situation is only exasperated when young boys do not see healthy adult interactions between men and women. This lack of healthy role models limits their ability to understand how men are supposed to be and behave with the opposite sex.

Kevin's mom was single, overbearing, angry, and verbally abusive. Anna had few good things to say about Kevin's father, who was rarely around and offered little instruction when he did see his son. As a teenager, Kevin learned some stuff about girls from the guys on the street, but at home he was mute and intimidated. By the time he graduated from high school, Kevin had only one clear vision for his future: get the hell away from his mother, as far and as fast as he could.

In college Kevin did not do well with the girls. They thought he was shy. The truth is, he was terrified of saying or doing the wrong thing. Watching his peers, he learned a few things about how to keep a woman in line, but he was not willing to pull the choke chain and risk the backlash of a woman's mouth or behavior. Then he met Vickie in English class, and they hit it off right away. Vickie was cute, sort of quiet, and very, very street smart.

Vickie would offer Kevin insights about how to be cool and how to modify his behavior without offending his sensibilities or his manhood. They had been cooing and courting for about three months when Kevin discovered that Vickie was the most popular female pot dealer on campus. Kevin couldn't imagine what Vickie saw in him. Or why she wanted to hang with him when she could have any man on campus. *How lucky am I,* he thought, *to have such a beautiful and smart woman who wants me?*

Vickie taught Kevin a lot about how to be, what to do, how to do it, and how to keep his business under wraps. While she didn't yell or call him names, Vickie knew exactly how to get Kevin to do whatever she wanted him to do by suggesting it to him as if it were his idea in the first place. She let him in on her little secret because she needed and wanted male protection. She also needed some help with her growing business. The inseparable couple was well into their junior year when Vickie got busted for dealing pot on campus. Her way out was to point the finger at Kevin. After all, he had the stash in his dorm room, and he had most of the money in his pocket. When confronted by school officials, Kevin refused to say that he was a delivery boy for his girlfriend or that he held the stash because she had three roommates while he only had one.

Kevin was expelled from school, placed on probation, and abandoned by Vickie, who told the college officials that the only reason she was dealing was because Kevin had threatened her life. She also told them that she loved him but was afraid of him. Kevin's mother had a few choice names for her son, reminding him how stupid he had always been, which was why she refused to come to court and would not allow him to come back home. He ended up living with his aunt in the city and falling back on everything Vickie had taught him about wheeling and dealing in the streets.

Graduating from pot to harder substances, it took only two years before Kevin earned himself a three-year bid for street-corner peddling of his product. In jail, he learned a great deal more about whom to trust, when to trust, and what happened when you trusted the wrong people. In Kevin's mind, anyone who asked you for anything could not be trusted, and those who did not ask were probably just waiting for the opportunity to take something from you. He learned that staying to yourself and speaking only when spoken to might make people think you were slow or crazy, but those were the behaviors that would keep you safe.

By the time Kevin was released from jail, his aunt had gotten married. Mr. Green was a quiet man, somewhat like Kevin, and he was very, very religious. He took a liking to Kevin, and on most evenings they had long and very interesting talks about life and women and God. Kevin had never experienced this kind of communication or relationship with anyone, let alone a man. He really liked Mr. Green, but he was also suspicious about what the man really wanted. He wondered what Mr. Green was up to by being so nice and accepting of who Kevin was and how he had lived.

Kevin's aunt, who was the total opposite of her sister, encouraged the relationship between her husband and her nephew. In fact, whenever Kevin would ask her something, she would respond, "I'm not sure. You should probably ask Mr. Green." In Kevin's mind, it felt like a setup, another form of rejection; he simply didn't understand why his aunt wouldn't tell him what to do and how to do it. He was confused and cautious about them both, just waiting for the axe to fall. He just wasn't sure who would be swinging the axe: Mr. Green or his aunt.

When you have lost your voice and don't know how to trust yourself, it's impossible to trust anyone else. When the people you love, care about, and trust violate you, distinguishing between loving care and a setup is difficult. Kevin had been taught that kindness was a weakness. He also believed that when you let people into your heart, they would hurt you sooner or later. These were the lessons he learned from his mother and Vickie. He had yet to master the lesson of knowing when to trust himself—or even that he *could* trust himself—or when it was safe to trust other people.

It had been almost a year since his release when Mr. Green told Kevin that a new condition for his staying in the home would be attending church. Wednesday night service was optional, but Sunday service was a requirement. *Okay! Here we go!* Kevin had known they were going to want something, and here it was! They wanted him to be something he didn't know how to be and to do something he didn't know how to do.

If he refused, they would kick him out, but if he did what they wanted, he would probably mess it up. Kevin was between a rock and a hard place. He knew he should take a stand for himself, but he didn't know how. He was afraid to give in and afraid not to at the same time. Thanks to Mr. Green's advice, he had saved up a little money, so instead of asking questions, making a counteroffer, or simply honoring the request, Kevin packed his bags and left their home. He had been staying with a friend from work for a few weeks, looking for his own place, taking the bus to work, and minding his own business, when he got the call from his aunt: Mr. Green had had a stroke. They did not know if he would recover. Could he please come, because when Mr. Green opened his eyes, he had asked for Kevin.

When Kevin got to the hospital, there were about 25 people in the waiting room. He recognized some of the men and women from his few visits to church. His boss was there, and so were Mr. Green's grown children, two sons and two daughters from a previous marriage. The other people were from Mr. Green's job. His aunt gave him a big hug, as if everything between them was just fine; Mr. Green's children also hugged him. One of Mr. Green's sons introduced him to Mr. Green's co-worker as his brother.

Kevin was totally confused. What was up with these people? What did they want from him? Why were they being so nice? Why had they even called him? He just couldn't figure it out. He sat with them, listened to them, and stood with them when the doctor came out to give them the prognosis. Mr. Green was awake. He had no mobility on his right side, but he could speak. He wanted to see just the family. Kevin's aunt went in first. When she returned, the sons stood up to see their father, and they invited Kevin to go in with them. Reluctantly, Kevin obliged.

Mr. Green looked fine, except for all of the tubes and machines. He put his left hand out to reach for his sons, each of whom bent down to hug his father. Kevin could not remember having ever seen one man hug another man in that way. He didn't know what to do, so he stood frozen by the door. When Mr. Green's eldest son invited Kevin over to "greet Dad," something hit him like a ton of bricks. *Acceptance.* Somehow in that moment he felt totally accepted and loved. It hit him first in his chest, then in his knees. After all he had done, everything he had said or not said, these people—including Mr. Green—were loving and accepting him just based on who he was. Kevin couldn't move. He felt as if he was about to faint. All eyes were on him. He tried to speak and could not. Mr. Green spoke for him. In a very soft voice, and with slightly slurred speech, Mr. Green said, "Trust me, son, all is forgiven." When he heard those words, Kevin fell to his knees and wept.

It is difficult for a broken heart to learn how to trust. It is particularly difficult when the heart that has been broken has never learned self-trust or the value of trusting others. When as children the adults we depend on for care and support unconsciously teach us that we cannot trust our own thoughts and feelings, we begin to rely on others to interpret what we feel and to tell us what to do. These are the seeds of co-dependence and people pleasing. When you have no voice and no independent thoughts, developing the depth of self-trust that is required to make independent and wise choices for yourself is almost impossible.

When as children we experience emotional alienation and/or abuse by domineering, intrusive, or emotionally unstable adults, learning to trust the goodness and kindness of others can be an insurmountable challenge. For many men, like Kevin, self-trust is undermined at a very young age by well-meaning, emotionally absent, or damaged parents who believe they are doing the best thing for the child. Then there are the many cases in which parents either don't know or don't care how their lack of child-rearing skills will impact the psyche of the young boys and adolescents in their midst. A boy who does not have a voice, or who has been taught that what he needs, feels, and thinks does not matter, becomes a man with serious trust issues.

WHAT GOES AROUND COMES AROUND AND AROUND . . .

Diane and Denise are identical twins. For most of their lives, they dressed alike and finished each other's sentences. Until well into their teen years, they did everything together. Then, a strange phenomenon entered their world—boys! When they entered high school, although each developed her own style of dressing, the boys couldn't seem to tell them apart.

The more difficult challenge was that Denise was never attracted to the boys who liked her. She was always drawn to the ones who fell for her sister, Diane. Although it caused some minor friction between them, Diane believed that Denise was being totally honest when she promised never to get out of line with a guy whom her sister was interested in. This pattern continued well into their young adult years, when the twins headed to two different colleges. They talked by telephone every day, sharing their most intimate secrets, particularly about the guys they were interested in. They were in their senior year when Diane announced she had found "the one," a medical student who simply made her toes curl. Denise could hardly wait to meet him when Diane said she was bringing him home for winter break.

Stephen, the doctor-to-be, was a cutie! He was pleasant, was well spoken, and had a great sense of humor; for the first three days, he really could not tell the twins apart. They kept reminding him that their hair was different, but when he impulsively grabbed Denise's hand under the table, she began to think he wasn't really trying to remember that they were different people.

On New Year's Eve, the twins thought it would be fun once again to dress alike. They each bought the same dress and shoes. Although Diane's hair had blond highlights and was slightly longer, they managed to achieve the same hairstyle. They knew their parents would be delighted, and it would be fun to tease and trick the rest of the family.

As the clock approached midnight, Diane was standing next to her beloved and Denise was standing behind him. When the clock struck 12, he turned away from Diane and planted a sloppy wet kiss on Denise's lips. Pushing him away and screaming, Denise ran to her sister and began to apologize. Diane was stunned, as were her parents. Stephen made a very weak excuse that made absolutely no sense to anyone, but rather than challenge him, Diane just laughed it off. Denise, on the other hand, felt that her sister needed to pay closer attention to what was going on with her beau.

Fast forward! Diane and Mr. Doctor-to-Be had been married for four years and were expecting their first child when Denise traveled to spend a week with them. Five minutes into the visit, she knew that something was off, but her sister was being overtly cagey and kept mum. Her husband was doing his residency at a prestigious hospital and was therefore rarely home. Maybe that was it. Diane talked briefly about being lonely, and she said how glad she was that her mother had committed to coming for three weeks after the baby was born.

It was when Denise witnessed how her brother-in-law talked to her sister that she became intently concerned that something was really off in her twin sister's world. What she could not figure out was why her sister would not confide in her. Was it that she didn't trust her? Or was she just too embarrassed to tell the truth?

Diane went into labor three weeks early, on the day Denise was scheduled to leave. Their mother arrived later that day, and the baby came the next morning: a beautiful little girl. That evening, as Denise was leaving the hospital, euphoric over her sister's little angel, she was accosted by a young woman dressed in scrubs. The woman called Denise all manner of names and vowed that she would do everything in her power to "get her man back."

Denise tried to explain to the woman that she was making a mistake, but when her attacker mentioned her brother-in-law's name, Denise realized that she had stumbled into the truth she had been feeling all week long. The rest of the conversation took place in the parking lot, at the rear bumper of Denise's car. Beverly had been in and out of a relationship with Stephen since college. She had left him, gotten married, then divorced, but they had rekindled their relationship the previous year when she finished nursing school and found herself working in the same hospital where he was a resident. No, they had not been having an affair. They had been involved in a long-term relationship. Stephen told Beverly that he was with Diane only because he and Beverly had broken up, and he promised that he would leave his wife. In fact, Stephen *had* briefly left Diane over a year before, but he had gone back home because he thought Beverly was mentally unstable. Beverly did not know that Diane was pregnant, which is why she had mistaken Denise for her sister.

We have a few things going on here: The first is that you can love and trust someone and still not share your deepest darkest secrets with her. You may love and trust your mother with your life and still not tell her that you have two lovers or that you smoke marijuana or that you stole change from her purse when you were ten years old.

As humans, we are often challenged with trusting someone and disappointing them. Everyone thrives on approval and acceptance. When we believe that something we have done or have been involved with would disappoint someone we love, chances are we will withhold the information. Does this mean we are untrustworthy? Or does it simply mean we are human? Does it mean we believe the person from whom we withhold the information cannot be trusted? Or does it mean we are attempting to control or maintain her opinion of us? These are some of the common pitfalls we face when it comes to trusting others. It is a choice we make in response to our needs in that moment.

Back to our story:

Stephen had demonstrated a propensity toward shady behavior with Denise early on. Diane was unaware of, or choosing to dismiss or deny, the early signs that she had fallen in love with Slim Shady. From his grabbing her hand under the table, to his New Year's Eve kiss, to that feeling she could not shake four years later, Denise had known that something was off with her brother-in-law, but she had chosen not to say anything. Why? Because nothing is more difficult than to suspect or accuse someone of being untrustworthy when his surface behavior and communication contradicts what you know to be true within yourself.

We want to believe the best about people. We always want to give others the benefit of the doubt, and as human beings we are reluctant to move or speak without cold, hard evidence that substantiates what we're feeling. When the evidence is missing and those around us do not seem to support our suspicions, more often than not we will deny what we know in fear of being wrong. Why didn't Denise tell her sister that Stephen had grabbed her hand under the table? Does this omission mean that she is untrustworthy? Why didn't Diane tell her sister what she was feeling rather than waiting for Denise to spill the beans and confirm her suspicions?

How do you raise questions about someone's trustworthiness when everyone else seems to be blind to what you see? Are we willing to risk upsetting people or being wrong about our suspicions when it has an impact on our intimate relationships? In more instances than we care to admit, rather than run the risk of being wrong, we will remain deaf, mute, and blind, even when we have clear evidence that what we *think* is true is, in fact, true. In the end, when others discover that we knew or had reason to know the truth, they are disappointed that we did not tell them. In fact, they may feel that we betrayed their trust.

Denise explained to Beverly that Mr. Doctor-to-Be was and had been married for the past four years and, as far as she knew, had never discussed leaving her twin sister. She asked Beverly to back off because her sister had just had a baby, and she promised that she would deal with Mr. Doctor-to-Be herself.

She kept her word. That night Denise confronted Stephen about the young woman she had met and their conversation. She demanded to know his intentions with regard to both his wife and his lover. When Stephen tried to play it off as if Beverly were crazy, Denise reminded him of the New Year's Eve kiss and the other slips of integrity he had demonstrated to her.

Although Stephen eventually admitted his infidelity and promised to clean it up, Denise didn't believe a word of it. Stephen had already proven his ability to live a double life, and she did not trust that he would honor his word or her sister. *When people show you who they are, believe them the first time.*

Denise was torn about whether or not to tell Diane what she had discovered, but wondered whether telling her would be a violation of her sister's trust. They had always taken care of each other. They had always looked out for each other. How could she protect her sister from any future heartache? It just wasn't fair that she should be the one to break her sister's heart and shatter her dreams.

Diane was in her room resting with the baby when Denise asked her mother what she knew about what was going on between Diane and her husband. Mom knew everything except that the other woman was still in the picture. Mom knew that Diane and Stephen had separated briefly, but she thought it was because he was never home, and when he was, he treated Diane with utter disregard. Diane said he was mean and had, on several occasion, threatened her, but he had never made any physical moves. Mom had told Dad, and Dad had given him a good talking-to.

According to Mom, Stephen came home after a two-month absence, and Diane said things were much better now. Denise's first response was anger. To think that her sister didn't trust her with the truth just made her mad; then she was sad to know that her sister didn't trust her.

Why? What had she done that would make Diane think she couldn't tell her the truth? Why would her twin sister lie or hide the truth from her? It wasn't until her mom reminded her that perhaps Diane had felt the same way when Denise had waited until the last minute to tell Diane that she was going to a different college and later that she was not moving back home after college. Then her mom hit a really raw nerve when she asked if Denise had ever told Diane about the pregnancy she terminated the year before. Mom said it best: *"What you do and how you do it will come back to you, even when what you do is done to protect or help or spare someone else."*

Even when you have the best intentions, demonstrating that you do not trust someone with the truth, your feelings, or specific information will come back around, sooner or later.

TENDING THE GARDEN OF TRUST

Learning to trust someone is a process that grows over time. It requires that we really get to know people; that we remain open to moving through their mistakes and our own; that we allow people to grow, change, and heal in our presence while we grow, change, and heal in theirs. And when the evidence is clear that a certain person is simply not trustworthy, we must accept that, make a choice about the nature of our relationship with them, and move on.

Nothing impedes our ability to trust someone more deeply than not recognizing and accepting the truth that is revealed through their communications and behavior. Acting as if we don't know what we know about someone, or as if he did not say what we know he said, will only get us into deep trouble.

By spending time with someone, we gain knowledge and insight about their motivations, their character, their needs, and their fears that will support us in recognizing who they are and what motivates them. Noticing how they treat others and what they say about others provides insight and information that gives us silent clues as to how they may treat us. A prudent, wise, and self-aware person will catalog this information and avoid the trap of thinking: *They did that to everyone else, but they'll be different with me!*" They may be different. They may have grown and changed; however, you still need information as a yardstick to determine whether or not your assessment is true. Learning to trust someone means taking the time to observe who they are and being honest about what you discover.

Really learning how to trust others and how to forgive them when they fall short begins with taking a good, long, honest look at yourself. Ask yourself:

- Do you always keep your word?

- Do you always tell the truth about what you need and want?

- Are you always respectful of the feelings and needs of others?

- Have you always lived up to the trust and confidence others have placed in you?

- Most important, have you forgiven yourself for the instances when you have fallen short in your relationship with yourself and with others?

We are all human. We have all had days when we are less than our best selves. Acknowledging that and telling the truth about it is the key to learning to trust others. Giving ourselves the benefit of the doubt, understanding and acknowledging what motivates us and what throws us off track, and being real about what we have done that has hurt and disappointed others—whether we meant to do it or not—gives us a sense of compassion and awareness about the shortcomings of those around us. Raising ourselves above the human fray by believing that we are always right, have always been right, and have never done anything to hurt, harm, or disappoint anyone else can only lead to unrealistic expectations of others.

One important aspect of trusting others means knowing what you are capable of, remembering what you have done during your less-than-great moments, and being willing to recognize that the same is possible for every other human being. When you are serious about being able to trust others, you are willing to adjust your expectations. One way to think about this is the following: consider how many people have been or may be lying on the therapist's couch as a result of their relationship or interaction with you. No one is perfect! And by some miraculous means, we have all survived one another.

EXCUSES

This was not the first time; Max had violated Cece's trust and then denied having done so on several occasions. He had stolen money from her and tearfully protested her accusations at least three times. And he had failed to honor her boundaries or to respect the rules of the house more times than she cared to remember.

Each time Cece made excuses for her brother. She told herself that Max was young, that he was still learning, and that he needed repeated instructions to get the gist of what was being offered to him. Each time she wanted to believe him, but doing so meant that she had to diminish, deny, or dismiss her gut feelings. In order to trust him, she had to distrust herself and disown her intuition. Because the truth about Max was simply too difficult to accept, she chose to violate herself instead.

This time, Cece told herself that things would be different, that Max would be different. He had been out of her home and partially out of her life for over a year. When he contacted her, asking if he could stay for a few days, until he could get in touch with a friend, he sounded different and it felt different. This time he had a plan. He wanted to save some money, make a final break from his co-dependent girlfriend, and get his own place. He talked about some of the things he had learned since his last departure and finally acknowledged his previous wrongdoings by asking for forgiveness.

Cece wanted so desperately to believe that Max had changed that she failed to consult with her own internal guidance system. His words had warmed her heart, and the truth was, she missed him. This time, in an attempt to take a hard line, Cece gave Max clear boundaries and a time limit. He had three weeks to figure everything out; during those three weeks he would have to work to earn his place; and he was not to have any guests in the home. Three weeks turned into three months because he really toed the line. He was supportive and helpful in everything she asked of him.

Well . . . there were a few slips here and there, but nothing major. The slips were caused more by mindlessness than intentional bad behavior. Things got a little rocky when Max reengaged with his girlfriend, Meagan; however, after their temporary separation, even she seemed different. Meagan was more polite and attempted to be helpful when she did come around. When the two of them got into an argument, they would both back down and correct themselves as soon as they were challenged or questioned. Shortly thereafter, one or both of them would apologize, and things would return to a peaceful norm fairly quickly.

In Cece's mind, all of this was concrete evidence that things had changed and that she could trust that Max was doing better. It was this process, the signs of humility and his willingness to make corrections, that allowed her to believe that he could be trusted.

Cece stopped challenging the little things Max said and did that felt off. She relaxed her defenses. She ignored her concerns. She placed her trust in what she wanted to believe about Max rather than checking in with herself and holding fast to her boundaries.

The surprise birthday party that her family organized shocked her. Without warning, what had started out as a quiet Saturday evening morphed into people everywhere—dancing, eating, and celebrating her on this special day. No one ever knew what to give Cece as a gift, so they all gave her money. Each person came to her and offered words of love and gratitude as they stuffed some amount of money somewhere on her body. When it was all said and done, she had money glued, pinned, or taped everywhere on her body and on her clothing, and there wasn't a dry eye in the house. Like a stripper, she peeled the bills off and threw them into a basket. It was hilarious, the highlight of the party.

After Cece said good-bye to the last guest, she took the basket and placed it in the most sacred place in her home, her prayer room. Believing that it would be safe there, she closed the door and went to bed. After the party, Max left the house to spend a few days with his cousin. The next morning, as scheduled, Cece left her home for a three-day business trip. As she buckled her seat belt, she had a brief inclination to go back in and move the money, to hide it. But being too lazy to walk back and thinking that no one was home anyway, she ignored her gut feeling and took off as planned.

On the morning Cece was scheduled to return, she got a telephone call from her sister, who had forgotten she was away. Her sister had gone by the house looking for Cece to join her on a brief shopping trip. Her sister said that when she got to the house, she found Max in the kitchen counting money. At first, she didn't think anything about it, but then something just didn't feel right.

Cece's heart dropped. She asked her sister to go into her prayer room and see if there was any money in the basket next to the vase of flowers. Her sister wanted to know where her birthday money was. "Just go," she instructed her again. As Cece waited, her stomach went sour, and her head began to ache. Her sister reported that there was $77 in the basket. "Is that your birthday money?" she asked.

Cece wanted to hang up and throw up. Instead, she asked her sister to check the guest room to see if Max was there. He was not in the guest room but outside with the dog. Heartbroken, Cece told her sister to call all of the men in the family and ask them to come and deal with the all-too-familiar situation. Cece's brother, Max, whom she had trusted enough to allow to stay in her home again, after too many betrayals, had stolen all but $77 of her birthday money. Because she didn't trust herself not to cause him severe bodily harm, Cece had to turn the situation over to the men in the family, who had vowed the last time that if Max betrayed her again, they would set him straight.

How had this happened? Why had this happened? Cece lamented. In truth, it was painfully simple. Max had violated his sister again because she had wanted to believe that he had actually changed. The first time she had discovered him smoking in his room after she had asked him not to smoke in her home *was a sign* that he could not be trusted to honor his word. Cece had been violated again because she put more stock in Max's smooth talk than she did in her own gut feelings.

She remembered that once when she had returned home after a shopping trip, she had felt that something was not quite right, but she ignored it. Max had been just a tad too friendly, and he seemed restless. Later, when she heard him talking on the phone, she decided to pursue what she had first ignored. In their conversation, she discovered that he had invited his friend into the house to use the restroom after she had specifically asked him not to have anyone in the house in her absence. Cece let her annoyance go after he swore the guy had been in the house for only five minutes to pee.

If Cece's antennae had been up then, she could have prepared herself for the even deeper desecration now. She was violated because she couldn't accept the unpleasant thoughts she had about her brother and the unsettling feelings that keep surfacing. She beat them down when they came up, because Max's behavior seemed so different this time and his words sounded so sincere. In reality, though, there had been warning signs that she had refused to listen to. These signs—plus the small, seemingly insignificant violations—were mounting evidence that her trust had been misplaced.

Cece knew that Max was impulsive, that he often acted without thinking or considering the consequences. She knew that he had no sense of self-worth and therefore could not value their relationship—or any relationship. Max said what he needed to say and did what he needed to do to get what he needed in the moment. The fact that this was the result of his childhood and life experiences was none of her business. She knew that he had been abandoned and rejected by both of his parents, and as a result he had no self-esteem. She knew who he was and what he was capable of, and yet she expected him to behave differently.

Max had spent the better part of his adult life sleeping on other people's sofas and living out of black plastic bags. For all intents and purposes, he was homeless. Every place he stayed was temporary because he knew that it would be only a matter of time before he did or said something that would get him put out. Max would try for as long as he could to toe the line and live up to the expectations. Now Cece realized that Max didn't have the understanding or capacity or perhaps even the desire to do better. She accepted that he was okay knowing that sooner or later he would need to hustle up another temporary sofa or corner in a back room.

Cece was betrayed because she did not trust what she knew about the mismatch between her expectations and her brother's capacity. She expected Max to do what she knew he could not do and to be who she knew he was not . . . and finally the bill came due.

To Trust or Not to Trust

It is impossible for people who are untrustworthy to become trustworthy simply because you want them to be that way. Trust is a matter of character. Some folks are untrustworthy because of the belief patterns that are tied to their past experiences. They may have learned or come to believe that trustworthiness is not important. Others are untrustworthy as a matter of conscious or unconscious choice. People show you who they are in what they do. This is not to say that people cannot change. They can. Nevertheless, you must trust what you see people do and build your self-trust muscles until you have the capacity to say no to their inappropriate or unacceptable behavior the first time you encounter it.

While it is possible to love untrustworthy people, continuing to place your trust in them is not wise. Trust grows from and deepens with intimacy. Trusting others requires that you first and foremost learn to be intimate with yourself. The more intimate you are with yourself, the more truth you can tell yourself about yourself. The more time you spend in contemplation of what makes you tick, the more you know who you are, and the more you will learn about whom you can trust. When you are not intimate with yourself, your attempts to trust others will always fall short because you will overlook key elements and important signs revealed in their behavior.

Self-intimacy fosters understanding. An understanding of yourself supports you in learning to see and understand other people. Understanding people is essential to your ability to trust them. This level of understanding is the result of the many small interactions and connections that occur over time. In the process, you learn to trust people's way of being: how they show up in the room, in the community, and in the world.

SELF-PROTECTION

There is always an element of risk involved with trust, so you must be willing to risk being wrong about what you feel and sense. That means you must take precautions. If protecting yourself by trusting what you know means hurting other people's feelings—so be it. They can and will recover. However, when you trust yourself, your first thoughts will not be about anyone else, they will be about you and what feels right for you.

Remember, when you do not trust yourself, you cannot and will not trust anyone else. Instead, you will ignore your inner voice and intuitive inklings and tell yourself that what you feel is wrong. Why? Because your suspicions will not hold the other person in a good light. When you cannot face the truth, you'll find yourself making excuses for the demonstrated bad behavior that provides a clear indication that the person cannot be trusted.

Often, you will ignore the warning signs because they are simply too stressful or too difficult to acknowledge. Or the circumstances go against what you want to believe, and accepting the truth would create a domino effect in your life. So you dismiss or deny the very clear intuitive and explicit messages you receive by expecting people to live up to a level or capacity of trustworthiness that they simply cannot or choose not to honor.

When you do not trust yourself, what you feel, and what you know, you will expect people to be who they are not. You will hope against hope that they will do things you already know they cannot do. You will expect them to be who you want them to be rather than trusting what you know about who they are and what they are capable of doing. *This is not trust.* This is magical thinking, and engaging in it will set you up for a big letdown. Trusting yourself is important when dealing with others because it protects you from repeated violations and devastating heartbreaks.

When you do trust yourself, you are able to read situations, environments, and people in a way that supports your personal boundaries and keeps you safe. Self-trust also equips you to communicate to others clearly regarding what is and is not acceptable. You know what feels right and what does not, and you do not question what you feel in response to what others may do or say.

Never measure your inner clarity in response to what someone else may say or do. When you trust yourself, people cannot talk you out of what you know from within. In fact, tell others what you know as a demonstration that they cannot and will not put one over on you. You then have the ability and willingness to alter your behavior in a way that protects you and promotes an environment in which you feel safe, an environment you can trust.

When you trust yourself, you know that it's okay to see people as they are without feeling bad when what you know does not put them in a good light. When you know certain people have a propensity for dishonesty, there is no need to feel bad about it. Trust yourself enough to take precautions about how you participate in their stories and activities and adjust what you expect from your interactions with them accordingly. When you trust yourself, you don't feel bad about knowing the truth about yourself or anyone else.

As human beings we want to think the best about everyone. But the truth is, not everyone can be trusted. Some people are at a place in their own growth and learning where they do not honor themselves enough for you to trust them. It is also true that some people, at their current level of development, do not deserve to be trusted. Yes, people can change. Yes, people do deserve a second chance. Yes, there will be those instances when you'll think everything seems fine, only to discover later that it was not. When you trust yourself, you will take clear, definitive action the moment you feel an inkling or see a sign that something is off. In learning to trust others, you must learn how to distinguish between your current inner knowing and your judgments about people's past or past behaviors.

Trusting others requires a level of intimacy, a depth of understanding, and clear evidence that the people being trusted have the capacity to honor and live up to your expectations.

PERFORMANCE DATA

Trusting others is both a logical and an emotional experience that requires that your head and heart come into agreement. Logically, you learn whether or not you can trust people by calculating the risk involved. You may have faith in human nature and potential; however, you must also trust what you know based on what you have seen and experienced. In business, this is called performance data.

Trusting others requires that you gather and assess the data being provided through communication and behavior *before* you invest your trust. This logical assessment has nothing to do with expecting people to "earn your trust." To do that is to ask others essentially to guarantee to you that they will not make any mistakes as they learn to live up to your expectations. That is not going to happen! People will make mistakes, and in doing so, they may hurt your feelings or sensibilities. This does not mean they cannot be trusted.

The logical assessment that is required in learning to trust others means that you must determine, through intimate contact and communication, whether or not *who they are and what they do* keeps you safe. And whether or not the way they are being with you feels honorable and honest. When people never show up when they say they will, or when they always have an excuse or reason for not doing what they say they will, you can draw the logical conclusion that they probably cannot be trusted with more important things, like your heart. This brings us to the emotional experience of trusting others.

We all have valid reasons not to trust people. People lie. People forget. People will do whatever they think they need to do to get what they want from someone else. People make mistakes. People are emotionally clumsy and negligent. People will consciously and unconsciously hurt our feelings and then deny or become defensive about what they have done.

When it comes to trusting others, it requires that we are willing to be vulnerable and risk being hurt. For average card-carrying human beings, allowing ourselves to be vulnerable and then being taken advantage of is one of our greatest fears. This great fear, coupled with the fear of rejection, the fear of abandonment, the fear of failure, the fear of disappointment, the fear of being wrong, the fear of being ridiculed or of looking stupid, and the fear of losing love makes trusting others an almost impossible task.

Yet as humans, we crave companionship, connection, love, and intimacy with others. These cravings can and often do make us hypervigilant about managing and controlling what others do and how they do it. You will not grow emotionally and learn to trust others if or when you are attempting to control them. Instead, you must be intimate with and understanding enough of yourself to know that, no matter what happens, no matter what other people do or don't do, you will be okay.

BLOOD TRUST

It made everyone cringe when Grandma said it, but Jess had proven time and time again that Grandma was right: "If you will lie, you will steal."

No one understood why she did it. Spending quality time with her, listening to her speak, or involving her in any project that required hard work or consistent support made the truth indisputable. Jess was a liar and a thief who had hit almost everyone in the Porter family. Her mother, her siblings, her cousins, and her aunts and uncles all had a horror story they could tell about something Jess had stolen or something she lied about that involved the resources of other members of the family.

No one could figure out how to convince Jess that her felonious behavior wasn't necessary. They all loved her. All she ever needed to do was ask for their help or support. They had each, over time, forgiven her and let her back into their homes and lives. Things would be fine for a little while, and then—BAM! The cash would disappear. The credit card would have charges. The jewelry would be gone, and Jess would actually help you look for the missing item. Then you would discover who had invaded your account, and Jess would deny, deny, deny that she had had anything to do with it, only to be caught in another lie.

Everyone in the family shared a jaw-dropping moment when they discovered that Jess had cleaned out her grandma's bank account. All the money that Granddaddy had left her was gone. This time, however, Jess had covered her tracks so well, it took them almost a year to discover what she had done and how she had done it.

Aunt Belle was the first to raise suspicions about whether or not Jess had reformed her thieving ways. After Jess had written a string of checks on her mother's account and bought a computer with her brother's credit card, she had been all but banned from the family home. She was allowed to visit on Thanksgiving and Christmas, and that was it. At all other times, she could call and folks would speak to her, but she was not allowed into anyone's home. Those who let her in on holidays did everything in their power never to leave her unattended.

Jess's sister Candas was the hardest on her. She constantly reminded her of what she had done and attached a few choice names to those memories. Momma Porter would not allow bickering between siblings, so she would rarely tell Candas when she saw or spoke to Jess. She loved her daughter and actually felt guilty about her bad behavior, believing there was something she had done or not done that caused Jess to betray and violate her loved ones the way she did.

Jess was a teenager when her fingers first became sticky, which is when Momma Porter put her in therapy. From the age of 16 until she was about 22, Jess seemed to have been reformed. She made peace with her father and how strict he had been with her and her siblings. She came to understand how the experience of deprivation as a child gave her an insatiable thirst to have things that she did not need, could not afford, or was simply attracted to as an adult. The strange thing was that she didn't steal from stores or strangers; instead, she went to great lengths to steal from those who cared the most about her. But stealing from Grandma! Come on, Jess! *That just ain't right on any day of the week.*

Momma Porter had bought Grandma Porter a new computer for Christmas. They all wanted her to join the family's online page so she could keep up with family news and information. Jess was the geek in the family and agreed to help Grandma become familiar with all of the new technology so that she could always be in touch with the relatives who lived at a distance. Momma Porter helped Grandma set up all of her online bill-pay accounts, and, at a time when everyone thought Jess had reformed, she gave Jess the passwords.

Jess showed Grandma where to go and what to do to store her passwords and how to change them. When Candas discovered that Jess had Grandma's passwords, she went ballistic! She told Jess, Momma Porter, and everyone else who would listen that they were crazy if they thought Jess would not rip Grandma off the way she had done with everyone else. At the time, it had been well over a year since Jess had invaded or violated anyone in the family, and it even appeared that her tall tales about her life had come to an abrupt end. Candas didn't believe it, would not believe it, and she told them all: "Don't even call me when this S*&%$ goes down! I don't want to hear it!"

How do you know when you can trust people again after they have violated your trust? The short answer is, you may never know. People can and do change; however, it is only if and when they violate you again that you can know for sure whether they have been reformed. Trusting people who have a history of being untrustworthy is a risky business, because you just never know for sure what they will or will not do.

THE MISTRUST-GO-ROUND

People, in general, will use their past experiences to determine whom they can or cannot trust. In this sense we all have some reason or another not to trust people. In fact, being mistrustful is more often than not a default setting in the mind of those who have experienced any level of betrayal or abuse in their lives. If people are too nice, we don't trust their motives or intentions. If people seem cagey or guarded, we believe they are up to no good.

It doesn't take much to push a person from being open, vulnerable, and trusting into a pit of fear, where their defenses are high and their guard is always up. Mistrust takes little or no effort. With enough internal or external evidence to support the plausible theory that this will protect you from future or abuse or betrayal, you will have a valid reason not to trust anyone. The questions are: Does that really work? Does it really keep you safe? My experience has been that it does not.

I once heard that trust is about believing and seeing yourself and others as worthy, while mistrust is about seeing the opposite. When you do not see yourself as worthy of peace, joy, love, and all sorts of other good things, you will see others in the same light and, in doing so, will believe they are capable of all manner of wrongdoing. Following this line of thought and reasoning, we forget that life is like a mirror or an echo chamber, where what you send out comes back. When you see, hold, or believe yourself to be unworthy, you will attract people who believe the same about themselves and you. They will undoubtedly treat themselves and you with dishonor and disrespect. A violation of trust is as much a sign that people do not respect themselves as it is a sign that they are out to get you. People who honor themselves will more often than not honor you, too.

The key to trust is to remember that in this life we do not get all that we ask for, but we always get what we expect. This does not in any way excuse people for their bad behavior. Nor does it make you responsible for the misdeeds of others. However, if and when you find that you are repeatedly attracting folks who seem to abuse your trust, violate you in some way, and prove themselves to be untrustworthy, it may be time to scrutinize your thoughts and belief system.

The other possibility that can lead to an unsuspected betrayal or violation of trust is refusing to see what you see and know what you know. Life is filled with people who can be trusted and people whom you should never trust. The trick is learning which club you belong to. If you are a member of the trustworthy-people club, this does not mean you throw all caution to the wind and throw open the doors of your life to everyone who passes by. You must live life with a healthy sense of caution and awareness. You must do your due diligence to make sure that the people you are associated with are carrying the same club card that you carry. Folks who move from one club to the other, depending on the circumstances and situations in which they find themselves, may not be members in good standing of your group.

Watch! Listen! Learn! Do not be fooled by appearances but rather be educated by experiences. Do not act like you do not know that people are capable of crossing lines. Do not hope against hope that your club is so attractive to them that they will remain a loyal and dues-paying member. Remember that liars lie, cheaters cheat, and thieves have a bad habit of stealing. This does not mean that you don't trust them or believe they can never change for the better. It means that until you have clear evidence that the shift has occurred, you should not trust them with your wallet or purse or believe that they are working late every night.

Back to our story:

No one, including Jess, understood why she lied and stole, but more important, everyone had a difficult time accepting that she did, except her sister Candas. Candas, who had been sexually abused as a young girl, married a man who cheated on her and lied about it. She didn't trust anyone and was totally self-righteous about her suspicions. Momma Porter never told her children that Daddy Porter had been an alley cat, because learning how to forgive him after he left her had saved her life and opened her heart.

Jess, who had been Daddy's little princess, had never quite recovered from her father's departure. She loved her mother and sister dearly but also revealed in therapy that her father's absence, which she secretly blamed on her mother, left her with a void that she could never quite fill. She was 16 when he passed away. After many discussions, family members determined that it was about then that the spirit of dishonesty seemed to take hold of her. Although Jess came across to everyone as a kind and thoughtful person on her good days, Candas believed it wasn't safe to leave her alone in a room with goldfish. Then there was that time when Momma Porter couldn't find her ring, and everyone blamed Jess. Three months later when Momma found the ring under the washing machine, no one could apologize enough to make it up to Jess for the months of ridicule and isolation she had experienced as punishment for the missing ring. Instead, they all began to act as if they didn't know what they knew about her past behavior.

The first time the bank called to inform Grandma Porter of irregular activity on her bankcard, Jess was the one who took her to the bank to get a new card and then back home to change her passwords. The second time it happened was around Christmas, so no one became suspicious. By the fifth time it happened, though, even the bank and Candas believed that Grandma Porter was a target because of her online purchases and bill paying.

When Momma Porter asked Grandma for a short-term loan of $2,500, they discovered that the trust account had been almost cleaned out. Over the course of seven months, the balance, little by little, had been depleted from $42,000 to $5,800. At first, no one suspected Jess. It was only after the bank did a thorough investigation that they determined that most of the withdrawals had gone into another bank account that was linked to Jess's social security number.

When you know people are prone to be dishonest and they have not demonstrated that they have reformed their behavior, this does not mean they should not be trusted with *anything*. It does, however, mean it would not be wise to trust them to tell the truth. Jess had previously demonstrated that she was capable of jumping from the trustworthy club to the untrustworthy club. The challenge was not only her repeated violations of trust, it was also the difficulty everyone, except Candas, had in accepting and acknowledging the truth.

In the end, the family determined that no one had ever really trusted Jess. It was that they felt bad for her and about acknowledging that she was, in fact, someone who lied, stole, and had repeatedly harmed them. They felt guilty about the times they accused her only to learn over time that there were wrongs she was accused of that she did not commit.

Grandma realized that she never wanted to come across like Candas, who was very vocal and very committed to her total distrust of Jess. It was not attractive nor did it feel loving. The bottom line was, after Jess's first major infraction, everyone expected and suspected her of being exactly who she had demonstrated herself to be; but because they loved her, they didn't want to talk about it.

As human beings it is our nature to want to be connected to our loved ones, to live in peace rather than pain, and to seek safety rather than fear. We have a difficult time accepting that the things we believe should be good for us are not and that the people who should be good to us are not. For this reason, mistrust is almost as painful as having our trust betrayed, because it goes against our natural inclination. We have to work hard to maintain the line of mistrust, to be suspicious, to hold on to the past as the evidence that keeps us alert to the possibilities of violation by someone we love. Because we want to trust, we find ways to ignore the signs, to excuse behaviors, and to deny our internal alarms and warning signals.

We want people to be who we believe they are, and in doing so we open ourselves to opportunities for them to prove they are not full-time members of the trustworthy-people club. Learning to trust others means paying attention internally and externally without guilt or shame in knowing what you know. It means telling yourself the truth about yourself and others to the degree that you are willing to protect yourself without injuring or insulting them. It means having boundaries that are solid and consistent. It means choosing how to be in relationship with others in a way that honors them and honors what you feel and know. There are times when drawing a hard line in the sand will not only protect you, it will also protect people from themselves and their untrustworthy behavior that they cannot seem to control.

When it comes to trusting family members, we walk a tightrope that many of us struggle with. For some reason, logical or not, we believe that because we are related to someone by blood, they will not or should not have the same human frailties as the rest of the human race. We want to believe that parents will not betray or disappoint us; that uncles, cousins, or grandparents will not violate us; and that our siblings, whether older or younger, will keep us in a special place in their hearts.

Millions of us have learned from experience that nothing could be further from the truth. Fathers and mothers can lie. Aunts and uncles will sexually molest. Siblings do abandon and disappoint. Knowing this, it's important to recognize and understand that although we share a bloodline with people, we also share in the human condition. We all have lessons to learn, weaknesses to overcome, strengths to develop, and temptations to avoid.

Overcoming a family betrayal or violation is a very bitter pill to swallow—so bitter, in fact, it sometimes comes back up on us. My suggestion is that you gain some additional perspective by neutralizing the blood relationship ASAP. Start by removing the "relative" label from the offense and deal with it as if it were just another person. In doing so, you can expect the negative ego to fight back, giving you every plausible reason to be extra outraged or damaged and to hold on to the hurt because . . . *they should have known better.*

Here I would offer you what Byron Katie says in her work, "When you argue against reality, you will suffer." The reality is that whatever was done was not done because the person was related to you. The reality is you experienced it and they did it . . . because somewhere in your shared humanness, there was something each of you needed to learn or heal.

Family betrayals are the result of opportunity converging with human weakness to produce a human condition that requires healing and forgiveness. They are no more or no less devastating than any other violation or betrayal of trust. It all boils down to this: You have a choice. You can use the trust violations within your family as a reason not to trust anyone, or you can look for the lesson, employ forgiveness, heal, and grow. In making the choice, consider this self-supportive and self-honoring questions. *Do I want to be right about how wrong they were? Or do I want to find and claim peace?*

| # TRUST IN OTHERS
IS TRUST IN SELF

Americans have long embraced the national mythology that we are tough and strong and able to handle anything and everything. After all, we are the most technologically advanced nation on the planet. We are educated and, for the most part, enjoy a quality of life and a wealth of conveniences that make us the envy of the world. Yet if we sit around a table long enough with a group of America's finest, someone will start to tell the truth: *We thought we had it all together. . . . What happened?*

We no longer trust ourselves to make it through what we're going through. We do not trust that people will be there for us if and when we need them. We no longer trust that life is a benevolent process designed to help us grow.

Being human sucks! we lament. Beyond the bills and bad habits, the threat of terrorist bombs, the unfulfilling and dysfunctional relationships, and the fear that a pink slip may take up residence in our pay envelope, we seem to be experiencing a loss of meaning, direction, and life satisfaction in monumental proportions.

Workers who have launched their careers are so afraid of losing their jobs that they are trampling over one another in word and deed. Those who do not have careers or meaningful work, fear that they will never find it. Young people are putting tattoos on and holes in parts of their bodies that should not be seen in public. And when they flaunt these symbols publicly, we are no longer sure what to say. Those who are considered middle-aged are afraid of everything on the love front, from whom they are sleeping with to never having someone to sleep with again. Seniors are being stockpiled in nursing homes, while the homeless are being stockpiled in armories. Whether you are 17, 27, 47, or 87, if you live in America, you are probably trying to figure out, *What's next?*

TRANSITIONS

Whether you are an adolescent heading toward young adulthood, a college graduate looking for your first job, a newlywed just getting settled, a first-time parent, an aging hipster staring down the road to a midlife crisis, or a senior praying that social security won't retire before you do, in order to navigate life's transitions—and flourish in the face of the unknown—you will be forced to trust other people.

Today, 28 percent of the total American population consists of baby boomers—people born from 1946 to 1964—of that population, 51 percent are women. This means that at least one-eighth of the American population is perimenopausal or in the throes of menopause. Menopause is a physical, mental, and emotional transition that takes you from one stage of life to another. When the transition begins, there is absolutely nothing you can do to stop it. You learn, either painfully or willingly, to go for the ride. You do what you can to make it easier. If you have ever had a hot flash in the middle of a business meeting, or been reduced to tears at the sight of fresh, crispy broccoli in the supermarket, you are painfully aware that life's transitions will humble you.

Women have many more options for handling life's transitions than men. Women crying publicly will stop traffic and raise concern.

Men doing the same thing will evoke stares, smirks, and even contempt. Menopausal women can take hormone replacements. Although men experiencing andropause, or male menopause, have the same option, the challenge is getting them to confide in someone that something is amiss in their minds or their lives.

Women have no problem writing in a journal, joining a support group, or crying on a friend's shoulder. Men, on the other hand, tend to frown upon such "girly" activities. They get busy, get drugged, act out, or drop out. They hide or camouflage their feelings and, in some disturbing cases, release their frustrations on vulnerable women, children, or total strangers.

The point is that the entire world is in a state of transition. The changes are coming hard and fast. If you do not have something within yourself to hold or grab on to, you can be knocked down. Whether you are male or female, black or white, wealthy or barely making it, when you find yourself in the midst of a transition, *you must consciously seek out people around you whom you can trust.*

This was a circumstance that John struggled with deeply after an unexpected betrayal.

. . . NEVER SAW IT COMING

John grew up in a two-parent household in which both his mother and father were active in his life. As the youngest son, he often heard the family tale of how his mother desperately wanted a girl after three boys. In fact, as her three sons grew up, John's mother, Madeleine, seemed to take a strong liking to all of the girlfriends John and his brothers brought home. When John and Val started dating during his junior year in college, Madeleine took to Val right away. By the time they got married, Val and John's mother were BFFs, which all but cut John out of the wedding plans, the purchase of their home, and the naming of their first child.

At first John thought it was wonderful that his wife and mother got along so well. But by the time he and Val started having some upset in their marriage, John became increasingly aware that his mother was more involved in his personal business than was normal or necessary. It was when John and his wife separated that he realized he had a serious problem: he discovered he had essentially been married to two women—his wife and his mother—and now they were both working against him.

John loved Val, he really did. Their biggest problem was that Val never felt that anything he did was right or good enough. She constantly criticized him and always wanted something else or something more. In their last year together it seemed that no matter what John did, he couldn't satisfy his wife. During their most intense arguments, she would always bolster her complaints against him by saying, "That's what your mother always says about you. You don't . . ." When John asked why Val always brought his mother into their arguments, she would respond, "Because she knows you better than anyone." John didn't think that was true, but he never had a fast comeback to counter Val's judgment.

Over time, Val's relationship with and reliance on Madeleine created distance between John and his mother, but it was his mother's e-mail to his wife that finally pushed him over the edge. In a detailed correspondence that Madeleine sent to him by mistake, John said he got "bitch-slapped" with the truth. His mother, an accounting wizard, was giving Val tips on what to do and what to say to get the most money from John if they were to divorce. Madeleine knew the laws, and she expertly instructed Val on what she needed to ask for in alimony, living expenses, and child support. Apparently, she had already helped Val with some investments that John knew nothing about, and in the e-mail she explained to Val how to list them in court documents so that they would not accrue to Val's list of assets.

John felt totally betrayed and devastated. His trust in his mother, in his wife, in women in general, and in himself died that day. When John confronted Val and his mother about their plot against him, they both said that he was crazy and stupid and that it was their job as women to protect themselves against men like him.

Throughout their separation, which eventually culminated in divorce, Val and Madeleine seemed to wage an all-out assault against John that impacted the entire family. His brothers and their wives, his father, and even his grandparents all seemed bewildered, yet nearly everyone remained mute about what John felt was his mother's covert behavior and overt betrayal.

How could his own mother side with his ex-wife against him? How could Madeleine support, even encourage, Val to keep the children away from him and use them as pawns? *What the heck was going on? How could this happen?*

More important, John thought, how come nobody in the family was taking up for *him* in the midst of his battle? John was angry as hell, but more than that, he was hurt. He was his mother's baby boy. She had been his world, yet it seemed as if she had turned against him. Why? Madeleine claimed John was too sensitive. She also gave him a shopping list of all the ways he had destroyed his marriage and said she had valid reasons for providing Val with her counsel.

As his children grew older, John drifted in and out of relationships, never quite able to trust or commit again. He rarely spoke to his parents, and his relationships with his brothers were cordial but strained. Rather than actually deconstruct what happened and why—and live with the heartache of it—John chose to bury his pain deep inside.

As his marriage to Val unraveled, John learned from his great-aunt a good deal about his parents' relationship and his mother's betrayals of his father, including her two affairs. *Who knew?* Children seldom are privy to the intimate details of their parents' relationships. They make up what is going on based on how they see their parents interact.

Over time, in bits and pieces, John came to understand that Madeleine was an angry, bitter woman and that his father had stayed with her because he refused to leave his three sons. Dealing with John's mother became a game of chance that John's father had learned to navigate. John never healed his feelings of betrayal because he flat out refused to forgive Val or his mother. Instead, he denied, dismissed, and ignored his feelings and stood his ground.

He would never trust another woman again. He was 54, single, and drinking way too much when his mother passed away. He did not attend her funeral.

John's mother's meddling may have accelerated the disintegration of his marriage; however, a truly solid relationship cannot be destroyed from the outside. Madeleine never honored her son's transition from boyhood to manhood, and so it was easy for her to ramrod her way into his "personal" affairs. After all, she did not trust her son's judgment. When you are stuck in seeing someone through the lens of *who they were* rather than as *who they are*, it is easy to blame them—and betray them—for not living up to *who you want them to be*. But Madeleine's betrayal was no match for John's ultimate self-betrayal, because even her death did not set him free.

TRUSTING OTHERS: AN INSIDE JOB

In the midst of betrayal, it's hard to remember that people do what they do as a function of who they are, what they need or want, and the information held in place by their belief systems. How their behavior impacts or affects others ain't personal! It is a sober reflection of how they do relationships and what everyone involved in those relationships has signed up to learn.

When we learn to trust others, it supports and eases the difficulty of life's most challenging experiences. Trusting others gives you something to hold on to when it feels as if change is sucking the life out of you. Knowing there is someone whom you can trust to share your most intimate thoughts and feelings may be the very power surge that you need. To those who think calling out trust violations is just another excuse designed to provide whiners and complainers with temporary relief from painful life experiences, may I offer—as Dr. Phil McGraw would say—"*Get real!*"

When you do not know or believe that you can trust yourself enough to trust other people, life's experiences will beat you to a pulp. Even when you believe you are clear, things happen that demonstrate how much *you don't know* about what you *think* you know. Because thinking can be hazardous to your progress in life, as you try to figure out the "what's next" and "how come," it's always important to have someone you can trust to bounce ideas off of before you make your move.

Without friends, companions, family, and people we can trust in our corner, we are prone to make up stories about what's going on, what to do, and what not to do. In the process, we delude ourselves by making up new names for old problems, and approaching those problems with solutions that do not and cannot work; we then become exhausted, bitter, and deflated, all the while believing there is no one we can turn to or lean on who will not disappoint, abandon, or hurt us.

Learning to trust others is a deeply internal process that seems frightening and difficult to master or comprehend. Many of us float from one deflating experience to another, lost and afraid to admit it, hurt and ashamed to acknowledge the pain. We work for money that we are afraid to spend. We save money that we are afraid to lose. We go in and out of relationships carrying our unmet needs, afraid that if we put them down, someone will come along and steal them.

I believe that until and unless we open our minds and hearts to a new awareness and understanding of what trust is, and how to trust others, we will continue to be lost in space. We will suffer from the effects of unnecessary loneliness or inertia and beat ourselves up about being unwittingly victimized. We will miss the beautiful sailboat of life because we insist that it is normal to swim alone in a teacup. Trusting others in the midst of a painful transition or through normal daily experiences of life is a divine privilege that teaches us how powerful, and durable, we really are and can be.

We are living in a time when our interpretation of what is going on in our lives and in the world does not provide answers that allow us to sleep at night. There is no disgrace in breaking down, falling down, or falling apart. It is, however, disconcerting not to have a path or process that allows you to pull yourself back together.

Trusting others and allowing them to support you when you feel weak or vulnerable or confused is a workable and viable option. Trusting yourself is a loving, self-supportive, self-nurturing process that will open your mind and heart to a way of being that merges the edges of the soul into a courageous and cohesive demonstration of character. Learning to trust others is the way that your character gets its daily strength training.

PRISONERS OF THE PAST

Daphne expected men to lie to her because her father had a bad habit of breaking promises and telling her lies about why he had done so. She learned that he was lying from her mother, who constantly harangued, "Don't believe a word he says! If his mouth is moving, he is probably lying." By contrast, Daphne's brother, Sean, learned that he constantly had to prove himself to women in order for them to actually believe what he was saying. He learned this from his mother, who constantly told him, "I hope you don't grow up to be a liar like your father." He also learned it from his father, who told him, "Just say what you need to say to keep their mouths shut."

Both Daphne and Sean had a very difficult time establishing lasting intimate relationships with others as adults. Daphne would accuse people, particularly men, of being dishonest, even when this was not the case. Sean went out of his way to prove himself to be trustworthy, which often meant that he gave more than he received and accepted less than he wanted or deserved—from women in particular but also from all people in general.

Things came to a head for the siblings when Sean promised Daphne he would pick up her daughter's birthday cake. He called her several times to make sure he had the correct address for the bakery. The only reason Daphne had asked for her brother's help was because she could not trust that her husband would get the cake and arrive at the party on time. Sean had taken on the lifelong role of doing for his sister what she did not trust her husband to do. He frequently did things for her, and yet Daphne very rarely said thank you or acknowledged his support.

Sean left work 30 minutes early on the day of the festivities to ensure he could pick up the cake and get to his sister's house on time. On the freeway, his car was struck by an 18-wheeler. Sean had to be cut out of the car and spent three days semiconscious, with two broken legs and a severe neck injury. When Daphne received the call that her brother had been seriously injured, she thought it was his way of making an excuse for not getting the cake to her on time and hung up the telephone. Thirteen days later, when Sean had the strength to call his sister, she went into a state of shock. He wondered why she had not come to see him and why she had not responded to the calls from the hospital. Daphne admitted that she thought it was his way of making excuses and covering up for not doing what he had promised to do.

Sean was dumbfounded. Had he *ever* let her down? Had he *ever* lied to her? Hadn't he *always* done what he promised to do? Daphne apologized and made her way to the hospital within hours. While she was on her way to the hospital, Sean listened to the stream of god-awful, foul messages Daphne had left him. Devastated and heartbroken, he refused to see his sister when she arrived at the hospital. They did not see or speak to each other for the next four years.

REFRAMING THE SCRIPT

In order to trust others, you must know deep down that you are a good person, that they are good people, and that you all have good intentions toward one another. This will be extremely difficult when you are framing your present experience with childhood wounds and disappointments. If you judge and evaluate your current experiences through an outdated filter, you are living in the past.

Daphne's filter was that men lie. Sean's filter was that he was obligated to do what was asked of him so that people would know he was trustworthy. Daphne and Sean had never learned how to trust themselves or anyone else. Neither one of them had accurately assessed the other's character or trustworthiness. They were not intimate, understanding, or vulnerable with each other. Instead, they did everything within their power to control the other's impression and experience of them.

You cannot trust and control. You cannot hold others hostage from the platform of your past experiences or lessons and expect to have a healthy, fulfilling, or loving relationship with them. Learning to trust others means that you must forgive and release your childhood wounds, see people for who they are as they are right now, and be willing to be wrong about who they are or are not.

Sean was not like his father, but neither he nor Daphne knew that to be true. Daphne's lack of trust in men had nothing to do with Sean; however, he did not understand that he could never do enough to make her change her mind about him, nor was it his responsibility to change her mind. Both Daphne and Sean had to learn that trusting others requires that you live in the present moment. Unless you are able to free yourself from your past filters, you will not know or trust whether the person you are with right now has good intentions.

In learning to trust others, it is important to recognize and understand that disappointment, rejection, abandonment, and seeming failures caused by bad decisions are all a part of being human. We will all face each of these human conditions at some time or another at the hands of others, not because we are inherently untrustworthy but because we are human. This is where forgiveness plays an essential role. Forgiveness will clear your channels.

FORGIVENESS

Until and unless you learn to forgive, you will have difficulty learning to trust others. Forgiveness is your ticket into the willingness to be vulnerable and your ticket out of the pain when your vulnerability is exploited. As your first step, you must be willing to engage in deep and compassionate self-forgiveness for the mistakes, errors, and poor choices you believe you made in the past. As *A Course in Miracles* counsels, "All things are lessons that God would have us learn." (W-pI.193.1:1) The choices, decisions, and missteps in everyone's life are simply the building blocks of our individual life curriculum. By forgiving what you think was wrong, you open your mind and heart to the learning you need.

Your next step is to forgive all others for what you believe they have done to hurt or harm you. From your overprotective parents to your first-grade teacher, who may have shamed you about the shape of the circles you drew, to the abusive boss who tried to make you the team scapegoat, everyone must be forgiven. *In order to trust others, you must forgive.* There is no other way to free yourself and others from bondage to the judgments you have made in the past. Without judgments, you are free to stand on the moment-to-moment experience of right now rather than referencing everyone and everything through an outdated filter, like Daphne and Sean. When you forgive, you clear the decks, you learn the lesson, and you set yourself free. When you forgive, you open your heart and mind to a new depth of understanding about who you are and why certain people and experiences were necessary in your life.

MISTAKES WILL BE MADE

Trusting others means remembering that people will make mistakes, that there are times when you will get hurt in the process of their mistakes, and that your hurt feelings are not a sign that people cannot be trusted. Instead, they are a sign that you must pay closer attention to what you do, what you ask for, and what you expect from yourself and others. When people repeatedly fall short or disappoint our expectations, we will lose trust in them. More important, we lose trust in ourselves for trusting them in the first place. As a result, we will not want to risk trusting again because of what happened last time.

The key here is to recognize that when you do not take the time to develop the intimacy required to keep yourself safe and deepen your understanding of other people and experiences, you are not trusting. You are engaged in repetitive, self-defeating behaviors that will ultimately lead you into trouble that you can blame on someone else. In some instances, people simply cannot do the thing we are expecting them to do. In these situations it is not because they are untrustworthy. Instead, it is because they simply haven't learned how to do what is required. This means they do not have the capacity to meet our expectations.

In other instances, people have not learned the self-discipline nor have they defined and developed the requisite personal values that would move them beyond their destructive or harmful behavior. This is clear in their "performance data," that is, what you observe how they do what they do. When their personal performance data provide you with evidence that they cannot or are not meeting your needs or expectations, it is not logical or appropriate to continue to expect, require, or trust that they can or will change. Some of the nicest people in the world will demonstrate that they do not have the capacity to meet our expectations and . . . *that's okay*. Do not continue to trust or expect them to fulfill your expectations. Instead, redefine and re-create the type and parameters of the relationship you choose to have with them.

MISMATCHES: EXPECTATIONS VERSUS CAPACITIES

When you are intimate with a person you have an opportunity to observe their actual capacities. When there is a mismatch between the expectations of one person and the capacity of the other person to meet those expectations, the result will feel like a violation of trust. To hold someone to expectations beyond their demonstrated capacity is not a violation of your trust. It is the result of your not trusting what you know and insisting that it be different.

There are times when we trust others, when we believe that they know what we think they know, when the truth is that, they do not know. We trust them based on our belief that they know and understand what we want; that they know and recognize what is important to us; and that they know what we expect and how they should behave in a given situation or under certain circumstances.

We put our trust in them based on our perceptions. Unfortunately, there has been no meeting of the minds, no spoken agreement, and no clear communication about what we are thinking. As a result, the other people have no way of fulfilling what is expected of them.

In an intimate relationship, it is always important to know and clarify what the other person is agreeing to do or agreeing to be for you. Pat learned about this in her last relationship. She also learned that what she first thought was a betrayal of trust on Jim's part and a mistake of trusting the wrong person on her part was actually a mismatch between her expectations and his capacity.

Jim was a kind, generous, loving, and intelligent man. But in retrospect, Pat recognized that he had a totally different perspective of *what to do* and *how to be* in a relationship from the one that Pat held. When it came the three C's of a committed relationship—*communication, cooperation,* and *collaboration*—Pat and Jim were on different channels. Unbeknownst to them, they had totally different awarenesses and understandings.

After being single for more than five years, Pat rekindled her relationship with her ex-beau. They had remained friendly throughout the years, which is how she determined that they had both changed and grown. Throughout the course of their intermittent communications, Pat discovered things about Jim that she hadn't known, and she learned to be comfortable sharing and saying things to him that she had previously withheld.

Pat and Jim never really *decided* to become a couple; they grew closer over time, and then Jim moved in. Once they were living together, Jim asked Pat to marry him, but she wanted to wait. The truth was that something in her gut was screaming, *No! Wait! Don't do it!* And, because Pat trusted herself, she acted accordingly.

Throughout her life, Pat had held a lifelong dream of being in relationship with a man she could talk to about anything and everything. And that's how she approached Jim once his clothes were in the closet; she talked to him about everything she did, everything she thought, and what she planned to do. It took her a minute to recognize that while Jim always listened intently and would offer her his thoughts and opinions, he never really told her anything about his *own* life or plans.

Pat also held a vision for all they would be able to achieve by working and planning together. Yet after a few months, she noticed that whenever they talked about doing something mutually beneficial, either it never got done or Jim would go off and do some or all of it on his own without inviting Pat to participate.

These experiences confused Pat, because Jim always showed up to support her when she was working or running a community event. However, he never invited her to participate in any aspect of his work or life. Though Jim would always tell her what he was doing, he never asked her to participate. As she thought about it, all of these omissions were small red flags; then there was a huge, glaring, and flashing yield sign that she could not ignore.

Over the course of their first year together, Pat realized that what she had regarded as their meeting of the minds was actually two minds orbiting completely separate planets. Pat increasingly suspected that Jim had a tendency to tell her what she wanted to hear rather than to respond to what she asked of him. And by the time they had been together for two years, Pat recognized that Jim simply did not have the capacity to meet her expectations or needs. He was wired quite differently than she was and seemed unaware of how or why he was missing the mark.

Eventually, Pat began to realize that what felt like a betrayal of the trust when Jim responded or did not respond in certain ways could, in reality, reflect the fact that Jim was at a different level of awareness, had a different kind of life experience, and was working from a very different frame of reference. Because his frame of reference was so different from hers, when she raised an issue with him, he would dismiss it or diminish it because it had no meaning to him.

At first, Pat was tempted to believe that Jim didn't care and that he had intentionally broken trust with her. However, she soon discovered that Jim actually believed that he understood what she wanted and simply proceeded to make everything happen from his point of view.

Because Jim worked three hours away from where they lived, he would frequently stay at his home in the city where he worked. This meant he could be gone two, three, even four days a week. As he left for his weekly trek, Pat would bid him farewell and say, "Let me know you got there, okay? Check in."

"I'm good," Jim would respond. "God is my guide. I'm protected and covered. You don't even have to worry or think about me not being safe."

"Yes, I know you will be safe, but it's good in a relationship to check in. This way if something happens and you are lying in a ditch bleeding, I can send out the Mounties. Instead of thinking, *Jim's fine, he just doesn't call me when he's gone,* I'd know that something was wrong."

"Why are you worried about me?"

"It's not about worrying about you. It's about communication and making sure that we have a pattern and a process of regular habits so that we can be alerted if anything goes sideways."

Jim would leave on Thursday, and Pat would not hear from him until or unless she called him.

After several months of no calls from the road, Pat began to feel that she could not trust Jim to honor her feelings. Even after she expressed how important the calls were to her, Jim refused to comply because he simply did not see the necessity. After many tearful and heated conversations, Pat began to accept that there was a major mismatch between her needs and expectations and Jim's capacity to fulfill them.

Pat finally accepted that Jim just didn't really understand how important staying connected was for her or that honoring her request would establish deeper connection and trust between them.

This same kind of disconnect can happen in any relationship, whether among friends or relatives. In instances where there is no meeting of the minds or common frame of reference, what results can often be construed as a trust breakdown.

Communication can strengthen willingness, expectations, intimacy, and understanding, but without a clear and definitive meeting of the minds, there can be no trust. And only with clear communication can you determine if two minds are really aligned.

In relationships between men and women or between intimate partners, even as one person says, "I want what you want," how the two individuals go about getting their respective needs met may be very different. The difference can often be mistaken for a sign of indifference or a violation of trust. We are not referring to the liar who cheats. We are talking about the small things, the day-to-day infractions that may have serious implications to one person but do not register at all with the other.

When there is no meeting of the minds, no communication or explanation of expectations, and no clear-cut agreements, it can look as if people have broken trust when the truth is they are just *doing what they do the way they do it*. While there may be no general intention to break trust, the small, repetitive infractions and failures to meet expectations can over time be more damaging than an outright betrayal.

EMOTIONAL VOCABULARIES

An important step in learning and practicing how to trust others is taking the time to assess others' communication style and competence. It is critical to determine whether you and another person have a common emotional vocabulary and a well-stocked emotional library. This is generally easy to assess through open communication and the sharing of experiences. Yet too often these touchstones are overlooked. A person who went from high school to college, college to work, and is now 25 and has never been in a relationship for longer than six months may have a very different emotional vocabulary and library than a 25-year-old who was raised in a series of foster homes, worked her way through college, got married at 20, and has been divorced for two years.

While both may be 25 chronologically, in psychological and emotional terms, they are likely on very different wavelengths. It's very easy to have your trust violated by people who function on a different emotional wavelength than you do. I witnessed this level of disconnection being played out in living color when I worked with Jay Williams, a man who fathered 34 children with 17 different women.

Jay Williams and I first connected when he wrote to *Iyanla: Fix My Life* about his desire to bring all of his children together for a family reunion. He had arrived at a place in his life where he recognized that it was important for his children to know one another, and it was important for him to learn how to be present for them. I was not as intrigued by Jay's desire to bring his children together as I was about how he had engaged with and impregnated 17 different women, some of whom had borne him children of nearly the same age within months of each other.

In working with Jay, I discovered that he had many unmet childhood needs and a great deal of unclaimed baggage related to trust. While he believed that most of his issues stemmed from his encounters with his mother, I recognized that his father had equal if not greater responsibility for Jay's behavior and sexual recklessness. Jay had a hole in his soul in the shape of his father that he had tried to fill with women. As one observer commented, "Jay was a boy who wanted a toy, and he was willing to do whatever he needed to do to get it."

What Jay wanted was the love and acceptance he had never fully experienced with either of his parents. Jay attempted to fulfill this desire through women who had similar unmet needs.

I met only one-fourth of the women who had children by Jay. Each of them was beautiful, articulate, and very attentive to her children. After my conversation with each one I found myself asking, "What did she know? When did she know it? And why did she stay with a man who seems to have no regard for violating her trust?" While Jay had lied to and betrayed each of them, these women were still willing to be in a relationship with him. Even after they had become fully aware that Jay had violated their love and their trust, they were hard-pressed to tell him how they felt or hold him accountable for his behavior.

Some of the mothers even went after each other for their involvement with Jay. Others just accepted his sometimes love and sometimes presence as a father to the children they shared. Jay's life story was a classic example of how, when people with unmet needs attract each other, they only deepen each other's pain. *What you draw to you on the outside is a function of what you are holding inside.*

Jay's relationships with so many women were a glaring demonstration of how people on different wavelengths, with different emotional vocabularies and libraries, engage in ongoing trust violations that are excused away with the currency of false promises.

HOPE VERSUS TRUST

Learning to trust others means that you not only have an awareness of your own unmet needs, you also possess a consciousness of how desperate you are to get those needs met. When you are *desperate* to meet a need, you can be easily swayed by the promise of something better than what you have previously experienced. When you are unaware of the need, its origin, or how it motivates your choices and behavior, you are no longer working with trust. You are holding on to hope.

Hoping that someone will meet your needs and trusting his capacity to do so are two very different things. When you are hoping, you ignore, dismiss, or diminish all of the physical and logical signs that are presented to indicate whether or not you can or should trust the other person. You downplay or reject the signs that suggest that what you want and the other person's capacity to give it to you are as separate as oil in water. When you are *hoping* to get your needs met with someone, more often than not you know it will not happen with this person, but you hope you are wrong. When, on the other hand, you *trust,* you see clear evidence that what you need is possible and that the person you are involved with is willing and able to fulfill the need.

Remember that trust requires knowing that you are involved with a good person and that they have your best interests at heart.

You trust yourself enough to be vulnerable, and you trust the person enough to believe they will not take advantage of you. While trust may have been present with some of the women in the beginning of their relationship with Jay, what I heard in their stories was that, when he violated their trust, they then fell headfirst into hope: hoping Jay would change, hoping they were not wrong to wait for him to change, even hoping they would simply survive their encounter with him. In the end, for all but one of them, these women gave up hope and chose to see Jay as he really was—they arrived at a rational and honest response to his consistent behavior.

RISK

When someone does not keep his word or promise to you, that experience creates a crack in your trust wall. This wall is a protective device, constructed largely by your intuition, that governs your ability to make conscious choices that ensure you will get your needs met. Once the wall is cracked, you will have a difficult time knowing and trusting who to let in or what to do to avoid further damage. When your trust wall is cracked, self-trust is the first thing to leak out. Unfortunately, when you have a self-trust leak, establishing intimacy, developing understanding, or having meaningful communication with others becomes difficult. When you are so busy trying not to make the same mistake again, listening between the lines and looking over your shoulder for clear evidence, you will more often than not miss the subtle clues that the person you have attracted to you is untrustworthy.

For all of us, but particularly those who have a crack in their trust wall, it is important to ask, *"For what reason am I trusting others?"* If you trust them to meet the unmet needs created throughout a disappointing childhood, chances are you will be disappointed again. Your needs are *your* responsibility. Expecting others to fulfill within you needs that someone else has not fulfilled does not require trust. It requires deep and effective therapy.

If, on the other hand, you are trusting that they have good character and intentions, that they will do what they say they will do, and that what they say to you is the truth as they know it in the moment, then your work is simply to assess their performance data through communication, intimacy, and understanding. This does not guarantee that you will not get hurt or be disappointed, because as humans we will make mistakes. What it means is that even with a crack in your trust wall, chances are you will come out less bruised and smarter.

In life and in love, the ability and willingness to trust ourselves so that we can trust others is one of our greatest strengths. This requires that we remain willing to take the risk of trusting and that we get a handle on our fears. When we do not have a solid sense of self-trust, or when we are afraid to risk our hearts, we erect emotional walls instead of healthy boundaries. These walls create a sense of isolation and separation that fuels loneliness. When we are afraid others will take something from us—physically, mentally, or emotionally—we develop the need to control everything and everyone. When we cannot gain or maintain control, we become suspicious and cynical. We live from a very intellectual space that makes it almost impossible to know or follow our hearts.

Trust: An Openhearted Experience

Real trust is a heart-centered, heart-expanding experience. While logic is a necessary process that is helpful in developing trust in others, rationality alone will not deepen your ability to trust. To trust, you must learn how to feel your way through certain experiences. Without feeling and an open heart, you are more likely than not to live your present experiences through your past. Without the openhearted space that trust requires, you will experience the worry and anxiety that can rob you of the joy of the present moment. Trusting others is a decision that you must make moment by moment, knowing that there are no guarantees when it comes to dealing with other people. Sometimes you will make the right decision, and other times you will be way off. And no matter what happens, trust in yourself is the only guarantee you will have that you will be okay no matter what happens.

As you work through the process of learning to trust others, it's important to recognize and understand that trust is not about finding the perfect person or the perfectly trustworthy person. Trust is about having faith in yourself, faith in others, and the willingness to work through the pain and disappointment that occur when your trust is violated. Equally, just because a person violates your trust or disappoints your expectations does not mean that they are rendered totally untrustworthy. Nor does it mean that your relationship with them must come to a screeching halt.

Remember Pat, who experienced a mismatch between her expectations of Jim and his capacity to meet her expectations? If you recall, she landed in a space where she did not feel that she could trust Jim with her heart and did not feel safe emotionally because he seemed indifferent to her needs and requests. After many long and intimate conversations, Pat considered that Jim simply did not know how to hear her and honor her requests because he was working from a different perspective and a different bank of experiences.

In contemporary conversations, it's quite common for people to say "okay" without you—and even them—ever having a clear understanding of what they're saying okay to. Are they saying okay to the fact that they heard what you said? Are they saying okay to acknowledge that there is an issue that you want to have addressed? Are they saying okay to what they think you mean?

Like Pat, Jim had been single for a long time. An ex–Air Force man, following his years in the service he was not naturally inclined to report to anyone about his movements or whereabouts. He'd had enough of that in the military. What Pat and Jim discovered was that Jim heard Pat's check-in requests as a way of monitoring his movements. Pat trusted that Jim was being faithful. She knew that his work required him to be in many locations throughout the day. But she also felt that because of the distance between them, if they did not establish a routine, they would grow apart.

Through committed communication, they recognized that Pat's fear of abandonment was driving the intensity of her check-in requests, and Jim's fear of being controlled was fueling his resistance. Pat acknowledged that she had to trust that when Jim left he would be back. Jim acknowledged that he could be responsive to providing Pat with what she needed without feeling controlled. Together, they worked through what each of them really needed and wanted in order to feel safe and able to trust the other.

When past experiences are used as a filter to determine whether or not we trust someone, we can end up hurting ourselves by misreading a person's behavior and intentions. The way we usually avoid being hurt is to withhold our trust until the other person proves himself or herself to be trustworthy. When, however, there is a mismatch between expectations and the capacity to fulfill them, determining what a person is doing and why can be difficult.

In many cases, when a poor response is viewed as a violation of trust, people aren't even aware of the hidden needs that drive their request. Even when they are aware, they often really fail to grasp what's going on. Pat's case is a classic. Little girls who grow up without a daddy, who sat on the porch waiting in vain for their daddy to come, often have a really hard time with people, especially men, who are tardy or unaccounted for. Tardiness or an unexplained disappearance can trigger the memory of sitting on the porch, sitting at the window, sitting at the kitchen table, dressed and waiting for the daddy who never comes. Then when someone is late or makes an innocent mistake in the relationship, the rejected child gets triggered and is prone to go off the deep end, believing the other person is being dishonest or manipulative and therefore "I can't trust what you do or what you say." However, the real underbelly of the upset is caused by one person's childhood experiences and has nothing to do with the other person's trustworthiness.

In situations like those related to trusting others, there is the overwhelming "exchange challenge." Trust requires that you give something without knowing what you will get in return. When you give your trust, you expect that your needs and expectations will be met, even if you don't know when or how or even if that will actually occur. Often this results in a hypersensitivity to what gets done and how it gets done. When you add to this equation a mismatch of perceptions, unmet needs, the human factor of poor communication, and the propensity of human beings to make mistakes or be less than diligent in their speech or actions, trusting others can be a gut-wrenching, nerve-racking experience.

LIVING IN TRUST

Learning to trust others means developing and mastering your ability not only to think but also to feel your way into and through experiences and relationships. Living with trust means living with feelings that you recognize and honor. Feelings, in this context, does not refer to emotional mood swings that can render you a basket case. I'm referring to feelings that alert you to when it is safe to trust and when it is not safe, that unfold as internal whispers that open your heart and propel you toward what "feels" right in the moment.

When you live with trust and walk with trust in your heart, what you hear from others is irrelevant; it is your inner knowing that determines what you do. What you see and experience with others is grounded in a deep personal integrity anchored in your heart that allows you to see, feel, and accept the truth about everyone and everything. Learning to trust yourself is the key to living with and walking in trust that you can extend to others. Self-trust gives you the stamina and fortitude required to deal with the human mistakes, painful disappointments, and letdowns. Until and unless you faithfully trust yourself to take care of yourself and handle your own needs without controlling anything or anyone else, trusting others will be very challenging.

TRUST MAINTENANCE

Like many people, when it comes to saying something we know may upset people or hurt their feelings, the temptation is great to avoid, withhold, and lie. I will be the first to admit that this is quite a dilemma. When the truth is unpleasant or difficult, we are confronted with that added layer of challenge: to be honest and tell the truth when it's really uncomfortable to do so. I have been in this situations often. For years I would default to "sacrificing myself and saving them" at any cost to my integrity and trustworthiness. Then my spiritual godfather gave me the perfect solution.

Once when I was faced with the gut-wrenching dilemma of telling someone something I knew would both upset him and hurt his feelings, I asked my spiritual godfather for his advice. He asked me, "Is this an important relationship in your life?" I told him it was. He then instructed me as follows.

1. Tell the person that your relationship with him is a valuable and important aspect of your life.

2. Tell him why he matters to you and the kind of relationship you want to continue to have with him.

3. Offer him your belief that sharing the truth as you know it or sense it is an important aspect of the relationship you want.

4. Ask if he feels the same way.

5. If the response is yes, tell him that you have something difficult to share with him and ask his permission to do so.

6. Once you get his permission, share the information and then ask him what he heard you say.

7. If necessary, offer clarity about what you have said by offering correction to his feedback.

8. Check in again to make sure you have been heard.

9. Once you know you have been heard, ask him how he feels about what you have shared and go from there.

This is a life-saving practice that I continue to use today whenever telling the truth is difficult but necessary. This practice has also taught me that I can trust myself to tell the truth if I do so with compassion and with no expectation that people will receive my message the same way I hold it. Please know that in some situations, certain people will resist hearing the truth. Also know that telling the difficult truth to difficult people does not make you wrong.

There is something else that you may want to consider when you are faced with sharing a difficult truth or sharing the truth with a difficult person. In his book, *Legacy of the Heart: The Spiritual Advantages of a Painful Childhood*, author Wayne Muller writes about the dangers of re-creating our parental relationship in all relationships. In "Busyness and Stillness," he addresses the issue of gossip and people who gossip with the teachings of Buddha.

We should choose our words carefully, speaking only what is most loving and true. Right speech is to refrain from using language to tell lies, to harm another, to create disharmony, or to engage in useless babble. Right speech is benevolent and gentle, meaningful and useful. We should speak only at the right time and place, and if what we have to say is not useful, we may keep noble silence.

In keeping with this teaching, Muller offers four steps of right speech that can be used when addressing useless babble. According to Muller, before presenting your concerns or issues to someone about the way she is being or about something she is saying, you must ask yourself, "Is what I am about to say kind? Is it loving? Is it necessary? Can I say it in the way I would want to hear it?"

On the journey to trust in others, right speech means that you must be willing to release people and situations in which truth is not welcomed or honored. In life you will encounter people who choose to be right rather than truthful. You will find yourself in situations where you can or will be punished for telling the truth. You may find yourself in circumstances where telling the truth can cost you something very valuable or even everything you hold dear. In those moments, I encourage you to let wisdom prevail. While this may seem contradictory, what I am trying to convey is that with prayer, the right intention, and trust, whatever you choose to do will be the right thing for you. No matter what happens, remember that you will be okay.

As long as you are safe from mental, emotional, and spiritual harm, as long as you are not repeating a childhood pattern attached to fear or survival or abandonment, as long as you do not willingly compromise your values or integrity, as long as the choice you make does not put anyone else in danger, you will instinctively know how much truth to tell, when to tell it, and how to tell it. You have an imprint of wisdom on your soul that knows exactly what you and everyone else involved needs. *Trust it!* Do what feels most appropriate for the highest good of everyone involved.

HONOR YOUR AGREEMENTS

When people do not know they can depend on you, they become suspicious and frightened. Suspicious people are hard to get along with. Frightened people attack! When *you* do not know if you can depend on you, you lose confidence in yourself and become suspicious of everyone and everything else.

One pillar in the foundation of developing trust in others is confidence. The other is dependability. The quickest way to build confidence, and to develop self-trust and trust in others, is by honoring your agreements. In other words, do what you say you will do, when you say you will do it, even when the agreement is with yourself. In this way you and others know that you are dependable. If for any reason it is not possible for you to keep an agreement, renegotiate it before the time it is to be executed.

Even small agreements are important. When you disappoint yourself and others about small things, you create little cracks in the wall of trust you are building within yourself. One small crack connected with a bunch of other small cracks eventually leads to a collapse of confidence and a major fracture in your trustworthiness internally and externally. Here is how not honoring an agreement can play out.

You tell your friend Mark that you will support him or go somewhere on a particular day. The details are loose, but you agree to it anyway. As the time approaches, you change your mind, or you make a competing commitment to do something else. Unfortunately, you fail to communicate your change of plans. The day before the time of the first agreement, Mark calls you with the details. You tell him that you cannot go because you forgot or you made other plans, or you lie and tell him you will do it because you feel bad that you forgot.

Saying that you cannot go will probably upset Mark. Why? Because he was depending on you and you failed to communicate the change. You can earnestly be sorry and communicate that to Mark, but chances are that will not be enough to ward off an upset. If breaking agreements is a part of your history with him, chances are nothing you offer will matter. If this is the first time, you may get away with it, but know that you have created a crack in your dependability with Mark and within yourself.

The last scenario—"telling a lie"—is probably the most common and the most detrimental. When you are consciously dishonest, offering a lie as an escape or an excuse, you teach yourself that you cannot be trusted. This has a tremendous impact on your self-confidence and your personal integrity. More often than not, when this is the course of action, the next step is to "create" an emergency that prohibits you from honoring the agreement. In this case, while it will be difficult for Mark to get mad at you, it requires that you tell yet another lie, creating another breach of confidence and integrity.

There will always be small temptations that peck away at your integrity. Being dishonest, breaking an agreement, and then being dishonest about why you are breaking an agreement are not small things. They are major cracks in the walls that can destroy the foundation of trust.

Because trust is an internal exercise that is demonstrated externally through our behavior, it is important to be as trustworthy with yourself as you expect others to be with you. In other words, be the truth that you desire to experience. One way to honor your promises and agreements is to practice, practice, practice keeping your word to yourself and others. For many years I've kept a small notebook in which I outlined, day by day, the things that I said I would do whether they were promises, agreements or commitments. As I completed or accomplished something, I would check it off. When I felt myself becoming resistant to something I had agreed to do, I would stop and get still long enough to figure out the origins of my resistance. I discovered that the things I was most resistant to were things I committed to unconsciously without checking in with myself. They were either things that didn't really matter to me but I felt obligated to do, or they were things that I thought I had to do—needed to do—to gain approval or acceptance from someone else. It became like an internal push-up for me to slow down long enough to think about what I was committing myself to do before I agreed to do it, and then to learn how to say no to certain invitations and people. Building trust with others requires strenuous exercise.

The biggest challenge I faced was learning that I could renegotiate an agreement or commitment with another person. Talk about getting triggered! I had made up in my head that if I didn't do something I was committed to doing, people wouldn't like me, or would be mad at me, or would talk bad about me. These thoughts were the ramblings of my unhealed inner girl child, whom I could not seem to control. So instead, I would make up excuses or stories (i.e., lies) to elicit sympathy and ensure the other person would not be mad at me. Thanks to my little notebook, I eventually discovered that every story I made up, every lie I told to wiggle out of a commitment, was like putting a dagger in the heart of my personal integrity. I also realized that what I was doing to myself was far worse than having someone be upset with me, or not like me, or talk bad about me. So one day, I put on my big-girl panties and I told the truth. When you really want to heal and prove to yourself that you can trust yourself to withstand your greatest nightmare, simply tell the truth.

After realizing that I had committed to attending an event that had absolutely no meaning or value to me, and that I was planning to attend only because I thought my date for the evening would think badly of me if I didn't go, I made another choice. Hours before I was expected to be there, I called my date and said that I would not be able to attend. I said that I had done everything else that I had committed to do, and realized that all of that was enough for me. My date replied, "Oh my God! Me, too! I really wanted to stay home tonight, but I was going because I told you I would and I didn't want to disappoint you." We both laughed at ourselves and made a new commitment: to trust ourselves.

You may not be able to share as openly and honestly with everyone you know. Let's face it, there are times when we all must do things that we would rather not do for one reason or another. This scenario may not be appropriate when it comes to certain personal or professional obligations. Trust yourself enough to tell yourself the truth about what you need, what you want, what you do, and why you do it. Be honest with yourself because it gives you the strength and courage you need to be honest with other people.

MASTERING THE 4 ESSENTIAL TRUSTS

Trust in Self
Trust in God
Trust in Others
Trust in Life

Chapter 11 | # THE CHICKEN AND THE EGG

> YOU MAY BE DECEIVED IF YOU
> TRUST TOO MUCH,
> BUT YOU WILL LIVE IN TORMENT
> UNLESS YOU TRUST ENOUGH.
>
> —*Frank Crane*

I once heard my friend Reverend Michael Bernard Beckwith preach a sermon that created a major shift in how I viewed the difficulties of life. He used the example of a chick in an egg to make the point about the process of moving from one experience to another. Reverend Michael explained that for as long as it was useful, the egg with its hard shell was a safe place for the chick. However, as the chick grew, the egg no longer provided the chick with the space it needed to continue to develop properly. Over time, what had once been a safe haven became cramped quarters where the chick was forced to wallow in its own filth while navigating its continued growth and development.

Eventually, the chick came to know that it had to leave the cramped, poop-filled space of its once-safe haven and venture out into the unknown. But how was the chick to escape its discomfort? Instinctively, it starts pecking and breaking the shell of its protective covering. The process takes 12 to 18 hours, but I am sure, for the chick, it feels like forever. As Reverend Michael explained it, the process is the same for humans. We can live in a particular situation, under certain circumstances, for a long period of time; then we have got to get out. Unfortunately, human beings are not always as courageous as the chicks. We fear the unknown. We learn how to accommodate all manner of discomfort. We become so deaf, mute, and blind to the poop or mess in our lives that we will stay where we are and suffer rather than risk venturing into the unknown. Can you imagine that a chicken has more courage than a human being? Or is it that the chick intuitively trusts the process while humans want to control it?

Life is a process. It involves beginnings and endings. It ebbs and flows, with highs and lows. The process of life includes thinking and feeling, giving and receiving, winning and losing, living and dying, and so much more. As a process, life requires us to live in a perpetual state of preparation for the known, the unknown, and the inevitable. There are no guarantees about anything in life. You cannot assume that what's good in your life will last or that what's bad and unpleasant will ever go away. There is no guarantee that what you put out you will get back when you need it or want it, or that who you give to will reciprocate in kind.

Life is a process that requires living moment by moment, doing all that you can, the best that you can, while trusting that the rewards you receive will be just and plentiful. The only thing you can know for sure is that if you do not fully participate in as much of life as you can, and trust in the process, life will not be easy for you to bear or manage.

Learning to trust in life is also a process. This process involves knowing and being okay with not knowing; exercising awareness and listening; understanding and remembering what you learn; trusting your intuition and behaving logically in response to where your intuition leads you. The most important aspect of learning to trust yourself and the process of life is honoring what you feel and aligning your behavior to match what you know. To trust the process means you must learn how to be still, even if just for a moment, until you can get your bearings or zero in on an intuitive direction about where to move and how to get there.

In stillness, more often than not, you do not need to know or do anything other than trust. When you are trusting, you are actually banking on the unknown, which feels absolutely terrifying in most instances. Yet by its very nature and definition, trust means knowing that no matter what is going on or what happens, everything is working toward something beneficial and new for your good. When you are in the process of life, knowing there is a Giver and Creator of life, you may need to remind yourself that the unknown is a temporary condition that unfolds in just the right time and, always, in just the right way.

At some time or another in the process of life, we are all like the little chick pecking out of the egg. We simply must grow and change and leave what is familiar. For humans, the eggshell represents the heart. As difficult and painful as it may be to bear or accept, it is not until our hearts are broken open that we become aware of the wonder and expansiveness of life. Even when our breaking open includes loss, pain, and betrayal, there is something wonderful going on. A broken heart will take you beyond the limits of who you imagined yourself to be in life. Death or loss can transform how you value life and those who share it with you. Betrayal and violation can and will give birth to an inner wisdom and truth that can and does guide how you do what you do for the rest of your days. When we learn through difficulty, pain, loss, and hardship to trust in life, we come into the realization that living in poop is only one choice among the many choices we can make if we trust the process and ourselves.

VILLA NOVA REDUX

Let me remind you about the story of my new home, Villa Nova. I was broken. Filing bankruptcy had destroyed my credit. My income was stabilizing but was nowhere near stable yet because my financial obligations surpassed my income. I was riddled with hidden shame, guilt, and fear. What kept me moving toward the fulfillment of my vision to own a home was trust.

Day-by-day, step-by-step, I had to trust myself enough to peck through the shell of being a renter for the remainder of my life. Trust is a process that unfolds within you and around you. I had to trust the inner voice that said, "This is your house." I had to trust that I would be blessed with grace when I made the application to prequalify for a mortgage. I had to trust that by the time I needed the down payment, the money would be there. I had to trust that there was no one and no thing in the world invested in my not having my own home. Along the way, I had to keep whipping myself into shape and allowing myself to see and recognize that it was all working out. I had to allow the process to unfold in spite of my fear.

In the book *The Amazing Power of Deliberate Intent*, the mystic Abraham offered, "I ask. I allow. God Becomes." This is where an intimate relationship between yourself and God comes in. Intimacy is what creates the connection. Intimate relationships open the heart. God can enter an open heart. Intimacy with God leads to an understanding of God. When you understand what God is and the nature of Him/Her, you become aware that nothing can remain unknown. Everything is a possibility waiting to unfold. Learning to trust the process of life teaches you how to bank on the unknown possibilities with courage and patience, knowing there are no guarantees, and expecting to endure some bumps and bruises along the way to get right and mo' better.

TRUST GRACE

Karen spent the innocent years of her childhood searching for God. She had an inexplicable thirst and hunger to see and understand Source, and she longed to know herself as a spiritual being. Even as a youngster, Karen understood that knowledge alone could not sustain her. And while she recognized the presence of God in the world around her, she harbored a secret fear about the mysteries of the spiritual world.

Karen came from a dysfunctional, spiritually vacant childhood. Although her grandmother prayed and said the rosary ceaselessly, the family dysfunction—which included substance abuse, child abuse, domestic violence, and poverty—outweighed her grandmother's influence. Abandoned by her drug-addicted mother, abused by her drug-addicted aunt, and sexually violated by various relatives and family friends, Karen became an angry and lost teenager. Until she met her first love, Jesus.

When Karen met the tough guy in the neighborhood, she was 17 and he was 20. Jesus understood Karen's anger because he had lived with it and through it for most of his life. His mother had often left him with his grandmother so that she could work. Then, when she met a man who did not want a ready-made family, she completely abandoned her son to the care of his grandmother. Jesus's grandmother had a massive stroke and was confined to a wheelchair when he was 12. This transformed Jesus into the man of the family with the responsibility of taking care of himself and looking after his grandmother. Although she could see and speak well enough to direct Jesus in what needed to be done, she could not keep her eyes or her grip on the angry young man Jesus was becoming. They needed money to survive, and Jesus learned how to get it.

By the time Karen met him, Jesus understood how to navigate the mean streets of Spanish Harlem. This information he readily shared with Karen. He taught her how to boost clothes and play three-card monte. She did well on the streets because people did not think that such an attractive young woman would swindle them. Jesus also taught her how to work the drunks in bars. She could get them to give her money without having to give them anything in return. The biggest lesson Jesus taught Karen was how to live beyond the pain of her reality with a joint and a hit of coke just before bedtime. What she was really learning was how to stuff her feelings and check out, and it felt better than anything she had ever felt before. What Karen taught Jesus was that in spite of their history and their less-than-stellar lifestyle, they both needed an education. So they got their GEDs in a night-school program.

By the time she was 19 and he was 22, Jesus had his own corner. In fact, his corner was so busy with drug traffic that they both had to carry guns. Everyone knew that Karen was Jesus's woman. They also knew that he was crazy as hell. Jesus had a volatile temper that Karen had encountered on many occasions. But because she believed he loved her, she believed he would change. Each time she threatened to leave him, they would have a two- or three-month truce. The quieter he got at home, the crazier he got on the streets.

It was during those quiet periods when Karen talked to Jesus about their future. She wanted to be a cop. He told her she was crazy. He wanted to be a wealthy businessman. Karen encouraged him to pursue that dream by taking classes at the local community college. They made big plans, believing they would always be together. Jesus wanted Karen to have a baby, but she told him there was no way she was doing that without the benefit of marriage. Besides that, who in her right mind would bring a baby into the kind of life she was living? She told Jesus that if he wanted a family, they needed to save enough money to buy a house and he needed to go to school so he could become legit.

Jesus was 24 on the day he enrolled in college and signed up to take two classes. That was also the day he asked Karen to marry him. Two days later, when his crazy met a bigger crazy, Jesus was shot dead on the very same corner where he had controlled the drug trade. Devastation does not describe what Karen experienced. At 21, she had lived the life of someone 15 years older. She had seen and done things she would never reveal to anyone, but she had done them with Jesus at her side, guiding and directing her path. He had orchestrated the process, and she had trusted him with her life. Once Jesus was buried, his family and friends encouraged her to keep the business going, because they were benefiting from the work she and Jesus had done.

People respected Karen because she had been able to keep Jesus in line. Everyone knew her, and out of respect for Jesus, they allowed her to continue selling. Karen could not see beyond the loss of her love. Her pain was unspeakable. She remembered the lesson that Jesus had taught her about a joint and hit of coke before bedtime. A year later, bedtime had become 6 a.m., noon, midday, and dinnertime. She had become her own best customer.

Toni had once been one of Jesus and Karen's most loyal buyers, and she knew that Karen was desperate for money, because she watched and participated as Karen ruined her reputation and the business on the corner. Toni, trying to help out another woman, introduced Karen to a new possibility for working the corner.

Seven years can pass quickly when your mind is clouded by grief, anger, a history of family dysfunction, and drug addiction. At 29, Karen was one of the most sought-after ladies of the evening. She used everything that Jesus had taught her about business. Her body was her product, and she knew how to package it, market it, and sell it to the highest bidder. Through it all, she held on to her dream of being a cop. She had never been arrested or had any run-ins with the law. As strange as it seemed, the other runners and hookers on the street looked out for her. She had the distinct "honor" of remaining Jesus's woman. For this reason, people felt as protective of her as they had been of him.

Karen knew it was time to leave the street life when she met Mr. Townsend, whose crazy trumped Jesus's crazy to the third power. She prided herself on never being attracted to her johns. But somehow she let her guard down with Mr. Townsend, and he always left her smiling. He encouraged her to leave the streets. He bought her nice things and offered her even more. After their third time together, he refused to sleep with her anymore. Instead, he would take her to dinner and listen intently as she talked about her dreams.

The only problem was that Mr. Townsend, like Jesus, had a violent temper. Karen never knew what would set him off. She walked on eggshells and lived in a constant state of fear that if she did or said the wrong thing, he would choke her. Or if he didn't like what she was wearing, he might punch her. Even worse, she had to be on constant alert, because she never knew when he would pull out the razor-sharp knife that he kept in his suit pocket and cut her clothes off, leaving tiny little marks on her back or buttocks. It was her friend Toni, who had given up the streets for church, who helped her make sense of Mr. Townsend. One day when Karen was sharing her fears and concerns about how to get away from him, Toni said matter-of-factly, "Baby, he ain't treating you no worse than you have treated yourself."

Life—and the process of living—creates echoes. What you put out consciously or unconsciously will come back to you. Moment by moment you are living the echoes of what you believe. You are living the consequences of what you think, what you expect, and what you do. Some consequences are immediate. Others are long term, in that it takes time for them to come around. Karen's belief system established in childhood was the echo that created her adolescent and young-adult life. Mr. Townsend was just the mirror that arrived to show her what she had become and who she believed she was.

Karen had loved and trusted Jesus. When he died, she felt that she had been betrayed by life and by God. Betrayal, abandonment, and abuse were not new experiences for Karen. Both of her parents had abandoned her. The males in her family had betrayed and abused her. Mr. Townsend had been the first and only person she was willing to trust since Jesus, but he was too unstable. Karen knew that she had outgrown the life she was living, but she did not know how to change, get out, or move away from what had become so familiar.

It was Toni, the former drug-addicted streetwalker, who tried to steer Karen in a new direction. She asked Karen if she had ever considered why it was a man named "Jesus" who had protected and taken care of her for so many years? Karen had not made the connection. Toni told Karen she would like to help her build a relationship with another man named Jesus. Karen told Toni she was crazy! How could she ever trust "the real Jesus" after all she had been through? Toni asked her one question: "How can you not?"

Beneath every experience of mistrust there is an unresolved pain and the belief that it is not safe to trust. Karen, like so many of us, was never taught and had no awareness that the difficulties she experienced in life were tools for her transformation. She became lost in the pain, disappointment, and hurt she had experienced. Without the proper guidance, instruction, understanding, or support, Karen could not make sense of her childhood or her life. I mean, who teaches us this stuff? Who teaches children that dysfunction can be turned into a blessing, or that hurt and pain are useful and essential to your personal growth and development? Without this information Karen fell into the very common human default: a pit of anger and blame. She was angry about what she had been through and blamed others for the pain she felt. Yes, others were responsible, but Karen also needed to take responsibility for some pivotal choices she had made. She talked about those choices and so much more with Toni.

Karen never knew that she had a friend she could trust until she spent time with Toni, the same woman who had taught her how to walk the street and make the money she needed to support her drug habit. It was the same Toni who took her to rehab and visited her almost every day for the entire 90 days she was an inpatient. And it was this very same reformed Toni who allowed Karen to sleep on her couch for 14 months until she was strong enough and clear enough to take the police academy entrance exam.

On those days when Karen was down on herself and ready to throw in the towel, Toni would first offer her three words: *Trust the process!* Karen says she cannot count the number of times Toni told her, "The only thing that can stop you now is you." It was Toni's loving counsel to Karen to "trust the process" that kept her police academy dream alive even though she blew her first exam. Karen wanted to know how she could live beyond the pain, the loss, and the betrayal she had experienced. Toni explained that Karen had to be willing to trust God's grace to take away the pain and help her change. And she had to trust herself enough to know that she could change.

It took Karen almost nine months before she realized that the woman who was helping to save her life had nothing in common with the woman she had known from the streets. This woman was a Sunday school teacher who worked for the telephone company. This woman was dating a man, a minister, who absolutely adored her; by association, Karen also benefited. This woman was kind and gentle and sure of herself. When Karen became fully aware that the old Toni and the new Toni were two completely different people, she asked her how it happened. Toni gave her the lowdown.

"I learned to trust in life," she said. One day Toni realized that every difficult situation, every hurt, every betrayal, every disappointment had a purpose, but she could not see the purpose because she was stuck in the pain. In fact, Toni said she realized that it was not the events but her holding on to the events that caused her to suffer. One day, after a john had beaten her to within an inch of her life, she decided to let go of everything. That was the day she went into rehab and got clean. That was that day she made an agreement with herself to trust that she could change. That was the day she realized that if the life she had lived and the things she had been through had not killed her, there was still hope. Hope and trust took her off the streets and into a women's prayer group.

Toni's next step was to believe she could change. There is nothing worse than a woman who loses her self-worth and dignity to pain and suffering. Toni said that she had lost sight of who she was but that she believed she could get back to a place of being proud of who she was as a woman. She didn't know how, but she was determined to find a way, so she prayed. The final and most difficult step was forgiveness. Toni realized that she had to forgive herself, her parents, her pimp, and every john whom she had ever slept with while she was out of her mind with anger and blame. She had to forgive the pushers who sold her drugs, which included Jesus and Karen. She had to forgive the other addicts who had shared their drugs with her. Finally, she had to forgive herself for being so angry with herself for things that were not within her control. Toni believed that forgiveness taught her to trust and that trust gave her hope.

Karen listened and wept, knowing she had held on to a past that had caused her to suffer. She wept because she did not understand fully the source of her pain or how to heal it. She wept because in that moment, she didn't believe she had the courage to change. Her broken heart did not feel like the opening it could be and would become for her. She wept because she was afraid and because she didn't know if she could ever forgive herself. Toni listened and let her weep for hours and then for days. Over time Toni helped Karen get a job and study to retake the police academy exam. This time she was admitted!

By the time Karen finished her basic training, Toni had set her wedding date. Karen spent weeks planning every detail of Toni's bridal shower; it would be the day after her swearing-in ceremony. As Karen took the stage to receive her badge, she noticed that Toni was not among her friends in the audience. When she called her home, Toni did not answer. When she called Toni's office, she received the news that Toni was discovered dead in her bathroom that morning. They suspected she'd had either a stroke or a heart attack. Later, after eight years on the police force, Karen resigned to become a stay-at-home mom with her first child at the age of 39. She named her daughter Trust Grace.

LIFE PROCESSES

According to the Oxford dictionary a process is a "series of actions or steps taken in order to achieve a particular end." Cooking, for example, is a process. In order to make a meal, we must start with the end in mind. Depending on the dish you are preparing, you must purchase the ingredients; chop, season, mix, blend, or combine them in a particular order; and wait a specific amount of time until the ingredients are baked, broiled, fried, or so on.

Education is a process. We know that in order to be educated, we must attend school on a consistent basis, pay attention to what is being taught, do the work assigned to us, and take the required tests. Hopefully, at the end of the series of mandated requirements, we will graduate and complete the process of our formal education.

Our days and lives are filled with countless processes, the steps we are required to take, and the systems we are required to follow in order to achieve a desired result. Likewise, life is a process. It is a series of experiences and steps that must be taken in order to achieve a particular end. The key to being able to relax, enjoy, and trust in the process of life is knowing and understanding that no matter who you are, or what you do, the end is coming. The other important perspective about being able to trust in the process of life is recognizing that you are not the chef . . . you are the carrot!

Though you are aware of some of life's processes, most you are not aware of. There are a series of processes going on in your brain and body right now as you read and decode the words on this page. You are not thinking about that process; you simply trust that as your eyes scan these words, your brain will do what is required for the words to take on meaning. Every time you eat something, there is a process that goes on which supports you in utilizing whatever you take in for the purpose of fueling your body. Most of you don't know how these processes work, and even if you did, you wouldn't spend your time thinking about them. You would simply trust that if you take a bite of food, it will end up going where it needs to go and doing what it needs to do.

When you drink liquids, the same thing happens. You trust that what you take in will do an appropriate job of creating energy so that your body will continue to function.

Life works in much the same way: everything you take in is processed so that it can be used to support you in continuing to function in all aspects of your life. The distinction between eating a sandwich and moving through the full process of life is that in the first example, you don't think about what is going to happen next once you eat the sandwich, whereas in the latter process, you think, overthink, and strain to analyze exactly what life will throw at you next.

While it is true that we are not "in charge" of the process of life, we make our participation more enjoyable and the process easier by putting in good "ingredients" and maintaining the "machinery."

Healthy, whole foods will create a smoother operation than those that have already been processed. We must understand that processed foods are not necessarily designed to nourish our bodies; rather, their end game is to grow their producer's bank account. While there is no inherent harm in this, we must be mindful of allowing another's process and end game distract us from our highest and greatest good.

Likewise, when we attempt to process the ideas, beliefs, and information offered or given to us by others, we must be mindful that although these things may carry a certain amount of "nutrition," they are no substitute for what we can get directly from the Source. In learning to trust the process of life, it would serve you well to have a relationship with, understanding of, and direct connection to the Source of your life. Not having any or all of these things can and often does cause the process to go awry. Think of it this way: a carrot does not know what to do with itself until the chef puts it where he wants it to be. Once the carrot has become an ingredient, its only job is to be a carrot and do what carrots do: add texture, color, and flavor.

One of the more difficult challenges we face in learning to trust the process of life and living is to think we do not know what we are supposed to do or be, and, more often than not, we rely on information we've received from another "carrot." Included in these details may be some misinformation about the dangers and downfalls of being a carrot, the unacceptability of being a carrot, and why it is better to be a clove of garlic or an onion. Worst of all, we might learn that some other carrots out there are bigger and better than we are, so we had better figure out how to shape up. With these ingredients in the mix, we are prone to spend a great deal of time trying to figure out why we ended up being a carrot or, worse, how to be something other than what we are.

It is hard to trust the process you are in if your mind is fixated on how to get out of it. The truth is that who you are and what you have come to do is etched into the fibers of your being. You can choose, consciously or unconsciously, to postpone, delay, deny,

217

avoid, or attempt to steer the process of your unfolding in another direction, but eventually, who you are will show up and take hold of you. In this unfolding and taking-hold process, your job is to trust that the chef knows what he is doing and that no one else or nothing else can or will misappropriate the chef's plan or purpose for your participation.

DESIREE

For 23 years Desiree had been married to Tom, who was, according to his wife, a good provider, a conscientious father, and a total control freak. Together, Tom and Desiree had five children and a family-owned business. Desiree was the chief cook and bottle washer in the business, meaning she did everything to keep it running; however, her husband controlled what she did, how she did it, and when she did it, and he kept all of the proceeds that resulted from her hard work.

When I met Desiree, she did not have her own bank account, and she had not bought a new dress in more than 20 years, because her husband demanded that she shop in thrift stores. She could not drive the car without his permission, and when she left the house she had to give him a detailed account of where she was going, why she needed to go there, and when she would be back—plus she had to take all five children with her.

Desiree was the sweetest, kindest, and most loving person I had ever met. She was also nothing short of brilliant. When you could get her to speak, you would be remiss not to have a notebook and pen handy, because the words that came out of her mouth were nothing short of golden nuggets of wisdom. Unfortunately, getting her to speak was difficult. She had lost her voice after so many years of Tom shutting her down and shutting her up if he did not agree with what she had to say.

All of the women in our posse tried to convince Desiree that she did not need to live this way and that, if she continued to do so, she would lose herself and her mind, in that order. She would say simply, "Tom is a great father and provider. He doesn't mean to be the way he is. I keep praying for him, and I know it is going to get better." Collectively, we would sigh and scratch our heads, mumbling, "When, Lord? When?"

Without a single word to anyone, without a plan that had been reviewed and approved by the posse, one morning Desiree got up from her marriage bed, packed a small suitcase, and left her home, her husband, and her children. We were all shocked! Stunned! And, secretly, delighted. Desiree asked only one thing: "May I spend a few nights on your sofa?" Who would say no?

Although three of her children were already grown and out of the house, she left behind at home one who was a senior in high school and another who was a freshman. The senior, a son, told her that he would be okay. The freshman, a daughter, was nothing short of devastated. Desiree tried to explain to her daughter that she had nowhere to go and that if she even attempted to take her daughter out of the home, her husband would systematically destroy what little life she had left. The child simply could not conceive of living with her father without her mother, and she was damned angry to have been left in a place where her mother would not stay. Without a visible tear in our presence and very few words about the heartbreak she was experiencing, Desiree stuck to her guns and stayed gone. We all did the best we could to keep her safe and comfortable. She rarely asked for anything. She refused to speak about what she was really feeling. She slept on sofa after sofa for several months, until finally things got better.

For Desiree, things getting better came in the form of a friend who, upon hearing the news, gave Desiree the keys to her empty rental property and a credit card with a five-figure limit. Desiree got a job outside of the family business for the first time in 23 years. She worked, she saved, she prayed, and things really did get better, until suddenly they got worse. One day, Desiree came home to discover that there had been an unexplained fire in her home. She lost everything, which wasn't much.

Overnight she was back to sleeping on sofas, yet she never complained, she never worried, and still she said very little. By the time her daughter graduated from high school and went off to college, Desiree had her own place and her own car. Little by little, she began to open up and talk about how she was rebuilding her relationship with her daughter. What she refused to discuss was her husband. Not a word! Not a sound! Not a peep!

The day she filed for divorce, we all breathed sighs of relief that quickly turned to gasps of horror when she told us she wasn't asking him for anything. We were sure that she had lost her mind when we were not looking and prying into her business! Twenty-three years of working like a slave from sunup to sundown, giving birth to and raising five children, without even one new dress, and she asks for nothing? Desiree said it was not worth the fight because she had everything she needed. Some people wear insanity very well!

The divorce proceeding took all of 20 minutes, and Desiree was a free woman. All of her children were settled, and she rekindled a romance with her high school sweetheart. Within a year they were married. Several years later he retired. Today, she is a proud grandmother. All of her children dote on her. She and her beloved live a quiet, peaceful life of fun, work, and travel.

Many years later, I got up the courage to ask Desiree how she did it; her answer was simple: "I had to trust the process. I had given him my best, so in my mind there was nothing to fight about. The morning I left I was clear, and I knew that the time had come for me—not him—to change. I also knew in every fiber of my being that if I just took care of myself, everything would be okay. I wasn't angry and I wasn't afraid. I was clear and willing to sleep in the park with the squirrels if I had to."

I wanted to know how she knew. How did she know she could walk away from everything and still be okay? Again, in the loving way only Desiree could deliver the message, she said: "I refused to allow myself to believe anything other than the truth I knew in the moment, which was if I trusted myself and trusted God with my life, God would give me a life I could handle. It wasn't always easy or fun, but I knew I could handle it if I just leaned in to trust."

LEANING IN TO TRUST

Leaning in to trust means knowing that what you are placing your weight on is sturdy enough to hold you up. Trusting yourself, trusting God, and trusting that others have your best interest at heart are the pillars that you must lean on if you are going to learn to trust the process. It begins with being clear about what you are doing and why, without any concern for how anyone else is going to respond. Never judge your clarity on how you think others will respond. Leaning in to trust also means knowing that trust has good, solid friends that you can rely on.

Willingness is a friend of trust. You must be willing to do what is required, when it is required, without hesitation. You must be willing to risk falling flat on your face, and should that happen, you must be willing to get up and keep moving in the direction of your clear choice!

Truth is a friend of trust. It is a mistake to think that you can trust anyone or anything when you are not willing to tell the truth and face the truth. Without the willingness to tell yourself and others the microscopic truth without exhaustive explanations, you will be holding on to a wobbly pillar, and you will fall.

Clarity is a friend of trust. Few things make trust a more difficult prospect than the lack of clarity. Being able to see clearly even one inch beyond where you are is the first step. Refusing to give in to the human tendency to overthink, overanalyze, overquestion, and overplan is important because these things will take you headfirst into analysis paralysis. Be able to see it in your mind and feel it in your heart, even when there is no physical evidence that what you see is real, practical, or probable.

Vulnerability is a friend of trust. If you are afraid to take a risk or get sidetracked by the exploration of the exhaustive possible outcomes, you cannot be vulnerable. Without this friend by your side, trust is simply a word you banter around to impress other people.

The other friends that will support you as you learn to lean in to trust are faith, courage, focus, discipline, and commitment.

Just one of these is enough to keep you stable while you lean in; however, the more of these FOTs (Friends of Trust) you have on your side, the better the chances are that you will not fall down and make a fool of yourself. The bottom-line principle of leaning in to trust is this: until and unless you have the capacity to trust yourself, God, others, and the process, you are less likely to receive the benefits and the rewards of living with trust.

The realities of life are the same for most people, whether you trust them or not. You will experience heartache and heartbreak at some point. People are going to disappoint you some of the time. You are going to face hardships and difficulties because they are both a part of the process of living. You will have moments of astounding brilliance and foresight, and at other times, you will look, sound, and/or act like a plum fool—publicly! The people you love the best will probably betray or abandon you when you need them the most. You will have your mind and heart set on doing something or having something, only to have your hopes and dreams disintegrate right before your eyes. You can pretty much bank on one or all of these things happening, hopefully not all at the same time. However, no matter when they happen or how they happen, trust can, will, and does change your experience of them.

Leaning in to trust means learning how not to take any of it personally. It requires that you grow into a state of psychological, emotional, and spiritual maturity that supports you in recognizing that this and so much more are all a part of the process of life. Leaning in to trust, using it and its friends as the pillars you hold on to, will alleviate a great deal of stress, worry, and anxiety. Chances are that without trust, you are leaning on your own understanding, which also may mean that you consistently find yourself in the position of trying to figure out the what's, who's, how's, and how not's of life. Take it from one who knows . . . that is not going to turn out well for you.

Leaning in to trust and learning to trust in life requires that you become willing to slay all of the inner enemies. These include the inner judge, the inner critic, the inner naysayer, and the inner worrywart. These voices belong to the negative ego committee and the ensuing subcommittees of thought, belief, programming, and socialization that want a vote in everything you do. If you have a habit of remembering and rehearsing how you have been duped, manipulated, abused, or wronged in the past, you will avoid or reject trust and all of its friends. Instead, you will spend precious time beating yourself up, feeling stupid, and refusing to be vulnerable ever again.

BACKGROUND CHECKS

You want to feel connected to others and to blossom or flourish in their company. You want to love and be loved. However, you may also have issues of past betrayals that are more likely than not at the heart of all of your trust issues. Add to this the anger and hurt you feel when you are abused or abandoned as a child or betrayed by a loved one, and you have a cocktail for living that makes being vulnerable a bitter pill to swallow.

If you want to learn how to trust the process of life, you must first work through the issues of betrayal that support you in avoiding intimate connections, motivating you to keep others at a distance in order to stay safe. Leaning in to trust is the means by which you can create and hold healthy boundaries in order to let others in while still maintaining your safety. Telling people the truth about how you feel and being willing to ask for what you want are good places to start. Remember, however, that there are no guarantees. People will be people—clumsy, messy and prone to making mistakes. The alternative is to continue to depend on the inner enemies and deny yourself the possibilities of joy associated with connection and intimacy. The good news is that you get to choose.

———◆———

Tracey had been single and celibate for 11 years. She had dated a few really nice men, but none kept her interest long enough for her even to think about getting serious. She kept herself busy with overtime on her job, her church duties, and her volunteer work. Occasionally, she went out with the girls after work, but as an over-50 dater, the pickings were very slim. She had seen her neighbor quite often when she was walking her dog and he was walking his. They would smile and keep it moving, the way good neighbors do just to be friendly. She knew which house was his and thought it was interesting that a single man would be living alone in such a large house. Her home was the result of a divorce. She stayed in it because it was familiar to the children and because the neighborhood was nice for the grandchildren, who were arriving one after another.

It was the day he said "You cut your hair" that she realized how absolutely good-looking he was—nice face, nice body—and what a really sexy voice he had. She told him she was surprised he'd noticed. What had started as a compliment turned into a conversation and then an appointment to meet to walk their dogs together the next day.

Tracey and Kenneth really came to enjoy each other's company and their great conversations. After adhering to a strict 90-day, 'no sexual intimacy' rule—i.e., don't sign the contract before you read the fine print—she met his children.

When he met her children, they took to him right away—all but one, her oldest daughter. There was something Amanda just didn't like about Kenneth, but she could not give it a name. Tracey thought the name was Les, her ex-husband.

Tracey thought her daughter had gone off the deep end the day Amanda asked her if she had done a background check on Kenneth. It led to an argument that caused a three-week separation between the mother and daughter. Kenneth didn't seem moved by it all. He told her he would not be upset if she did the check, but he was willing to tell her anything she wanted to know. They talked about their divorces, their exes, and their plans for a future. They talked so much and so often, they were both shocked to realize it had been 18 months since he had first complimented her haircut and perhaps they should talk about taking the next steps.

Two weeks later Tracey and Kenneth hosted a dinner for all of the children. It was then that she revealed her engagement ring and invited them all to Bermuda, where they planned to have a quiet wedding ceremony. Everyone, even Amanda, seemed genuinely happy, and dinner was spent discussing and joking about what each group of adult children would call the other stepparent. They decided they would keep both houses. They would live in Tracey's home and Kenneth would rent his house to his oldest son, who was expecting his first child and needed more space. Things just seemed to fall into place . . . until they fell apart.

There was nothing particularly alarming in Amanda's voice when she called to say she was coming over. Tracey said great because she wanted Amanda to help her make some space in the closet for Kenneth's clothing, which he had begun moving in little by little. When she arrived they made small talk, but when Tracey suggested they go up to start working on the closet, Amanda broke the news to her mother. She had done a background check on Kenneth because of something she had heard from one of the neighbors. At first, she found nothing but she had been advised by the agency she worked with to try various spellings of his name. When she spelled his last name—Brown—with an *e* on the end, she found a criminal record from another state and a driver's license picture that matched the man Tracey was dating.

The fact that he was a convicted felon was one thing, but discovering that his conviction was for child abuse and child endangerment was a totally different thing. Amanda was sorry and sad, but she wanted her mother to know before it was too late. Tracey was grateful, because she knew her daughter had her best interests at heart. She was also furious, disappointed, and sad that Kenneth—whom she considered a great friend and even better love mate—had deceived her and violated her trust.

Kenneth didn't deny the results of the background check and said he could explain them. From his perspective, his ex-wife had coached her daughter—his stepdaughter—to say that he had beaten her when she rejected his sexual advances. He admitted that he had slapped and shaken the 14-year-old when he found her at home cutting school with a group of her friends, all of whom were lying around on various sofas and beds in their house.

During their many long talks, Kenneth had shared with Tracey how he held the girl responsible for the demise of his second marriage. She was rude, disrespectful, but her mother—his ex—seemed to turn a blind eye to the girl's potentially dangerous behavior and promiscuity. He had told Tracey that he simply got tired of fighting against the lies the young woman told about him and arguing with his ex when she took her daughter's side.

During the divorce the girl concocted a wild story about his touching her breast and offering to have sex with her in exchange for money. He said the allegations were not true, but since she told the story to a school counselor, there was an investigation. His wife sided with her daughter, and charges were filed against him. In order to prevent a long, drawn-out trial and to avoid the risk of being convicted, being sentenced to seven to fifteen years, and being labeled a sexual offender, he pleaded guilty to a lesser charge that carried a three-year jail term and two years of probation.

Tracey listened and asked a million and one questions, all of which he answered without a moment's hesitation. It was when she asked him why he had not told her any of this that he seemed stumped. He said he'd wanted to tell her but was afraid. He'd been going to tell her before the wedding, and his son had even offered to be with him for support, but he was just too afraid that she would not believe him and would call off their wedding. He apologized for withholding the information but would not apologize for lying. He had not lied. He had withheld information. In his mind, they were not the same. In Tracey's mind, they were exactly the same.

Tracey needed to decide what she was going to do, and she asked Kenneth for some time to think. She spent the next week crying her eyes out and not responding to his calls. The next week she spoke to him briefly but hung up when he began to cry. The following week was supposed to have been their wedding. She and Amanda went to Bermuda, and she spent most of her time weeping and asking why. When she returned home, she called Kenneth and told him that although she loved him, and she thanked him for everything, she was just not willing to move forward in their relationship. He didn't understand. He had made a mistake. He had apologized. Couldn't he please have a second chance? Tracey told him she was not willing to risk that he would withhold information or deceive her in the future, and she was not willing to have another conversation with him about it. This was her final good-bye.

Over the next month she was sad and shocked that Kenneth didn't call her, that he was honoring her wishes. She felt sorry for her dog, who rarely got to go out for long walks anymore. Tracey's son would come by when he could to take the pooch for a stroll outside, but otherwise the dog was confined to the basement to do his business. If not expecting visitors, Tracey wouldn't answer her doorbell in fear that it would be Kenneth and she would backtrack on everything she had told him. She missed him terribly; however, she simply would not allow herself to believe that she could ever trust him to be completely honest with her.

The issue for Tracey was not what he had or had not done. Had he told her from the start, she believed they could have worked things out. The issue for her was that he had not told her, knowing this was part of his history, yet had invited her to do a background check on him. For Tracey, that felt like conscious and deliberate deception. She had already married that and lived with it for 23 years. She simply was not willing to choose it again.

Tracey's first husband had not told her that he had a child until that child, at age 17, had shown up on their doorstep. He had not told her that he had a brother doing a long term in prison until he asked her if his brother come live with them when he was paroled. He had lived with them for two years before he made his first inappropriate advance toward her. She said nothing. By the time he did it for the third time, she realized that she should not have withheld that information from her husband. When she finally told him, he sided with his brother and told her she was imagining things. Tracey had a history with men who withheld information without any consideration as to how it would impact her life when she eventually found out. This history also included men who discounted and dismissed her feelings and her needs.

It had been three months since the breakup when she saw Kenneth walking his dog. He waved and she waved back, then she ran home and collapsed on the sofa. It had been seven months when she decided it was time to answer her doorbell again. The FedEx man looked vaguely familiar. When she signed her name, he asked her if she had gone to a certain high school. She said yes and cringed; those had not been good times for her. Being severely overweight, she had been the butt of cruel jokes and endless teasing. She had barely made it out of high school and into college because the emotional turmoil had sent her grades right down the toilet. He told her that he remembered her, and commented that she had lost a lot of weight. When he told her his name, she burst out laughing because he had been her secret crush.

What started with the delivery of a package from her son turned into another 90-day 'no sexual intimacy' process that wound up 14 months later with a background check, a pre-nup, and then a small wedding in her living room with his two children and her three standing as witnesses.

Tracey's story is a clear demonstration of how to address a betrayal of trust and what can happen when you do. It is also a very good demonstration of how to use what you learned from a previous betrayal to support you in avoiding mistakes in the future. It is very easy to open yourself to the possibility of repetitive betrayals by people you love or care about. Because you want to believe them, and because you know humans can be messy in their affairs, you feel obligated to accept their reasons and rationales for the small and large infractions. From her first marriage, Tracey had learned that she had a right as well as a duty and a responsibility to herself to say no to people, situations, and requests that did not feel right. In other words, she had learned to trust her gut.

INTUITION: THE GUT STOPS HERE

There are two fail-safe mechanisms that will support and protect you from violations and betrayals as you learn to trust the process of life. The first is a willingness to say no to whoever and whatever does not feel right for you. Saying no to what you do not want opens the door to what you do desire. As long as you hang on to things and people who have a slight tinge of dishonesty in their aura, even a minor breach of trust can keep you in a state of suspicion and make you vulnerable to possible victimization.

The second fail-safe mechanism to protect you from violations and betrayals is your intuition. Intuition means "the teaching from within." It is often referred to as the still, small voice that provides you with information, insight, and clear warning signs that can help you navigate through life. Everyone has it—that lingering, repetitive thought; a voice that calls out to you from within; the gut feeling that simply will not go away. It alerts you in various ways, at various times, with varying degrees of strength and accuracy. The challenge that makes it difficult to follow the guidance of your intuition is that you may not know how to interpret the messages you receive, and when the messages make you uncomfortable, you may be prone to taking the path of least resistance.

Often your intuitive messages are very subtle. It may be a thought or feeling that communicates, "Turn here," or "Don't go that way." If you overthink or ignore the message, it's likely that you'll soon find yourself in a situation that results in your thinking, *I should have listened to what I heard.* As you learn to listen to and follow your intuition, the more likely it is that you'll develop a level of self-trust that enables you to make self-supportive choices. Trusting and following your intuition requires practice, and it can only grow from facing real-life experiences.

Intuition grows from our internal value system. When what we believe in is clear, intuition provides us with the information we need to align with our values. Intuition also gives us a sense of inner wisdom as a basis for making choices and decisions that will not only restore your trust in yourself but will make it less likely that you can be influenced, led off track, or be betrayed by others.

One reason that we often deny or ignore our intuition is because we are taught as children to be overly dependent on others. The same intuition that helps us to be self-reliant and self-honoring as adults probably got us into a lot of trouble as children. In fact, we may have been taught to check in with or listen to others before we make a decision for ourselves.

Another intuition killer is that it is very common to dismiss, ignore, or deny your teaching from within because often, the subtle, vague "feelings" of your intuition go against the grain of what you have come to believe is common or acceptable in the world around you. As you begin to trust yourself more, listen to yourself, and act on your intuition, it will be easier for you to determine whom you can trust and what to do when trusting others is not productive for you.

The simplest way to say it is this: Pay attention to your gut feelings! Intuition rises from within you, from your solar plexus, at the center of your being. It may be a thought, a feeling, or just a sense that alerts you to pay attention and/or be careful. If you doubt what you feel or have not developed self-trust, deciphering the messages of your intuitive knowing will become a frustrating and confusing process. Unfortunately, the best way to learn how and when to follow your intuition is in retrospect. Each time you find yourself in a difficult situation, or after you discover that your trust has been betrayed, it is necessary to look back in order to discover the warning signs you missed or ignored. What were the thoughts? What signs did your body give you? What did you see or hear that you resisted or excused away?

Intuition is not only helpful to keep you safe from toxic people, it is also how you can detect when any situation is not right for you, even when on the surface everything looks fine and dandy. On the other hand, not only can your intuition show you the red lights and warning signs, but it will also confirm when you have a string of green lights and are ready to move ahead, free and clear. In learning to trust the process of life, it is absolutely essential that you develop and follow your inner guidance system—your intuition. In spite of all the evidence to the contrary and the commonly expected human response, Tracey trusted herself enough to follow her intuition, and what she gained was priceless.

BROKEN TRUST

I spent all of my childhood summers during the late 1950s and early '60s in the South—Virginia, to be exact. As I boarded the bus to leave New York City, I was sure of two things— that my name was Rhonda and that I was hopelessly, irredeemably wrong. When everything about you—that is, *who you are*—is seen as wrong, there is an assumption and presumption of guilt that covers not just who you are, but also everything you do. You feel it and others perceive it, whether they acknowledge it or not. And this unjustifiable rejection from the human family profoundly undermines your ability to trust others and to trust yourself.

My grandmother taught me that I was wrong. It was not intentional; it was the result of her attempts to make sure that, as a young black girl, I did what was acceptable to the world, in the world. She wanted to me walk, talk, speak, and, on some levels, think in ways the world at large wanted me to think as a person of color. My grandmother taught me to internalize and conform to the overt and covert tenets of racism, the black inferiority and white superiority equation that governed the social order of the era into which she was born. She had no idea that times were changing, and that the restrictions placed on her as a Native American/African American woman would slowly be disintegrated during my lifetime. While in many regards I have lived to experience this disintegration, I still regard the cruel and unusual punishment of everyday, socially acceptable racism as the worst form of soul murder.

Raising my son in Brooklyn, New York, in the 1970s was a daunting task, not only because I was a single mother but also because it was on the heels of the Black Panther, SNCC era, when young black men were often considered to be menaces to society. I taught Damon that he had to be different. If all of his friends were wearing sneakers, he needed to wear nice shoes. If the boys in the neighborhood had on T-shirts, his shirt should have a collar. I taught him that if a police officer stopped him, he should not talk back and he should never stand before a police officer with his hands in his pocket. I told him that he had two strikes against him; he was black and he was a male.

I told my son that police officers would kill him without a second thought, but I never told him why. Back then I didn't really understand why, but I knew it was a reality. Like my grandmother had done to me, I made my son wrong and guilty because that is what I believed the world thought about him. Back then I really believed that his appearance or behavior could save him from the overt and convert conditioning of the society. I have since learned that my fears for Damon in the 1970s were the same fears my grandmother had about me in the 1950s; that the people I did not respect or trust simply because of the color of their skin would not respect or trust my son because of the color of his skin. The issue of the lack of trust based solely on skin color and race was something that I inherited. Back then I was totally unaware that it was my experience.

As we headed south for the summer, we traveled from New York in the back of the bus with our shoeboxes filled with chicken sandwiches and our mayonnaise jars of sweet tea. We sat in the back because we were black. We carried our own food because we were poor. I'm not sure why we were considered dirty or dumb, but I had heard those things often enough by then from Southern white people to take them on. I remember the woman who thought it was cute that I had a book, and who was then shocked that I could read it. I also remember Grandma's insistence that I scrub all of my "tight places" extra hard so that I would not stink around other people. And I remember that when Grandma took me to work with her in the big houses in Scarsdale, New York, I had to wash my hands before I touched anything so I would not leave it dirty. I never quite understood how sitting on a box with my hands folded on my lap would make things dirty, so I concluded that my wrongness and blackness were interchangeable issues. When who you are is deemed wrong, you feel guilty about everything you do. If you are not careful, you will project your guilt onto others so they become wrong, too.

While my grandmother's naive attempts to make my wrongness as a black woman less offensive to the world left scars on my self-image, the racism I experienced in the larger world created gaping holes in my sense of value and worth. These two elements, self-value and self-worth, are absolutely essential in the process of developing self-trust, the ability to trust others, and the ability to trust the process of life. We have already established that if you do not trust yourself, you will not trust others. Therefore, it stands to reason that if you cannot trust others, you will not trust the process of life that brings you into direct contact and relationship with people.

When you are taught to think that you are inherently wrong, that something is wrong with you, and/or that you are guilty, you see others in the same light. These thought forms and the energy they carry not only make you suspicious, they become the filter through which you see everyone and everything. When these thought forms and thought filters of wrongness and guilt are then shaded by a belief system grounded in inferiority and superiority based on race, your instincts, reflexes, and reactions become knee-jerk rather than reality-based. When *you* think that *someone else* thinks you are wrong or guilty because of the color of your skin, your responses to or interactions with them are not grounded in reality. They are the result of programming and conditioning.

By the same token, when people think that who you are is wrong or that you are guilty of something simply by virtue of your race or skin color, their responses to and interactions with you will be knee-jerk and preprogrammed rather than genuinely appropriate to any specific situation. Unfortunately, whether you are reacting to your own internal programming or you are being reacted upon because of someone else's programming, in many, many cases, the reaction is unconscious and, therefore, difficult to acknowledge or correct. As a human being, you fight for what you believe, whether you know you believe it or not. When what you believe is unconscious, you may not be able to control or monitor the ways you fight to prove it is true.

I was about 15 years old when being black became "fashionable." Dr. King, Medgar Evers, and Brother Malcolm had been assassinated. Civil rights laws were changing the world. I was bused to junior high school, where I was quickly educated with a new set of descriptive nouns for my wrongness and my blackness. I was spit on and called names. I survived these experiences and worked hard to heal my heart and soul. What scarred me for life was being a witness to what happened to my brother when he got off the school bus or when he tried to play football or when he walked too close to one of his white female classmates. People who did not know us hated us; that reinforced our wrongness. The people who hated us because they did not look like us did not trust that all we wanted to do was go to school. We had not come into their community to infect them or pollute them. We were there by court order because change and evolution had become more important than private and public ignorance. It was a painful and degrading time that required a great deal of personal work from which to heal.

What triggers this pain all over again is when the men who killed Freddie Gray (4/19/15), Tamir Rice (11/22/14), Akai Gurley (11/20/14), Michael Brown (8/9/14), Eric Garner (7/17/14),

Trayvon Martin (2/26/12), Oscar Grant (1/1/09), Sean Bell (11/25/06), Amadou Diallo (2/4/99), and countless others walk free. Grand juries, prosecutors, and law enforcement officials are essentially saying they cannot or will not hold certain people accountable for their behavior based on the letter of the law. Those who hear such rulings then make up that someone was right and someone was wrong, according to the spirit of the law. The challenge with these two divergent views is that, without an understanding of perceptions, experiences, and the truth of one's intentions, there can be no accurate assessment of the individuals involved. This might lead you to believe that a process that pits the letter of the law against the spirit of the law is essentially flawed. It is difficult to trust something you believe is not only flawed but is also working against you. What is even more important to recognize is that you will ultimately become incapable of trusting the people who are tasked with maintaining the flawed system, and you will find it difficult to trust yourself for embracing the flawed system and its representatives.

What I have experienced in life as both a black girl and woman, both at home and in the world, has been hard, sometimes harsh, and often cruel. What my brother lived and experienced was downright ungodly and dehumanizing. His wrongness trumped mine, perhaps because he was a male, but surely because the world in which we live held an even lower expectation of him than it did of me. His presumed guilt and experience of always being wrong undermined his self-image to such a degree that he gave up on himself in ways that I never could or would consider. Perhaps he was simply not as strong as I was. Or maybe he just didn't have the extra grit that it takes to make it in a hostile world. What I know in my heart of hearts is that my brother died feeling wrong and guilty for who he was—both for what he had and had not done with his life.

Every day each of us enters every encounter and views reality through the lens of our individual experiences. These experiences are personal: some we have lived ourselves; others we have observed or been taught. In the same way that I was taught to believe and expect to be wrong, there are others who are taught to believe and expect that, no matter what, they are right. While our culture may not emphasize the tenets of rightness, it has surely assigned a face and a gender and a quality of life to wrongness.

No matter who you are or what side of the fence you grew up on, right is better than wrong. Right is *always* superior to wrong. Now, when you add gender and race to the equation of right and wrong, you are standing on a slippery slope. When you start sliding down that slope, it will be along the path of your own experiences, teachings, and beliefs. You will more often than not lean toward what you have seen, heard, and come to believe is true about yourself and others.

This problem is intensified when you have or don't have authority, power, money, and a weapon. The presumption of wrongness is deadly and costly and will continue to permeate our world until we become willing to face and tell the reality about what we have learned, been taught, and come to accept as truth about what is right and who is wrong. We must begin to unravel the myths about racial and gender equality. We are all taught things about who we are as it relates to race, gender, social class, economic standing, even the neighborhoods in which we live. Some of what we are taught is reasonable and real, based on our experiences. Some of what we are taught is absolutely false, faulty, and dysfunctional. The problem is that when a lie or misperception becomes truth in our minds, it also becomes the habitual and unconscious filter through which we see the world. This filter then becomes the foundation for the development of trust—who we trust, if we trust, and expectations we place on trust. In many, many instances our approach and the conditions we place on trusting others and the process of life has become unconscious, habitual, and highly dysfunctional.

We live in a world where there is an unconscious and often unacknowledged belief in the inferiority and superiority of individuals based on race. There! I said it! We want to believe that in response to our social and technological advances this is not true. White people want to believe that the racist programming of their ancestors has somehow been eliminated, and they are fully capable of seeing everyone, regardless of their race, as their equal. In some cases, because of the personal experiences and spiritual work, this may be true. However, we live in a social environment where the belief of superiority based on race has been concretized and practiced for so long, we have created laws to protect and punish those who have not shifted with the times.

On the other side, black people want to and strive to believe that we are seen and treated as equals. In some cases, we stand firm on the belief that we have moved far enough away from slavery to enjoy the fruits of the American dream so that the stench of racism cannot impede our movements. At other times, we just *hope* this is the case, but we constantly look over our shoulders for evidence that proves it's not true. The bottom line is, regardless of which side of the fence we live on, the *untrust* we experience today is more often than not our instinctual reaction to historical programs that reinforce racial inferiority and superiority, rather than our authentic response to our present-day social interactions.

Media stereotypes, social propaganda, and our growing fixation on social media that makes anonymous attack of personal reality acceptable keeps us from addressing the real problem head-on. Until and unless we become willing to do the hard, personal work required to clear our individual and collective consciousness of historical belief systems and racial programming, we will continue to act as if we trust each other when we don't; as if we can love all people, regardless of their race, when we cannot; and as if race and skin color are not the burning issues that underscore the ill-treatment of a vast majority of the human population. The underbelly of each of these situations is knowing that we can trust ourselves enough to tell ourselves the truth about what we really feel, heal those feelings, and begin to see one another from a place of love and acceptance.

When Trust Is a Collective Casualty

People have a need to be seen and heard. How we go about getting the attention we need or want in any given moment can be questioned or judged, neither of which lessens the need. If I whisper your name and you do not respond, my need to get your attention will grow. Eventually, I will call your name out loud. If you do not hear me or choose to ignore me at that point, my need to have you pay attention and acknowledge my presence will be further intensified.

People need to feel safe. They need to feel valued. When people do not feel seen, heard, or important; when they have needs that are dismissed, ignored, or denied, they will do whatever they feel is necessary to get the attention of those they perceive can give them relief. A whisper becomes a call. A call becomes a yell. When a yell does not yield a response, people may pump their fists in the air. When the fists do not get a response, something will be thrown. If you are hit by what is thrown, you will respond—not to the initial need, but to the fact that you got hit. The need that motivated the whisper still remains unaddressed. The attention has now shifted to *what I did* rather than *what I needed* in the first place

Unmet needs often reveal long broken trusts, and they give rise to a variety of emotions, many of which are toxic. These needs are often fueled by personal and collective history and experience. Unmet needs often clash with the energy of the society in which they live, giving rise to fear, anger, or denial. Whether we are looking at the Michael Brown case in Ferguson, the uprising in Egypt two years ago, or Rosa Parks refusing to give up her seat on a bus in Montgomery, Alabama, on December 1, 1955, when there is an outcry of unmet needs and the experience of feeling unsafe and devalued, those must be acknowledged and addressed.

UNMET NEEDS AND DIFFICULT EMOTIONS

When important needs are chronically unmet, people get angry. When they do, they act out, strike out, and commit acts which, if they are in their "right minds," they would not do and for which they often feel embarrassed and remorseful. Couples do it to each other when they feel everything else has failed. Parents do it to their children when they are stressed or overwhelmed. Supervisors and co-workers do it overtly and covertly in downsizings or layoffs that are indisputably hurtful and potentially dangerous.

We live in a world that has done a dismally ineffective job of teaching people how to channel or express difficult emotions. Those who experience or witness inappropriate emotional expressions often go into fear, then into judgment, then into the expectation of the worst from you. In fact, they prepare for it, escalating the stakes and diminishing or dismissing the initial need. Now their need takes priority. There is something they want from you. They want you to be quiet and go away. Now it's about power: who has it and who doesn't. More trust violations and difficult emotions to process, more unmet needs demanding to be met.

When fear is present and vision is obscured—*trust is a casualty*. When anger and rage cloud the mind and reasoning is faulty—*trust is a casualty*. When people are hurt and they fear it will get worse—*trust is a casualty*. When people are angry and they look for ways to defuse and disperse the energy—*trust is a casualty*. When people feel their power is challenged and they intensify their resistance—*trust is a casualty*. When people feel their power is stolen and they act out in anger and despair—*trust is a casualty*.

Human beings pushed to the limit of their experience and capacity to process what they are feeling *will* and *do* act out. They do it in their homes. They do it on their jobs. They do it in the public square. When people feel they are not being heard, they will do whatever they feel is necessary to get your attention. They did it in Ferguson and Baltimore. They did it with Occupy Wall Street. They did it in Selma. Such eruptions will continue to happen in overt and covert ways in a democracy until the needs of people are acknowledged and addressed. When there is no experience of justice, there can be no peace.

Individually and collectively, we can attach a variety of reasons, rationales, and judgments to the civil unrest that we have seen in Ferguson and Baltimore. We can agree or disagree. We can understand or not. What we must not do is deny that the needs of people in various pockets of this society are being ignored and dismissed. It is time to admit that we have broken trust in American society and that we are ill-equipped and often unwilling to address the difficult truths that are erupting in our streets. Many people are suffering. Many are in despair. Many can no longer trust the systems and institutions created to protect and serve the people.

You Always Get What You Expect

The institutions in Ferguson expected the worst from their people. They expected their power to be challenged. They got just what they expected. The people in Ferguson expected the worst from their institutions. They had experienced it long before the cameras arrived, and they knew it would likely be their fate when the news cycle moved on. Like a battered and abused woman, Ferguson residents had continued to place their distrust in a system that had already proven it could not, would not, respond to their need for justice. They, too, got exactly what they expected.

When trust has been systematically and continually violated, the only thing people feel they have left is to take sides. Anything that anyone says in this moment cannot be heard with an open mind or heart. Both sides are now looking at historical, social, and personal perceptions of right and wrong, guilt and innocence, fairness and unfairness. The broken trust in Ferguson no longer centered on the death of an unarmed black youth. The issue is no longer about the breakdown of trust between police authorities and the people they are entrusted to protect.

Can we, without fear of reprisal and attack, suggest the possibility of abuse of power by police authorities? Dare we mention the criminalization and demonization of African American males throughout this country? Can we even consider the difficult and sometimes impossible job of police officers in cities and towns around the country when it is known that they are not trusted and often despised—with or without good reason?

Are we to continue ignoring feelings of powerlessness, the need to be heard and seen, the need to feel valuable and important when you are poor or black or gay or elderly or just human? To heal means to make whole again—to restore to original purpose and value. Where exactly are we to look for healing? What exactly is it that we expect to be healed? How can the healing begin? Healing would require that everyone involved become willing to see, acknowledge, and address the unspoken truths that have resulted in more pain, more unmet needs, greater demonstrations of power, and a deeper sense of powerlessness and despair. It is possible that what we are witnessing is what happens when the very thing that makes us human—our capacity to think and respond with emotion—is taken lightly or not even considered.

Perhaps we are being confronted with what happens when trust is broken with an entire community and when people who are normally invisible are allowed to enter your mind, heart, and home at all hours of the day and night. One thing is certain, until we acknowledge that trust has been broken, until we dare to understand what history is saying and address it head-on, history will continue to repeat itself.

Few have broken through America's seemingly impenetrable wall of rightness and wrongness and systemic racism like Michael Brown, Jr., the 18-year-old black youth who was killed by Darren Wilson, a white police officer, on August 9, 2014, in Ferguson, Missouri. Michael's death sparked civil unrest and nationwide protests, and it ignited the Black Lives Matter movement. Marking his first Father's Day without his son, Michael Brown, Sr., recalled the tragic loss of his son on www.theGrio.com:

FATHER'S DAY

CLICK.

I'd just hung up on my son, Mike Brown Jr.

The day was August 7, 2014. I was at the hospital with my wife, Cal. We'd been married only three weeks. She had been diagnosed with chronic heart failure. Shortly after hearing the news, Mike called my cell phone. He told me Cal was going to die.

"Man, you need to watch your mouth!" I said before hanging up.

Those were trying times, and I was in a no-nonsense mood. A month earlier, our house had burned down. We'd lost everything. Literally.

I couldn't imagine things getting any worse.

They did.

Mike's predicting my wife's death came way out of left field for me. But that was Mike. He was a jokester, a dreamer, and an aspiring rapper. You know how it is with 18-year-olds; they think they're grown and can say whatever they want, whenever they want. Sometimes, depending on what you're going through, you just don't have patience.

To be honest, sometimes it took me a minute or two to get Mike's jokes or jive with his dreams. Like on April Fool's Day last year, when he called to tell me he had a baby on the way. He hung up, leaving me fuming for the rest of the day.

He got his dad good with that one.

Mike would say things that would confuse me or piss me off. Then, after some time, I'd realize that when he said something, it usually had meaning. For example, on the day we celebrated his graduation from high school, he announced that he wanted to be a rapper. "That's all fine and good," I responded, "but you're gonna stay in school and you're gonna stay focused."

He got angry and told the family, "One day, the world is gonna know my name. I'll probably have to go away for a while, but I'm coming back to save my city."

Like most parents, I wanted to support my child's dreams, but I wanted him to be realistic, too.

How in the hell was I supposed to know Mike's prediction would come true?

The same question applies to his call when I was at the hospital. After I hung up on him, Mike called another family member to explain what he had been trying to tell me: "Pop's mad at me. Tell him I said what I said because I've been having these visions and images of death. Tell him I keep seeing bloody sheets."

That was on a Thursday. Two days later, on Saturday, August 9, around 12:15 p.m., my cell phone rang. It was Mike's grandma on his mother's side. Mike was staying with her for a while before going off to college. She rarely calls me, so I answered quickly.

"Mike has been shot by a cop! He's lying dead in the street," she screamed hysterically.

I went into a state of denial instantly. No way! I defended. No! I could not possibly have heard what I thought I heard. My head exploded with one all-consuming thought: I've got to get to my son!

I don't remember much: a vague recollection of the dreadful silence in the car as we weaved and zigzagged through traffic; a muddled memory of a large crowd as we pulled close to Canfield Drive, the narrow street where Mike spent many childhood days. Like a linebacker on a mission, I pushed my way through the massive crowd, ignoring the comments pinging off my head:

"He had his hands up!"

"It was cold-blooded murder!"

"Why they leaving him in the street like that?"

To this day, I don't know how or why I didn't explode into a murderous rage when cops held up their hands to stop me from getting to Mike.

"That's my son!" I screamed over and over, as if those words would mean something.

They didn't. I had to stand there like everyone else. Mike's body was covered by that time. There I was, a semi truck's length away from my son, seething with impotence and telling myself he wasn't really dead. My mind insisted he was still alive under that ugly black tarp. I searched the eyes of policemen, praying that one of them—perhaps a cop with a child—would let me go hold my son's hand while his body was still warm.

I've heard about soldiers who block out the intensity of warfare until after the battle? I think I slipped into that state of mind. A couple weeks later, as my son's casket was lowered into the ground, I came out of my fog. Standing at that grave site, it got very, very real. My firstborn son—the kid I'd had when I was just a 17-year-old kid myself—was gone forever. Never again would I hear his voice, his often incomprehensible jokes, or his strange predictions.

Standing there, as they shoveled dirt on Mike's casket, our last conversations blasted loud in my head. My boy hadn't been talking about my wife's condition on that day he'd called me at the hospital. He had been having visions of his own death.

And I couldn't hear it.

Damn!

[. . .] Before he was killed, my son told us the world would know his name. That has come true. The name "Mike Brown" has become the national symbol of police shootings of unarmed Black men. Because of my son's death and the justice we're still seeking, hurting people, grieving people who've lost their children to gun violence or police brutality reach out to me.

[. . .] God forbid you end up like me.

[. . .] Don't be plagued by things left undone or words left unsaid. Reach out.

I recently spent some time in Baltimore, Maryland, working with the community in the aftermath of the death of Freddie Gray, who died as a result of sustaining spinal cord injuries while in police custody. Gray's death, following a string of similar incidents all around the country, left the residents I spoke to in a state of high "pissosity" and fear. The fear was understandable. What do you do when the people entrusted to protect seem to have little connection to you and even less regard for you? The rage and anger was palpable, bubbling just beneath the surface of our very civil conversation and interactions.

One woman spoke to the anger with such intensity that she began to cry. She asked me a series of questions:

- What do you do if, no matter what you do, the same thing keeps on happening?

- How are you supposed to fight against the things that are hurting you if the fighting gets you locked up or locked in?

- How do you make something better when the people who are creating the problem are unwilling to accept their role in it?

These were really good and really difficult questions for me to tackle. In the moment, I did what a good carrot is expected to do; I checked in with the chef. One thing we must understand about the process of life is that there are some things we will never understand. Instead, we must do what we can, when we can, knowing that if we trust the process and we trust ourselves, all things will work together to produce something better than what we started out with.

When I started to answer this courageous woman's heartfelt questions, I could only step forward in trust.

"Do you know and believe that God is in this process?" I asked. "Are you willing to trust that no matter how bad it looks or feels and no matter how long it lasts, there is something bigger, grander, better going on right beneath the surface?

Through her tears she responded, "I want to trust that, but I am the mother of three sons, and I am afraid if I just sit around trusting that this will get better, it won't."

I realized in that moment that what this woman, this mother, was experiencing is exactly what we all experience when it comes to trust. We hold the belief that certain things should be or look a certain way because of what we desire, what we think, and what we need. When our experiences do not mirror what we expect, we spiral downward into the belief that our trust has been misplaced or that it is not working.

As individuals we practice *micro-trust*; we see things from an individual perspective, grounded in our personal experience. Trusting God, others, and the process of life requires that we embrace the concept of *macro-trust*; we must learn how to assess and evaluate everything from a global perspective. We must recognize and embrace our importance in the world knowing that whatever we experience will have an impact on people we do not see and may not know. The lives of Michael Brown, Freddie Gray, Oscar Grant, and the others have had an impact on the world that is not more important than the loss their families have experienced, but it is one that has a great significance on the evolution of human consciousness. Their lives and the impact of their deaths is just as important as the lives and deaths of Medgar Evers, Reverend Martin Luther King, el-Hajj Malik el-Shabazz (Malcolm X), and Thurgood Marshall.

The grandparents who picked cotton or lost their lives in gas chambers or revolted against unfair taxation practices may not be remembered by or known to anyone who is living today; however, their sacrifices impact not only those in their lineage but also those in the world beyond their immediate relatives. The point is that we must learn to trust that God is in it all; that evolution and healing is a process; that what we live with or lose today will have an impact on tomorrow; that it is not necessary for us to like, enjoy, or agree with the process of life unfolding but that we must each learn to trust ourselves to get through it and serve a higher purpose.

When it comes to trusting others and trusting the process, it is foolish to think your personal and social programming and conditioning will not impact you. Who you are, what you do, and what you believe is both determined and impacted by what you inherit from the environment and lineage into which you are born. There are countless stories of people who have "overcome the odds" and "defied the circumstances of the birth" to rise to heights that were improbable and unexpected. I count myself among those people, and I will tell you from personal experience that what drove me from where I was at any given time to where I ended up—be it positive or not so much—was trust.

There were times I trusted myself and no one else. There were times I trusted God and not myself. There were times I trusted people, was disappointed by them, and was forced to trust only myself and God again. In the end, I stopped trying to figure out whom to trust and learned to trust myself as I trusted the process. Through it all I have learned that understanding and trusting the process of life are the only things you can really bank on.

People will disappoint you. God works in ways you can never fully understand. As a human being you are never quite sure what will push you over the edge into an instant of total insanity; however, life is fair and operating in your best interests, even when it doesn't feel that way. My prescription for sanity and surrender is what I found in *A Course in Miracles*, Lessons 25, 31, 47, and 74: "I don't know what anything is for" (W-pI.25.1:1); "I am not a victim of the world I see" (W-pI.31.1:1); "God is the strength in which I trust" (W-pI.47.1:1); "There is no will but God's" (W-pI.74.1:1).

I TRUST YOU.
I DON'T TRUST YOU.
I DON'T CHOOSE TO SAY.

Training to become a life coach, I failed miserably at most of the trust exercises. I was totally unaware of the ways in which my personal experiences, historical programming, and ancestral influences colored how I viewed others or myself. I had no idea that I was working through a filter that made me and other people wrong, guilty, and untrustworthy. I went into the ten-day training process with the intention of gathering information and developing the skills and tools I thought I needed to be a kick-butt coach. What I learned were life-altering lessons about trusting yourself enough to trust whatever process life presents to you. I also learned that as a coach every client who sits across from you is going to trigger your unhealed places and reveal to you what you need to know about yourself. Since coaching is a form of relationship, what is true about being a coach is also true about every other relationship in your life.

At first I thought I was being set up. As one of 3 African Americans in a class of 46, you could not convince me that the exercises were not biased. For most group activities, I was the only person of color in the group. In my experience and from my perspective, it felt as if everything I said or did needed to be interpreted and reinterpreted in order to be understood. Because of environment, experience, and social conditioning, there are some places and certain circumstances where people of different races and genders simply do not speak the same language. This creates a major barrier to establishing and exhibiting trust. The other reason I thought I was being set up was because at one point it began to feel as if the people in my group were analyzing me and my experiences based on *their* experiences.

It usually started with, "What I think you are saying is . . ." or "When you speak like that, it makes me think that you . . ." Internally, my responses were: "No. That is not what I am saying; that is what *you* are thinking!" and "When I speak *like what?* I am speaking English, fool!" By the third day of the training I had totally convinced myself that I had wasted my hard-earned money and that I would never be a coach. The process was not making sense to me. Then came the exercise that changed everything for me and within me.

The instructions were clear. We were to walk around the room, eyes cast downward, until we heard a chime. When we heard the chime, we were to stop, turn to the person closest to us, make eye contact, and hold it until we heard the chime again. On the second chime, we were each to respond in one of three ways: "I trust you," "I don't trust you," or "I choose not to say." Once we had each made our statement of choice, we were to walk away until we heard the chime again. The first few times the chimes were rung fairly close together. This meant there was very little time between the stop, the eye contact, the statement, and the walking away. There was barely enough time to see the person much less get an accurate read on her face to determine if trust were warranted.

In addition to my historical conditioning of always needing to say nice things to people, I made up that the best thing for me to do in that type of environment was to "choose not to say." That was not the truth. The truth was I was afraid to tell white people that I did not trust them. Not only did it feel like a mean thing to say, I did not want to spend another five days in the room with people who knew I did not trust them. Who was I not to trust somebody, especially if that somebody was white? The other truth was that I was afraid to look at them long enough to figure out if I should or could trust them. My summers in the South, my grandmother's stories, and her conditioning of who I was and who I should be had robbed me of my ability and willingness to know or stand in my own truth. However, as the time between the chimes grew longer and longer, the truth ushered me into my freedom from historical conditioning.

It must have been the fourth of fifth round of the exercise when I turned to face another black woman. Thank God! As I gazed into her eyes a disturbing feeling bum-rushed my entire being. The feeling was "I don't trust you!" But the nice girl in me refused to say that, so I lied. Looking right into her face, I said, "I trust you," and walked away. The next person I encountered was a white man. It seemed like hours between the chimes. As I gazed into his eyes, I could feel it coming, and I was horrified to find myself thinking: *I trust you.* Believing it was my duty and obligation to honor my ancestors, remembering all of the horrors and atrocities they had endured at the hands of his ancestors, I lied: "I don't trust you," I said.

The next person I encountered was a white woman, an elderly white woman with the kindest, sweetest eyes I could imagine. Standing at direct attention, my ego spoke to me: *Kind eyes do not make a kind person. She's white and you better not trust her!* While my instinct was to say, "I trust you," my ego was appalled that I would even consider such a thing. I lied again: "I don't trust you!" I said with a tinge of attitude. I could actually feel her heart sink as I walked away. This process was deeper than I could imagine, and it was taking me to places within myself that I had never dared to go.

After several corrective instructions by the facilitators and what seemed like hours of performing the exercise, two things dawned on me. The first was that I did have and could hear my own inner voice. It was clear; it was direct; and it sent a light ripple of energy through my body when I heard it. The second was that I did not trust my own voice, and even when I did, I would act to contradict it. This made me very sad. That sadness welled up in my throat and spilled forth from my eyes.

As the exercise dragged on, and I made eye contact with person after person, I became so intently aware that my lack of self-trust— not race, not gender—made it impossible for me to trust others. This awareness was so shocking, so devastating and freeing at the same time—all I could do was weep. And I wasn't the only one. All around the room, people were breaking down, weeping and wailing. It got to the point where we could barely see each other much less speak. I had begun to shake my head up and down to indicate trust or side to side to indicate the lack of it. People seemed to understand as we each walked away feeling, knowing, and reckoning with our own inner turmoil.

When the exercise was finally over, there were only a few dry eyes in the room. The facilitators then took us through a guided meditation in which we were instructed to gather up everything we felt and sort through it. Sifting through my piles, I recognized that not only did I not trust myself, I did not expect other people to trust me, either.

In one pile, I bumped into my lack of trust for women in general, and for black women in particular. This not only saddened me, it disappointed me. But I understood it. I became painfully aware that without trust in myself, I could not, would not trust anyone who looked like me: black or white. Since black women were my closest mirror reflection, they really bore the brunt of my self-loathing and mistrust.

Then I turned to the pile that dealt with men in general, and white men in particular. My father, my brother, my uncle, my first love, all of the disappointments, betrayals, hurts, and violations were in that pile and in the eyes of the men in the room. My grandmother's rapist, my mother's surly boss, the butcher who pinched my budding breast before he gave me the chicken on credit for my aunt—they were all in that pile. It dawned on me that while none of those men were present in the room, they were all present in the eyes that stared back at me, even in the eyes of those who told me, "I trust you." Weeping may endure for a night, but joy comes when you have the willingness and courage to allow yourself to know the truth.

As I thought it, the facilitator said it: "All issues of trust are a reflection of your willingness to trust yourself." Then, "No matter what you said or who you said it to, it is a reflection of your relationship with yourself and your level of participation in the process of life. Until you trust you, you will be suspicious, disconnected, and dishonest with yourself and everyone else. You will not allow yourself to feel, know, or tell the truth, and because of that you will lie to yourself and others. This means you know you cannot be trusted, and you will project that outward and onto everyone you meet. Unless you trust yourself, life will continue to walk you through the situations and circumstances that caused your first break with trust." All I had wanted was to become a certified coach. What I gained in the process was mind-boggling and eye-opening.

I wish I could tell you that my life changed drastically after that day. It did not. *I* am what changed. I changed the way I thought about myself, the way I presented myself in the world, and what I expected of myself and for myself. What changed was my willingness to hear, trust, and adhere to my own inner voice, even when what I heard meant that someone thought I was not being nice.

What changed was my perspective about life and the people who showed up in my life. Everyone, regardless of what they look like, provides me with an opportunity to see, hear, and act in a manner that demonstrates that I trust myself enough to recognize and act on the truth as I know it in the moment. What changed was the depth of my willingness to see and accept people for who they are, regardless of the color of their skin or their gender. More important, I learned that, in this process called life, if we are willing, we will be taken to the depths of our knowledge and experience in order to be pushed deeper into the process of learning how to see, know, and trust ourselves.

| # The End
# of History

> "TRUST THE PROCESS" IS A BEAUTIFUL
> PHRASE TO SAY, BUT ARE YOU LIVING IT?
>
> IT IS NOT UNTIL YOU ARE STANDING
> NAKED AND VULNERABLE WITH ALL
> THAT YOU THOUGHT YOU KNEW
> STRIPPED AWAY, THAT YOU ARE REALLY
> FORCED TO PRACTICE, LIVE, AND BREATHE
> THAT PROFOUND LEVEL OF TRUST.
>
> —*Connie Chapman*

Let's review the essential elements required to develop and deepen your ability to trust.

1. Understanding

You must understand the nature of the person or thing you are putting your trust in. Whether it's yourself, God, someone or something, or life itself, you must comprehend the essence of how the person or thing works, what you can expect based on what you know, and what is possible. It will be difficult to trust someone or something that you do not understand. And even when you think you understand it, you can be mistaken. This is what makes the second requirement of trust all the more important.

2. Intuition

Each of us has a spark of divinity within us. This is our connection to the ever-present, all-knowing, Infinite Intelligence of life. Our intuition is the great teacher from within that gives us the insight, information, and guidance required to walk through every experience. Learning to hear and believe your intuition is absolutely vital to the development of trust. When you do not trust your intuition, you become outer-referenced rather than inner-guided. The key is to trust that everything you need to know . . . you will know . . . when you need to know it. Intuition grows in direct proportion to the depth of your spiritual practice.

3. Vulnerability

Until and unless you are willing to be vulnerable, to make mistakes, to face difficulties with confidence, to keep putting one foot in front of the other, all while trusting that you are moving in alignment with your intuitive guidance, trust will be an impossible feat for you to master. Remember, vulnerability is not a weakness. It is a necessary requirement for the development of inner strength and trust in yourself, God, others, and the process.

4. Willingness

Regardless of who you are or what you have experienced, it's impossible for you to know everything about everything or everyone at first glance. Trust requires a willingness to admit what you do not know and to stand firm in what you do know. Willingness is an important prerequisite of growing, healing, and learning to trust. Willingness to be wrong, to be right, to know more, to unlearn what you have learned, and to learn something new builds your capacity to trust. There are no shortcuts when it comes to developing the willingness to deepen your understanding of people and things. Learning to trust your intuition when there is no logical or physical evidence that what you feel and know will pay off demonstrates willingness. Daring to be vulnerable and to exercise patience as you move through challenging or difficult experiences demonstrates willingness. Either you are willing to do these things or not. The choice is yours to make.

TRUST THE PROCESS

For the 30-plus years that I have been speaking publicly, I have never spoken from notes. My process is to stand before the audience and invite them to breathe deeply, then listen to what I hear internally and speak to whatever I hear using my own experiences for deeper explanation and exploration. Throughout the years I have learned to trust this process because it has never failed me. However, when I was new on the speaking circuit and heard that most "good" public speakers prepare what to say and write notes, I began to question my process and attempted to change it.

This is exactly what I did when I received a call from the legendary Susan L. Taylor, founder and CEO of the National CARES Mentoring Movement and Editor-in-Chief Emeritus of *Essence* magazine, asking me if I could accept a speaking engagement for which she had recommended me. This annual women's conference attracted more than 1,000 women from around the country. Ms. Taylor had been the keynote speaker the previous year. When the organizers asked her to recommend someone who could inspire and motivate the attendees, she gave them my name. I was honored that she thought I could do it—and scared to death that I would not be as profound and eloquent as I considered her to be. I did not trust that I could live up to the trust and faith she was placing in me.

Although I honored and respected what Susan Taylor represented in the world of women, at the time, I did not trust her impression of and regard for me. I decided that I needed to make her proud of her choice by ensuring that my speech was the best I had ever delivered. While I convinced myself writing out what I wanted to say was the right and professional thing to do, I now know it was an attempt to control what people thought about me and the process of how I used my gift. Two months out, I started preparing my speech, totally abandoning my usual process. Instead of trusting what I knew and felt, I made up that I could only be witty, inspirational, and motivational before that many people if I spoke from prepared notes. It was one of those moments when I abandoned my good common sense for doing what I thought I needed to do. It was a disaster!

My normal process was to pray for a title and speak to the title. The organizers gave me the theme they wanted me to address and I fashioned my speech to that subject. My first challenge was that I could not remember anything I wrote. I tried every speechwriting technique I knew, but what I was writing did not make sense; I could not feel it in my heart, so I forced myself to memorize it. The second challenge was that I was nervous and afraid. I had questions floating in my mind that I had never experienced. *What if they don't like me? What if I say the wrong thing? What if Susan's trust in me is misplaced? What if I get a run in my stockings?* Foolishness! Just plain old *craziment!* As the day drew closer, I became more and more frightened and less trusting of myself.

The ballroom of the hotel was packed: standing room only. Many of the women knew who I was because they had read the article about me in *Essence*. Others were just there to bask in the company of the other women, hoping to gain as much as they could. Internally, I was a wreck, praying that I didn't pee on myself and that I could remember what I wrote.

As the mistress of ceremonies read my introduction, a battle ensued in my head. I heard, *Leave those notes on the table.* What? I can't do that! *Leave those notes and trust yourself.* But . . . what if I forget what to say? *So what? So what if you forget?* I was supposed to move toward the stage when I heard my name, but I was in the midst of an internal argument, and I was losing. I picked up my notes to a rousing welcome and walked the three steps up onto the stage. I stood before a sea of women who were cheering, whispering, and embracing me with love. I heard, *Tell the truth and trust.* I could feel the pee running down my leg. I knew that this was a sure sign of growth. If you do not pee or want to pee when you are about to do something big in your life, you are not living big enough. On that day, the pee was actually sweat, but it had the same effect.

I started the way I always started, I asked the women to hold hands and take a deep breath. Then I told the truth. I told the women that the organizers had asked me to speak to the topic of finding faith in difficult times. I told them that I was there because Susan Taylor had recommended me. I told them that I had begun preparing what I was going to say weeks in advance. I showed them my notes. Then I handed my notes to a woman sitting in front of me and told the audience I couldn't remember a thing I had written, so I was going to speak to what I felt in my heart.

"Finding faith in difficult times means believing that there is Value in the Valley," I began. It was something that I had spoken to another woman about just a few days earlier. It was something that I knew a great deal about. The subject of that speech became the title of my second book. That book was my first *New York Times* bestseller. That day, that speech, taught me that trust is the only way to subdue the negative ego long enough to become vulnerable and stand in your authentic power, even if you don't understand how it works.

Life is a process, with processes within the process, designed to make us stronger, wiser, more loving, and more trusting of life and ourselves. Thus, as adults, we cannot afford to cling to our childhood expectations that we can have exactly what we want, when we want it, the way we want it—without having to face challenges and overcome obstacles. Nor is it productive for us to believe that people will be who we want them to be, or do what we want them to do, when we want them to do it. *Life just doesn't work like that!* When it comes to learning to trust the process, you must learn to have a grip on your expectations.

MASTERING TRUST

Mastering trust requires relationship challenges with both self and others. Challenges make us stronger. Until we become willing to face the challenges that help us develop the strength we need to face even greater challenges, we will not be able to master trust and grasp the possibility of joy or peace in life. Trust also requires that we make peace with time. Time is a key element of learning to trust. You must become willing to take the time required to understand yourself and others. Then you must be willing to walk through the process of interaction, challenge, and compromise to determine how to make relationships work or what to do if they do not work. These learnings and processes take time, patience, willingness, and trust.

STOP BEING A HISTORY MAJOR

There are times when your history can be a major deterrent to the development of trust. History is an exhaustive review of what has already happened for the purposes of examining and/or explaining certain motivations and behaviors. History can provide information and insight. Unfortunately, because history is the result of a particular perspective with a specific intention in mind, it may not always be an accurate estimate of what is possible in the future. In general, history is a good predictor of behavior and results. However, in our personal lives, when we rely on our personal history as the primary determinant of what to do and how to do it, we may miss the trust boat altogether. Why? Because you cannot use history alone to predict the future.

One lover who cheated on you does not mean all lovers will cheat. One friend who lied to you or swindled you does not mean all friends will behave accordingly. One win of the lottery does not mean you'll draw a winning ticket every week. Using history to determine what you can or will do more often than not keeps you stuck in the muck, mire, and pain of the historical perspective you are holding. The key to reviewing and using your history to support you as you learn to trust in life is to look at what you did or did not do rather than what happened to you because of what someone else did. Review your history and apply its many invaluable lessons in a way that helps you to move forward rather than as a reason to stay stuck where you are.

GET A CONFIDENCE GRIP

You, like every other card-carrying human on the planet, are going to make mistakes. You are going to choose the wrong love at least once. You are going to miss opportunities sometimes, and you're going to move too fast or too slow at other times. You will find yourself engaged in unexpected conflicts. You are going to be afraid or confused or plain wrong about something or some people. *Get a grip!* This does not mean that you are an idiot or that your life can be totally derailed by one or more of the mistakes you have made. Rather than getting stuck in how you messed up, use your mistakes, weaknesses, and missteps to build yourself up.

Confidence grows when you make a mistake, correct your course, and keep moving. Confidence in yourself, what is possible, and the process of life grows from your belief system. What you believe is possible gives rise to new ideas and a new sense of confidence from within yourself.

A Confidence Check

I once read a story about a businessman who learned a powerful lesson about having confidence from a most unusual stranger. The businessman, who owned his own company, was deeply in debt and could see no way out. He had done everything he knew how to do to attract customers and grow his business, but the creditors were closing in on him, threatening to sue. Suppliers were demanding payment for what he had already received, and he didn't have the resources he needed to stay afloat. Each day he came closer to the realization that he would need to shut his business down in order to survive. One day, he decided to just step back, get still, and figure out what he could and should do. He was sitting on a bench in the park, with his head in his hands, wondering if anything could save his company from bankruptcy.

Suddenly, an older gentleman appeared before him. "I can see that something is troubling you," the older man said.

In his state of desperation and confusion, the businessman told his newfound acquaintance everything. After listening to the man's tale of woe, the older man said, "I believe I can help you."

Then the gentleman asked the businessman his name. Once he heard it, he reached into his pocket, pulled out a small billfold, and wrote out a check. He pushed it into the man's hand, saying, "Take this money. Meet me here exactly one year from today, and you can pay me back at that time."

Then he got up, turned away, and disappeared as quickly as he had come.

When the man looked at the check in his hand, he saw that it was written for $500,000 and had been signed by John D. Rockefeller, then one of the richest men in the world!

This is it! the man thought. *I can save my business, eliminate all of my money issues right now, and still have something left over!* But instead of making the deposit, he decided to put the check in his safe. Just knowing it was there gave him the motivation, the strength, and the ingenuity he needed to work out a way to save his business. With renewed sense of hope, the man got busy. He negotiated payments, settlements, and better deals. He renewed and extended terms of payment. He closed several big sales. Within a few months, he was out of debt and making money once again.

Exactly one year later, he returned to the park with the uncashed check. At the agreed-upon time, the older gentleman appeared. But just as the executive was about to hand back the check and share his success story, a woman came running up and grabbed the old man.

"I'm so glad I caught him!" she cried. "I hope he hasn't been bothering you. He keeps walking away from the group and telling people he's John D. Rockefeller."

Then she led the supposed benefactor away by the arm.

Stunned, the businessman just stood there. He didn't know what to think or what to do. All year long he'd been wheeling and dealing, buying and selling, convinced that he had half a million dollars in his pocket. Suddenly, he realized that it hadn't been the money—real or imagined—that had turned his life around. His newfound sense of confidence had given him the power to save his business. And it was his confidence that had given him the strength he needed to trust the process.

KEEP IT MOVING

Failure is not fatal. The word *no* is not a life-threatening disease. In learning to have trust in yourself and to trust in life, you must be willing to fail, to be rejected or discouraged, and to have countless people tell you no. All people who have been betrayed or have succeeded against the odds will tell you that, at one point or another, they failed, were rejected, felt abandoned or worse, and, were told no! more times than they could remember.

For example:

George Lucas. The billionaire director, screenwriter, producer, and philanthropist spent four years shopping the script for *Star Wars* around to the various studios and racking up numerous rejections in the process. If he'd let his negative ego get to him, Lucas would never have ended up producing one of the highest-grossing films of all time.

Michael Jordan. As a young man, the NBA legend was cut from his high school basketball team. Known for his incomparable work ethic and determination, Jordan explained the secret to his iconic achievements, "I have missed more than 9,000 shots in my career. I have lost almost 300 games. On 26 occasions I have been entrusted to take the game-winning shot, and I missed. I have failed over and over and over again in my life. And that is why I succeed."

Harland David Sanders. The mastermind behind Kentucky Fried Chicken, Colonel Sanders lived in his car for more than a year and was told no 1,009 times by restaurants when he tried to sell his famous chicken recipe. The 1,010th pitch delivered "finger lickin' good" chicken to the world.

Walt Disney. This creative genius was fired from his newspaper job for "lacking ideas" and was turned down by more than a hundred banks and even filed for bankruptcy several times before he was able to manifest Disneyland.

Fred Astaire. After his first screen test, Fred Astaire posted a memo over his fireplace from an MGM casting director that read, "Can't act. Slightly bald. Can dance a little."

Vince Lombardi. The coach of the championship Green Bay Packers was told by an expert that he "possessed minimal football knowledge and lacked the motivation he needed to coach anyone about anything."

Tyler Perry. Actor, playwright, and movie mogul, Tyler Perry survived poverty and physical abuse and the failure of his first theatrical play in 1998, which left him homeless and living on and off in his car for six years. "I would not stop believing," says Perry, who was named by *Forbes* as the second-highest-earning man in Hollywood in 2011.

J. K. Rowling. Harry Potter's creator beat back poverty and depression as a single mother on welfare writing about Hogwarts in a coffee shop. The beloved author's refusal to abandon her dream made her one of the world's most successful writers. The magic of trust, indeed!

The point of each of these examples is that in order to get to where you need to be, you will be rejected by people, situations, and circumstances that are not right for you or that do not show up at the right time. If you give up after the first no, after the first rejection or betrayal, you will never find your rightful place. Every "no" you encounter is a trust-building opportunity. Every rejection you experience has the potential to deepen your capacity to trust yourself and the process of life. All too often you believe that you need the greatest amount of trust at the beginning of a new experience, but the truth is your trust grows as you walk through the challenges and difficulties of an experience. Muscles grow as you work them. Trust is a muscle that grows with the hard work required to stay the course. If you cut and run the moment you face a difficulty, your trust muscle will become flabby and dysfunctional.

TRUST THE PROCESS

While *trust the process* is a lovely and lofty phrase that we say and aspire to live, it is a difficult test to stand for and embrace. Learning to trust comes to us with all of its friends, asking us to stand naked and vulnerable, facing the unfamiliar without fear, surrendering everything we know and believe, all in order to receive what we desire and what life knows is best for us at any given moment. It is not until we become willing to be naked and vulnerable with the entire world watching that we will develop the skills required to practice and live trust when we have all of our clothes on.

Placing your faith in the unknown with no guarantee of the outcome is at the heart of learning to trust the process of life. It means that despite your history, despite the fear that history will repeat itself, you come to the place of surrender that allows you to give yourself over, knowing and believing that no matter what happens, you will survive.

At some time or another, we will all struggle through learning who, when, and what to trust: *Is this the right partner for me? Is this the right situation? Is this person or are these people telling me the truth? Is what I am feeling accurate? Is this the right time for this or that?* These are all-important questions that strengthen and cultivate our ability to trust. Sometimes we get the answer perfectly, exactly right; other times, not so much. Regardless of the circumstance or situation that brings us our trust-in-life showdown, it is never a good or productive practice to white-knuckle-grip what you already know—believing that you will be safe, will feel protected, or will have your expectations met.

Learning to trust the process is like closing your eyes in order to take your attention from the external in order to focus on the internal. It means learning to listen from within your soul to

267

what you heart is whispering. It means learning to recognize the sense of caution or support that wells up within you and acting in accordance and alignment with what you feel is right in the moment.

Growing, strengthening, and deepening your willingness and ability to trust cannot and will not happen until you know and trust yourself. Trust is a practice that must be built on a strong, loving relationship with who you are—your true and authentic identity. You cannot and will not trust what you do not know or understand. In order to trust in yourself and trust in life, you must know who you are, what you are capable of, and what you deserve.

Trust requires a gentle letting go. You must let go of the past and all of the grievances that are etched into your history. You must let go of the fear and all of its false images. You must let go of the need to know and the need to be right about what you think you know. When it comes to trust, the truth is, you do not and cannot know what is going to happen until it happens. A good place to start when you embark upon the journey of learning to trust the process is, *All is well*. From that point, link hands with trust and all of its friends. Begin the journey of trusting the process by holding on to the belief that life is actually on your side.

Trust Yourself

Trust yourself because you are worthy of your own time, energy, attention, and love. You—as a demonstration of and representative of the presence of the Creator in the world—deserve and are worthy of your own trust. Trust yourself because you are here to learn, be healed, and develop a greater appreciation for the process of life unfolding through you. Trust yourself because it is the way you demonstrate that you are willing to embrace, engage, and enjoy life. It also means that you understand that you will make mistakes; poor choices and unproductive decisions are a part of the process. And when all is said and done, your learning, healing, personal development, and unfolding will be a demonstration to others of what is possible for them.

Trust yourself because it is one of the most profound demonstrations of self-love and positive self-regard. Trust yourself because you are setting the example and creating the template for how everyone in your life must treat you. Trust yourself because when the rubber meets the road, when all else fails, when everyone else has fallen by the wayside, you will know that you have always been and will always be there for you. Trust yourself because not to do so is an invitation to feel suffering, experience sorrow, and submit to a waste of your precious time here in life.

When you trust yourself, you open your mind and heart to learn more, heal faster, and evolve into the highest possibilities that life has to offer. When you trust yourself, it is less likely that people will be able to deceive or disappoint you. When you trust yourself, it is a demonstration that you embrace your own divinity, nobility, and humanness with humility and respect. When you trust yourself, you acknowledge your weaknesses and become willing to address them without apology or defensiveness. When you trust yourself, you will spend less time looking back and running away and more time moving forward and growing into your life.

When you don't trust yourself, you become a victim of circumstances and time. You will miss the learning required for mental, emotional, and spiritual growth and the details of your personal and unique healing process. Without self-trust you will underutilize your personal power to make choices and facilitate change. When you don't trust yourself, life will become a treadmill of problems, difficulties, and challenges that you don't understand, fail to recognize, and become exhausted trying to manage or avoid. When you don't trust yourself, you will deny, diminish, or dismiss your own voice. This makes it highly unlikely that others will hear you when you try to speak up for yourself. When you don't trust yourself, you will become your own worst enemy, fighting against yourself and blaming everyone else for your perceived lack of power, choice, and capacity to create or re-create your own reality.

When you don't trust yourself, you are prone to giving too much, accepting way less than you desire or deserve, and repeating that experience over and over until the lack of trust becomes a loss of self-respect. When you don't trust yourself, you issue an energetic invitation for others to walk over you, to run amuck in your life, and actually to do to you the very thing you are unwilling to admit that you're doing to yourself.

When you don't trust yourself, you issue a statement of unworthiness that diminishes the presence of God within you. This ultimately destroys your sense of value, respect, and acceptability. When you don't trust yourself, you begin to demonstrate a covert level of self-hatred, self-loathing, and self-denial that breaks your connection with the presence of God and the experience of God's love within you and for you. When you don't trust yourself, life becomes a series of sad, traumatic, and spirit-breaking experiences that, if you are lucky, will push you to the point where you have no other choice but to run the risk of learning *how* to trust yourself.

TRUST IN GOD

Trust in God because it is your sole purpose for being on the planet. Trust in God because without that level of connection to the Source that gave you life, you will find yourself lost, alone, and searching for what you already have. Trust in God because God is the Source of everything you need and desire. Trust in God because you are a human being, prone to losing connection to and awareness of your good sense and sense of being amid the chaos, confusion, and deception of human interaction—and this turn of events almost never ends well for you. When that happens, you are out there on your own trying to figure out what doesn't make sense, what doesn't feel good, and why it is happening to you. Trust in God because it is the sure way that you will rise above your humanness into the truth of your authentic identity that is divine, purposeful, joy-filled, loving, and lovable. Trust in God because when you cannot do it—whatever it is—for yourself, God can do it through you and for you.

When you trust in God, it takes the pressure off and short-circuits the demands and deceptive practices of the negative ego that work through your unhealed places. When you trust in God, you give yourself the time and space you need to grow mentally, heal emotionally, and evolve spiritually without the internal doubts or external demands that can make you frantic and unsure about the process of life. When you trust in God, you have the freedom to just *be* who you are, learning, growing, and healing rather than trying to be perfect or prove to yourself and others that you are worthy of the space you occupy in life.

When you trust in God, you recognize the grace and mercy that allows you to give the best of who you are and what you have without fear that you will be depleted or that you will not have what you need when you need it. When you trust in God, you do not bargain with your dignity, compromise your integrity, or sell your self-respect in order to feel accepted by or acceptable to others. When you trust in God, you do not depend on people to repay you, acknowledge you, or complete you because you know, recognize, and understand that your Source is unlimited and readily available. When you trust in God, you can laugh at yourself, stand up for yourself, and be with yourself for as long as it takes to value, respect, and appreciate your divine nature.

When you don't trust in God, you will perceive your humanness as a fatal flaw rather than a divine opportunity linked to greater possibilities of learning and loving that being human requires. When you don't trust in God, you defend yourself with excuses and stories and threats against yourself and others because you fail to recognize that your own healing and growth needs require the exact people that have been offered. When you don't trust in God, you will undermine your purpose in life and underestimate the value of experiences and the role they play in the unfolding of that purpose.

When you don't trust in God, you attempt to manufacture your identity, determine your own destiny, and decide what is required and meaningful as you pursue both. When you don't trust in God, you are apt to attempt to make full choices and decisions for yourself with only a portion of the information required because you will not trust the voice and presence of God when it makes itself known to you, within you. When you don't trust in God and the divine purpose God has implanted in your soul, things will not turn out well for you. And if by some chance it seems that they will, you will soon find that what you thought matters really doesn't.

TRUST IN OTHERS

Trust in others because it is the only way to fine-tune your instincts, deepen your ability to trust yourself, and learn the depth of your capacity to love and forgive. There is, however, a caveat when it comes to trusting others. You must make a distinction between an unwillingness to trust and the wisdom *not* to trust under certain circumstances. You must also make a distinction between not trusting people without reason and not trusting people because they have demonstrated that they are untrustworthy. Trust in others because you need people to facilitate and support your mental, emotional, and spiritual growth. Even when your interactions and relationships are difficult, challenging, and uncomfortable, trust that you are growing. Trust in others because those whom you do trust—with or without good reason—will support you in recognizing the areas of your mind and heart that may still need loving care and attention.

When you trust in others, you expand your boundaries, both internally and externally. You learn what is and is not acceptable to and for you. This information, regardless of the circumstances that surround your discovery, will ultimately prove to be beneficial. When you trust in others, you are demonstrating that you trust yourself, that you can and will make good choices and decisions and that you are not allowing yourself to be limited by past choices and decisions that may not have worked out well. When you trust in others, you are offering them what you would want, an opportunity to demonstrate the truth of who you are and to be accepted in spite of your flaws, weaknesses, and history.

When you trust in others, it means that your mind and heart are open to greater possibilities of connection and interaction that may disprove your faulty or dysfunctional beliefs about trust. When you trust in others, it means that you are willing to be fully engaged in your life and the process of life, which requires you to take clear and calculated risks knowing and believing that no matter what happens, you will survive.

When you don't trust in others, you will spend more time looking over your shoulder than you do scanning the horizon. When you don't trust in others, you will be afraid most of the time, wondering who or what will happen next to threaten or destroy your well-being. When you don't trust in others, you will doubt yourself and what you know and what you feel, because you will be so busy worrying about the outside that you will miss the cues you receive on the inside. When you don't trust in others, you will become anxious, suspicious, and imbalanced, because you will never really know what anyone else needs, wants, or is capable of being and doing in or for your life. When you don't trust in others, it is a clear and present demonstration that you neither know nor trust yourself.

TRUST IN LIFE

Trust the process of life because it is an incredible journey of wonder, adventure, and evolution that you can experience only in direct proportion to your willingness to trust it. Trust the process because life is on your side. Life wants to encourage you, inspire you, and motivate you, moment by moment, and that can happen only when you trust that life knows exactly what you need, and exactly when you need it.

Trust in life because:

"You don't know what anything is for . . ."
A Course in Miracles, Lesson 3 (W-pI.25.1:1)

"You only see the past . . ." *A Course in Miracles*, Lesson 7 (W-pI.7.1:1)

"You are never upset for the reason you think you are . . ."
A Course in Miracles, Lesson 5 (W-pI.5.1:1)

"You are upset because you see something that is not there . . ." *A Course in Miracles*, Lesson 5 (W-pI.5.1:1)

"Everything you see has only the meaning you give it . . ." *A Course in Miracles*, Lesson 2 (W-pI.2.1:1-2)

"You do not perceive your own best interests . . ." *A Course in Miracles*, Lesson 24 (W-pI.24.1:1)

"You are not a victim of the world you see . . ." *A Course in Miracles*, Lesson 31 (W-pI. 31.1:1)

". . . Recognize the problem so it can be solved." *A Course in Miracles*, Lesson 79 (W-pI.79.1:1)

"You could see peace instead of this . . ." *A Course in Miracles*, Lesson 34 (W-pI. 34.1:1)

"Forgiveness is the key to happiness . . ." *A Course in Miracles*, Lesson 121 (W-pI.121.1:1)

"There is nothing to fear . . ." *A Course in Miracles*, Lesson 48 (W-pI.48.1:1)

"You are sustained by the love of God . . ." *A Course in Miracles*, Lesson 50 (W-pI.50.1:1)

"You are entitled to miracles . . ." *A Course in Miracles*, Lesson 77 (W-pI. 77.2:1)

"You are a miracle capable of creating in the likeness of your Creator." *A Course in Miracles*, Introduction (T-1,V.24:2)

When you trust the process, you'll find that guidance, direction, support, and grace are always available to you. When you trust the process, you will deepen your awareness and understanding of who you are and the meaning of every person and experience you encounter. When you trust the process, you can relax and have fun because you will be relinquishing your need to control and work on life. Instead, you will learn how to relax, surrender, and go with the flow. You will give yourself permission to stand for your hopes, dreams, and wishes without fear, trepidation, and doubt. When you trust the process, it pays off and it pays well. Trust brings you into alignment with the goodness and greatness that life holds in store for you.

When you don't trust the process, you work hard, gain little, and ultimately get pissed off and confused about why your plan and process are not working to your benefit. When you don't trust the process, it becomes increasingly difficult to figure out what to do, when to do it, how to be, or what does and does not work for you. More important, when you do not trust the process of life and living, you can be afflicted by the condition of analysis paralysis, in which you spend more time trying to figure out how to live and move forward than you actually spend doing what is required.

When you don't trust the process, you will find yourself in the midst of mistakes and missteps that make no sense and lead to nowhere. You will live way below your potential and blame life and people for working against you. When you don't trust the process, you will miss the goodness and fun and opportunities that may come your way to take you to exactly where you want to be.

SURRENDER CONTROL

You cannot and will not learn the value or power of trust as long as you believe you need to or can control the process of life unfolding within you or around you. Trust requires that you surrender the need to control people and events. Control is the number one human addiction. Control is the mental concept used by the negative ego to give the human mind a false sense of safety. Needing, wanting, and trying to maintain control is a sure way to avoid what is required in order to learn to trust the process of life. Control is what we use in an attempt to avoid a repeat of the dramatic and traumatic experiences we have had in the past. Control does not support you in learning to trust yourself, God, others, or the process of life. In fact, the more you attempt to maintain control, the greater are the chances that you will slip, fall, and hurt yourself. In order to trust the process, you must know that there is a loving, supportive, divine plan moving through you and in your life that you cannot control.

Even when you do not understand the plan or cannot see its path, trust is required. Any plan that is leading you along, attempting to control what happens and how it happens, will not be productive. At all times, in every situation, under all circumstances, you must know and trust that things are happening the way they are happening because life is rearranging your circumstances for a higher good. You cannot control what life chooses to arrange. Instead, you must learn to surrender. This does not mean you give up. It means you give yourself and your life over to something bigger, grander, and more glorious, even when you do not know what that is.

TRUST IS A CHOICE

Trust is not always this big thing we make it out to be. Then again, it can be. It all depends on your awareness and understanding of what trust is, how it works, and why you need it in your life. To become viable, trust begins with the little things: the prompting to take a different route home, to call someone you're thinking about, to ask someone you don't know for something you need or desire. Trust grows from doing the little things that make absolutely no sense in the moment.

I had no idea that when I wrote my book *Tapping the Power Within* and sold it from the trunk of my car that my work would ever grow into *Iyanla: Fix My Life*. *Tapping* started out as a workbook for women in a Life Skills program. They were moving from welfare to work. I created exercises for them that would support them in changing their minds and their lives. Someone said to me, "You need to make that a book!" I had never thought of it, but it felt right when I heard it, and I trusted that. There were hundreds and hundreds of steps between the day I took that workbook manuscript to Kinko's to get it printed and the day I filmed the first episode of a television show; that whole journey hinged on my trusting what felt right in my heart.

It is not wise or necessary to start out needing to trust something or someone for the rest of your life. You trust it for right now, in this moment, and you remain willing to grow and learn whether your trust is well placed or not. Each time you trust yourself you strengthen your trust muscle, your intuitive knowing, and your willingness to keep moving forward on your path, regardless of the outcome. Leaving the law, leaving an abusive marriage with no money and no place to go, starting my ministry in my living room, listening to the signals my life was giving me—day by day, moment by moment—paved the way for every successful opening in my life.

The only way to grow your life is to take one trusting step at a time; these acts of trust grow you. Everything you have done and everything you will do required and requires trust. Whether it is a first kiss or the start of a business or a move to a new city, each action you take requires that you trust something or someone. Start with yourself. Now I will admit that there is an uncomfortable rub with trusting; life and change will happen whether you trust or not. What trust can and will do is change the quality of the journey. How you do what you do and what you experience as a result will shift and change in direct proportion to the depth and quality of your ability to trust yourself, God, others, and life. When you don't have trust in your heart, you will have stress, anxiety, and fear.

We already know everything we need to know about the power of trust. It began when we were children, when we did not know what anything was for. Unfortunately, as we grew and developed, we were talked, programmed, frightened, and conditioned away from remembering and using what we instinctively knew. As children learning to walk, we all had to learn to trust our legs. We didn't know anything about legs until we tried to use them and fell for the first time. When we fell, it didn't have a meaning. We probably assumed that it was a natural part of learning to use our legs. Without preconceived notions or information about falling, we continued to stand up, take a step, fall down, get up, and try again until we fell again. In the process we learned to trust that our legs could move and that eventually they would hold us up. This learning came from our willingness to fall.

There were two things that disrupted the childhood trust-building process. The first was whether or not we got hurt when we fell. The second was the reaction of people around us. If we fell and hit our head or scratched our knees, there was pain and discomfort. This made an impression on us, but it did not deter us. After a few moments of crying, perhaps, chances are we took another risk to work with our legs, to stand and maybe fall again. More likely than not, it was the reaction of the people around us that gave the fall meaning, that made it frightening or acceptable. If the adults watching went into drama—screaming, crying, giving warnings and cautions—there was an imprint we had to navigate. Now the fall had a meaning. We may have come into the belief that there was something bad about falling. If the adults were screaming and crying, we may have believed that we should do the same thing—scream and cry—and that we should not trust that things would be okay if we fell. The good thing is that because trust is a natural, organic, internal process that grows with experience, we eventually had to override those outside influences and get back to the process of learning to trust our instincts and our legs.

Trust requires a willingness to fall without giving the fall a permanent meaning. Without outside influence or pain, children are willing to fall and get up. They focus on what they are going for. If the goal was to get the little red ball, the fall does not deter them. They never lose sight of their vision. They fall, get up, and try for the ball again. They don't make the ball or the fall wrong or bad. They trust that their legs will somehow, someday, help them reach the ball. And as they grow their legs get longer and stronger.

Unlike when our adult hearts get hurt in relationships, children who fall down and get right back up do not question the function of their legs. They don't become suspicious, they don't stop trusting their ability to walk nor do they abandon their vision of reaching the ball. Eventually, children learn to run and skip and jump. They trust themselves enough to push the capacity of their legs—

trusting anew each time, knowing full well there is a possibility of falling. They don't stop trying; they just keep trusting. As we learn to master trust, we must remember the value of falling and keep pushing ourselves, deepening our capacity to get up and try something new.

Ultimately, trust is a choice. You either choose to go for what you want, or you don't. If you don't trust yourself or the process of life, it's certain that you will never get what you really want. When you choose not to trust, when you decide that you are not going to give it your all, what you are actually saying is, "I trust that this is going to turn out bad." You are trusting in the worst possible outcome. When, on the other hand, you trust yourself, God, others, and your ability to align with the process of life, then a possible fall—aka wrong choice—means you're making an investment in yourself and your capacity to grow.

Every act of choice is an act of trust. Either you trust yourself and the process that helps you grow, or you trust in the negative ego-based defaults of fear and the worst possible outcome. In the end, you will trust what you believe because in the final analysis there is no surefire path to learning or deepening trust. There is no do-this or do-that formula. When you do not have trust or are afraid to trust, chances are you will endure hurt, suffer unnecessarily, and live way beneath your potential. Either you are willing to fall, get hurt, and get up again—or you are not. There is one inviolable truth about trust: When you have it, no matter what you go through, it will eventually pay off. The choice, beloved—*to trust or not to trust*—is yours to make.

GRATITUDE AND ACKNOWLEDGMENTS

At this point in my life, there is no way I can ever acknowledge all of the people who have loved, supported, and sometimes carried me, thus allowing me to be able to do the work God has given me to do in this world. This list is, therefore, recognition of what is in my heart today, at the completion of this work, and is in no way the sum total of the love and gratitude I have for all that I have received.

To the spirit of Orisha Sami, Gemmia Lynette Vanzant—who you were in life and what you are in spirit continues to be the light I follow and the rod that holds me up.

Cheryl Woodruff, my divine editor, for hanging in there with me, in the midnight hour, and trusting that we could and would get this project to the finish line. You have been the wind beneath my wings when I had the most difficulty trying to get them to flap.

Sir Rods, Rodney Scott, my manager, brother from another mother, and friend, for your willingness to go to great lengths to keep me safe and to remind me of the value of who I am.

Oprah Winfrey, Sherri Salata, and Eric Logan, for trusting your hearts enough to trust me in a way that has moved my life into a new and glorious trajectory.

OgunBi' Ide, Damon Keith Vanzant, my one and only son, there simply are no words to adequately express what your trust in me has done for me.

Nisa Camille Vanzant, my baby girl, just keep trusting yourself, my love. It is really starting to look good on you.

Robert Wesley Branch, for being a demonstration of what it looks like to trust yourself as you grow into your greatness. Your friendship and wisdom has been a rock upon which I stand.

Nora Reichard and Cindy Shaw, my *Trust* copy-editing and text-design angels, for your diligent work in putting this baby to bed.

Managing editor, Perry Crowe, for always keeping our train on the right track and Nicolette Young for proofreading magic.

Reid Tracy and the entire Hay House family, for always holding a place for me and offering me ways to share my gifts in the world.

My maestro and attorney, Kenneth L. Browning, you are simply the best—26 years and counting.

My posse: Almasi Wilcots, Sherman Wilcots, Helen Jones, Chinaza Deborah Lee, Lydia Ruiz, Laura Rawlings, Ken and Renee Kizer, who fed me trust tidbits; Yahfaw Shacor and Lydia Potter, for taking such good care of me; Elease Welch, Nancy Yeates, Deanna Mathias, Robert Pruitt, Jackie Smith, Peter Ripley, Lynn Barber, and the rest of the IVISD faculty, who continue to hold down the fort as I spread my wings wider.

My elders, Oshun Kunle (Alvaro Myrie), Awo Obara Ejiogbe, (Albert Oceguera), whose wisdom and support make it possible for me to continue to engage and trust the process.

To the guests and viewers of *Iyanla: Fix My Life* and the loyal and dedicated readers of all of my works, I am so grateful that you trust yourself enough to trust me to share with you all that I have learned and continue to learn about what is required to live in peace, joy, love, and excellence.

ABOUT THE AUTHOR

Photo Credit: Isaac Sterling

From welfare mother to *New York Times* bestselling author, from the Brooklyn projects to Emmy Award winner, from broken pieces to peace, **Iyanla Vanzant** is one of the country's most celebrated writers and public speakers, and she's among the most influential, socially engaged, and acclaimed spiritual life coaches of our time. Host and executive producer of the breakout hit *Iyanla: Fix My Life* on OWN: Oprah Winfrey Network, Iyanla's focus on faith, empowerment, and loving relationships has inspired millions around the world. A woman of passion, vision, and purpose, Iyanla is also the co-founder and executive director of Inner Visions Institute for Spiritual Development.

———

To receive a free issue of the *Daily Stimu-Mail Newsletter,* please enroll at **www.innervisionsww.com.**

www.Iyanla.com

———

INNER VISIONS INSTITUTE FOR SPIRITUAL DEVELOPMENT

*Where the Mind Meets the Heart and
the Soul Remembers Its Purpose*

Join Iyanla for

Online and In-Person

Classes, Workshops, and Seminars

Coaches Training

Ministerial Ordination

For More Information Visit Us At:
InnerVisionsWorldwide.com

Iyanla VANZANT

PRESENTS

GEMMIA'S
Master Peace

*Energy Clearing and
Balancing Body Washes*

MasterPeaceBodyWash.com

The MasterPeace Body Wash Blends are based on the ancient sciences of herbalism and aromatherapy, the use of plant extracts and essences to encourage and facilitate good health, equilibrium, and well-being. Herbal medicine and aromatherapy have been used by cultures around the world for millennia and MasterPeace Body Wash Blends take these two alchemical arts to the next level. Using specific combinations of herbs, essential oils, and African Black soap, each blend is designed to clean the body and clear subtle energies to restore balance to the mind, body, and spirit.

CLEARING AND RELEASING
Purging, Removing, Altering, Liberating

WELLNESS
Stabilizing, Calming, Balancing, Healing

ENERGIZE
Stimulating, Arousing, Activating, Expanding

PURIFICATION
Cleansing, Clarifying, Improving, Amending

PEACE AND CALM
Tranquil, Soothing, Stabilizing, Softening

SWEET ATTRACTION
Drawing, Reaping, Pulling, Magnetizing

For more information visit our website at:
www.MasterPeaceBodyWash.com
To place an order call: (301) 868-2837

SmileyBooks Titles of Related Interest

FORGIVENESS: 21 Days to Forgive Everyone for Everything
By Iyanla Vanzant

IF YOU CAN SEE IT, YOU CAN BE IT: 12 Street Smart Lessons for Success
By Chef Jeff Henderson

ALMOST WHITE: Forced Confessions of a Latino in Hollywood
By Rick Najera

THE RICH AND THE REST OF US: A Poverty Manifesto
By Tavis Smiley and Cornel West

HEALTH FIRST: The Black Women's Wellness Guide
By Eleanor Hinton Hoytt and Hilary Beard

PEACE FROM BROKEN PIECES: How to Get Through What You're Going Through
By Iyanla Vanzant

TOO IMPORTANT TO FAIL: Saving America's Boys
By Tavis Smiley Reports

BRAINWASHED: Challenging the Myth of Black Inferiority
By Tom Burrell

All of the above are available at your local bookstore, or may be ordered by
contacting Hay House (see next page).

We hope you enjoyed this SmileyBooks publication.
If you would like to receive additional information, please contact:

SMILEYBOOKS

Distributed by:
Hay House, Inc.
P.O. Box 5100, Carlsbad, CA 92018-5100
(760) 431-7695 or (800) 654-5126
(760) 431-6948 (fax) or (800) 650-5115 (fax)
www.hayhouse.com® • www.hayfoundation.org

Published and distributed in Australia by:
Hay House Australia Pty. Ltd. • 18/36 Ralph St. • Alexandria NSW 2015
Phone: 612-9669-4299 • Fax: 612-9669-4144 • www.hayhouse.com.au

Published and distributed in the United Kingdom by:
Hay House UK, Ltd., Astley House, 33 Notting Hill Gate, London W11 3JQ
Phone: 44-20-3675-2450 • Fax: 44-20-3675-2451 • www.hayhouse.co.uk

Published and distributed in the Republic of South Africa by:
Hay House SA (Pty), Ltd. • P.O. Box 990, Witkoppen 2068
info@hayhouse.co.za • www.hayhouse.co.za

Published and distributed in India by:
Hay House Publishers India
Muskaan Complex, Plot No. 3, B-2, Vasant Kunj, New Delhi 110 070
Phone: 91-11-4176-1620 • Fax: 91-11-4176-1630 • www.hayhouse.co.in

Distributed in Canada by:
Raincoast Books • 2440 Viking Way, Richmond, B.C. V6V 1N2
Phone: 1-800-663-5714 • Fax: 1-800-565-3770 • www.raincoast.com